Let's Go to Hell: Scattered Memories of the Butthole Surfers

BY: JAMES BURNS

DiWulf Publishing
EST. 2014

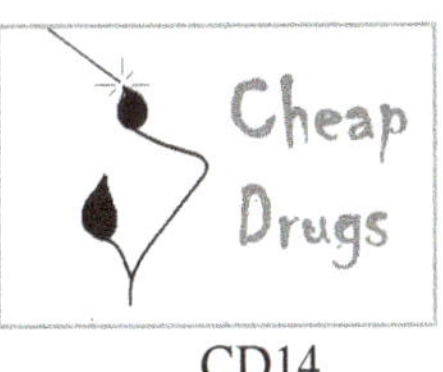

CD14

Let's Go to Hell: Scattered Memories of the Butthole Surfers, by James Burns
First published 2015 by Cheap Drugs
Republished December 2025 by DiWulf Publishing and Cheap Drugs

DiWulf Publishing
Morrisville, Pennsylvania
diwulf.com

Printed in the United States of America

ISBN: 979-8-9900264-3-8

for Loretta; and dedicated to Charles M. Young & Teresa Taylor

Chapters

Punks, not the Dead

FE: *It's not easy to figure out the chronology or personnel of the band's recordings since there's never any info on the record sleeves...that makes documenting the band's career pretty tough.*
King: *It shouldn't really matter. Who really cares?...*

- *Forced Exposure magazine, (4/18/86)*

The passage of time has a strange way of distorting the past. The lens through which we view people, places, and events becomes clouded over time. Memories get morphed and warped into some kind of strange alternate reality. We may claim that maturity and experience has made us wiser, giving us a new context to view the past with greater clarity and perspective, but this is not always the case.

It is through this warped lens that we might come to believe that a concert held in a sprawling, muddy field back in 1969 somehow affected anything at all, either socially or politically. To this day, there are throngs of people who make the pilgrimage to the town of Woodstock, even though the actual site of the concert is 70 miles southwest in the town of Bethel, NY. This distortion of reality is often better than the truth itself. Woodstock, the town, is a quaint village of shops and a bastion for artists and like-minded, eccentric individuals whereas, until recently, the spot where the Woodstock Festival took place remained little more than barren farmland (This, prior to the performing arts center and museum that opened on the site.)

Perhaps for that brief moment there was the hope that we could all live together as a community or perhaps segregate ourselves apart from the so-called normal man. But, as has prevailed in so many cases throughout the history of this country, violence and greed won. It wasn't enough to frolic naked in the mud. If any real change was going to take place in the minds of the masses, it seemed it would come via the route of the 1968 Chicago Democratic National Conventions, and not via the Marches on Washington, nor the huge festival concerts, for that matter.

Any chance at peace and love seemed lost on the balcony of the Lorraine Motel in Memphis, or laid bleeding to death on the floor in the kitchen of the Ambassador in LA. The last vestige of hope was murdered at the Altamont Motor Speedway near San Francisco, fittingly close to where the first cries for peace and love had emanated just a few years prior.

Still, the nostalgic show up in Woodstock each August attempting to rekindle some semblance of those three days of Peace, Love and Music. When their vacations are over, however, they return to their mundane realities. Like Benjamin Braddock and

Elaine Robinson in 'The Graduate', they stare vacantly into space wondering if the toil to attain The American Dream meant anything at all, or if the prize they sought was as fleeting as the 3 days themselves. 'After Hendrix, there's a huge traffic jam back to the Thruway, man...'

Punks didn't want to go out like their parents had. They didn't want to 'sit-in' until the cops came along with the tear gas and billy-clubs to restore law and order. They wouldn't be content to just sit wait for instant karma to get them or for The Man to come down in riot gear and shoot them dead. Never again to People's Park, or Kent State! Let's finish what Mario Savio started!

The hippies may have planted the seeds of a movement, but the farmers were too fucked up on brown acid to till the field properly. Idealism means nothing unless you've got the will to fight. Not just for three days, but for as long as it takes. Huey Newton, Abbie Hoffman and Malcolm X knew the score. Che Guevara's face spray-painted on a wall. That's what the punks took away from the 60's, and as much as their parents had abandoned the ideals of revolution, civil disobedience, and letting their freak flags fly, their kids began to realize their power.

And what better way to start a social revolution than through music? Elvis had certainly pissed a lot of folks off just by swinging his hips around. Before long, the youth were ablaze with frenzy and a new cultural revolution was underway. A decade after rock'n'roll changed the landscape of American society, the hippies got hip from the folkies and bluesmen and began to use it to make their own socio-political statements. A decade after the hippie movement had begun, the punks used the lessons of their parents' generation to try to institute their own brand of social change.

What many historians have failed to recognize, however, is the significance of this movement in the United States. Sure, the so-called 'punk movement' started in the UK, but just like the rhythm and blues music that spawned the British Invasion, punk rock is a uniquely American phenomenon. The Sex Pistols and the Clash (among others) used the American garage music of the Ramones and the Stooges (among others) to boldly challenge the political establishment of the time. The boredom-leads-to-self-destruction seediness of the lyrical content was replaced with anger at the political and social structure of British society at the time.

By 1976, one-third of all high school grads in Britain couldn't get a job and racial tensions lead to rioting in the streets. The government seemed completely out of touch with the working class. The time was right for an upheaval. It came, culturally at least, in the form of a 7" single by a bunch of teenagers who had just recently witnessed the Ramones on their first tour of the UK a few months earlier.

The Sex Pistols ignited the spark, and the countless UK bands that followed in their wake fanned the flames, but by the late 1970's the youth of America, themselves faced with a stagnant economy, an oil shortage, a hostage crisis, and the recent ousting of a sitting President, carried the torch forward onto U.S. shores.

Before long, punk bands were sprouting up in every major city, and many small towns as well. Like pins in a map, the landscape was dotted with scenes of malcontents who were not willing to settle for their parent's AmeriKKKa. The punks wouldn't be fooled, as the hippies were, into thinking they could change the fabric of society while working within its framework. Instead, they operated outside the mainstream and created their own underground social networks.

From artists who created posters and comics, to writers who published their own fanzines, to bands, to the few, brave club owners who booked them, to the ingenious kids who started their own labels and booked their local VFW halls when the clubs wouldn't have them; it took a total effort to fight the greed-heads and the war mongers. If hippie idealism was going to mean anything, it would take more than 3 days in a muddy field or a random march. It would take a 365 day a year struggle.

New York and Los Angeles naturally caught on first, but it wasn't long before punk scenes could be found in every major metropolitan area: Chicago, Detroit, Akron, Phoenix; it was inescapable. By the time the Sex Pistols played the Longhorn Ballroom in Dallas in 1978, a local band, the Nervebreakers, was opening for them. Soon after, punk bands started sprouting up all over Texas: The Dot Vaeth Group, Superman's Girlfriend, The Huns, and Terminal Mind among them. Shortly thereafter, bands like the Big Boys and The Dicks, both from Austin, became legends of their local scene. It was around this time in 1980 that two young men attending Trinity College in San Antonio decided to form their own band.

Like so many other kids, they were thrilled by the new wave of music bubbling up from the underground. They had been raised on bands like Grand Funk Railroad, the 13th Floor Elevators, and Moving Sidewalks but now, trapped in a world of AOR soft rock radio and bad local cover bands, were lost to find much of anything that captured that same kind of energy and excitement commercially.

Instead, they began listening to bands like Television, the Jam, the Fall, Wire, Surgical Penis Klinik, and Chrome, as well as records being pressed up by small, independent labels around the country. Labels like SST in LA, Placebo in Phoenix, and Alternative Tentacles in the SF Bay Area. Each label offered a glimpse into their own local bands and scenes. It turned out there was an incredibly diverse group of kids who shared, if nothing else, a similar belief that rock music was getting dull, art was becoming unchallenging, and anyone who had something to say should be given a vehicle to be heard.

By the mid-1970s, there was little room for experimentation in popular music. The idea of forming a band before the age of punk rock seemed almost futile. Major labels ruled the marketplace and Adult Contemporary music topped the charts. It was a time for Fleetwood Mac and the Eagles and for bands who were already well established and who grossed more in sales than many Third World countries' GDPs.

After Nixon's resignation in August of 1974 and the fall of Saigon less than a year later, the country was exhausted. There seemed to be a need for the familiar and the desire for a pillowy-soft complacency. The bands of the day seemed more than willing to provide the soundtrack to lull kids into that slumber. Rock music was becoming another commodity, and stadiums were filled with those who were buying into the banality of most commercial rock.

But there were many others who were drawn to the vibrancy of a new, emerging music scene. Among them were Paul Walthall and Gibson Haynes, and like so many other kids, they decided to form a band. They were actually a bit older than most who chose the vocation of punk music, as Gibson was already pursuing his master's degree in accounting at Trinity University, where Paul had recently stopped attending just one semester shy of his MBA.

Paul still had the guitar his parents gave him in the 3rd grade, and formed his first band, the Crowd Pleasers, in 6th grade, but he had barely picked it up since high school. He wasn't even sure he could still form a chord. But, Gibson's suggestion to start a band seemed like a pretty good way to blow off some steam, and the beauty part was that neither Paul, nor anybody, needed to be Jimmy Page to play punk rock music.

Gibson, who preferred Gibby, was on the verge of graduating after being named "Accountant of the Year" during his senior year at college. Everything seemed to come together when he scored a staff auditing job at what was the largest accounting firm in the U.S at the time: Peat, Marwick, Mitchell & Co. A golden future was sprawled out before him. He had been captain of the basketball team, president of his fraternity, and was a mere heartbeat away from the American Dream of a Cadillac in the driveway and 2.2 little tykes scampering in the yard.

But alas, most of us know at least *that* much of the story. Gibby Haynes did not go on to be the star accountant he seemed destined to become, and Paul Walthall would become known as Paul Leary, using his middle name instead of his last to avoid any embarrassing mix ups with his dad, Paul Walthall, Sr; Dean in the Business and Management school at Trinity.

They would go on to become among the most notorious figures in rock music: founders of the Butthole Surfers. And like microcosms of the movement itself, Gibby and Paul turned their backs on the establishment to create their own alternate reality, with its own set of rules: rules which were grounded in, but certainly not confined to, the punk rock movement itself.

And, as the passage of time has distorted so many memories, so too has it distorted the importance and significance of the Butthole Surfers within the realm of popular music. Today, we may think about the absurdity of a band with a name like this having a bona fide Top 40 hit song, or the unfortunate lawsuit with their former record label to obtain the rights to their old recordings. Perhaps some have heard about onstage sex shows or Gibby's stint in rehab with Nirvana front man, Kurt Cobain, but these facts and half-truths do little to divulge the true legacy of the band.

For those of us who remain in awe of the Butthole Surfers: the power and brilliance of their live performances, the originality and diversity of their recorded output, as well as their refusal to stay down despite the endless adversities heaped upon them, the Butthole Surfers are one of the most important bands in rock music history. They are not just a footnote in the histories of all the bands who have been influenced by their work, but worthy of a study all their own, and certainly worthy of more credit than they have often received.

At a time when the flame of what was the U.S. punk movement was flickering out and the alternative music scene was basically a non-entity, the Butthole Surfers were in their prime, keeping alive the last vestiges of independence long after many of the old punk bands had imploded or fizzled out. All this while the music industry floundered and wallowed in stagnation.

By 1988, they had become one of the highest grossing independent bands on the road, commanding by some accounts up to $15,000 per performance. Even before their breakthrough "hit" song, celebrity sightings at their shows were commonplace, and interns and A&R reps at major labels were wearing their t-shirts.

Their touring ethic during the 1980's was rivaled by no one. Even the legendary Minutemen, known to play 50 show tours in about as many days, had homes to return to when their tour was done. The Butthole Surfers lived out of their car for the better part of 3 whole years, with any home they had on paper merely a place to store the equipment they amassed while ping-ponging their way across the highways and bi-ways of America.

And it was in the live setting where the Butthole Surfers had you in their command. Like Ellen Ripley at the end of Ridley Scott's 'Alien', we the audience are assaulted by lights flashing and sirens wailing and the bottomless pit in our stomach as we realize that we might be eaten alive by this monster at any moment. Still, we tread slowly along hoping to reach safety, but never quite knowing what horror might lurk around the next bend.

The monster, in this case, is not some other-worldly being. The monster is us: sex, death, drugs, life, lies, neuroses, and politics. Not the politics of government, but the politics of the mind.

Certainly, the Butthole Surfers live performances were far more forms of social protest than those of just about any of the so-called 'political' bands of the era, but, there were no slogans or call to arms. Their shows were a shredding of the fabric of American society simply by pissing on the cultural norms of American society. They were a mirror held up to the faces of the guilty in power. 'You created this monster. You will be forced to acknowledge your part in this…you will feel the wrath of 10,000 Gods if you do not build us a bride!!'

Ahem…but, of the music, you say?

The Butthole Surfers' music is at once endlessly diverse while still being uniquely Texan. They are the amalgam of the multitude of musical styles their home state delivered over the previous 50 years or longer: from country to garage to psychedelia to classic rock. They owe as much to Roky Erickson as they do to the Dicks, and while their early sound resembled the latter, they would always, even in their earliest incarnations, pay homage to the rich musical roots that ran deep beneath the oil-rich soils of Texas.

Listening to the first EP, which the band released on Alternative Tentacles Records around July of 1983, one can hear everything from raging hardcore to delta blues to late 70's post punk and dime-store psychedelia. From bawdy sea chanteys to art damaged noise; the record a skewer a kabob of more genres than it has songs themselves.

And as the idea of what it meant to be punk in the 1970's began to give way to the narrow-minded view of what punk rock was supposed to be by the middle-1980's, the Butthole Surfers was one of the only undeniably "punk" bands that was able to maintain its fan base, even while the strobe lights pumped, the films rolled behind them, and 10 minute improvisational jams became staples of their live experiences.

Of course, their success, however modest, was not an overnight phenomenon. A long slog was traveled to garner even the humble amount of recognition they were able to achieve. The irony that the band was able to release their first EP may even overshadow the irony that a band so vehemently anti- establishment was able to score a Top 40 hit song.

Before they had time to ponder any triumphs, they were on to the next town, recording their next session, or cultivating their next incarnation. Just when you thought you could predict what was coming next you were left stupefied. By the time you were rising, they were in Phoenix.

And like history distorted by time and perceptions, the Butthole Surfers story has been based on as much legend as on facts: lost in a cloud of Dadaist ramblings and inside doody jokes. Few interviewers yielded any real information about the band and fewer still were left with any more of an understanding than that which they had upon entering the smoke-filled room.

As for the albums, they were released with no song titles on the sleeves, no liner notes, no studio information, no recording or engineering credits, no band member lists or photos or lyrics, and often with the suggestion that you play the record itself at 69rpm. Fans were left to fend for themselves for any iota of information they could gather.

In the world of punk rock where so many bands were attempting to change the listener's minds by telling them what they should think, with lyrics printed on the sleeves of records and inner sheets filled with political posturing, the Butthole Surfers never claimed to have the answers. They never tried to tell you that the world is fucked up. They simply created a fucked-up world all their own, and through that, held a mirror to society that spoke volumes about our own skewed norms and values.

By converting their own congregation of freaks, outcasts, and misfits who existed outside of "normal society", they themselves became a dangerous political movement. A certain secret society within, but separate from, the so-called normal society at large. And a secret society is far more dangerous to the AmeriKKKan way of life than screaming to change the political machine from within its confines. Certainly, the Attorney General and FBI believe this is true; ask David Koresh or

Randy Weaver.

It was a creation of an alternate society and alternate reality free from the confines of time and space…floating high in the air and rebounding down from the ceiling…like a voice spinning in endless repetition of a phrase over and over again, sped up to a high pitched chirp…with a bit of flange…zapping around the room…backwards and forwards, and high above your head before fluttering away into the stratosphere….fade out…

Fade In...

The sun finally began to emerge from behind the clouds in the afternoon sky. A crowd of thousands stood outside in a sprawling English field, drenched; their feet and trouser bottoms caked in mud. They had already witnessed the appropriately rain-soaked sets from many of their fellow countrymen at this festival event when the only U.S. band on the bill took to the stage. The singer, with more than a hint of irony, croons the opening refrain of Depeche Mode's "Sacred"

,.. To put it in words, to write it down, that is walking on hallowed ground, but it's my duty…I'm a missionary…"

The guitar player steps up to a mic:

"There's a time to fuck and a time to crave, but the Shah sleeps in Lee Harvey's GRAAAAAVE!!!!"

A wall of white noise screams out of the speakers; cymbals splash and drums pound; bass notes bend and groan. A guitar shrieks and wails before a final crash brings it all down into a solitary drone of feedback.

"There's a time to shit and a time for God, the last shit I took, was pretty fukkin' HAAAAAARRRRRRD!!!!!!"

The noise blasts out once again, only now it is joined by a scowling, moaning voice: looping above the bewildered crowd. Like Chris MacNeil listening from downstairs to that thing that used to be her daughter, locked away up in her room: ungodly. There is a manic scramble up and down the fretboards before the noise dampens, once again, down to a dull whine:

There's a time fer drugs and a time to be sane, but Jimi Hendrix makes love to the corpse of Marilyn Monroe!!" [sic]

The Gates of Hell crash open as people far in the back, many of whom had been in attendance to witness earlier sets by Jesus Jones and Voice of the Beehive, turn their heads to see exactly what in God's holy name is happening up on the stage.

There's a time to live and a time to die, I smoke Elvis Presley's toenails when I wanna get HIIIIIIIIIIGH!!!....

Screeching guitars. Inevitable laughter erupts. Some cheer. Some stand appalled, some in slack-jawed confusion as the noise becomes completely trance inducing...the last refrain repeats the first:

"There's a time to fuck and a time to crave, but the Shah sleeps in Lee Harvey's GRAAAAAVE!!!!"

Violence erupts on the stage ...the bass strap snaps off from around the bass guitarist's neck as the last few strums are raked across its strings...He swings it violently above his head and slams down, the strap cracking like a whip against the stage. The guitarist, too, slips off his guitar and joins along in the ritual. Bits of bridges and volume knobs shatter into the crowd...another swing and the instruments finally crack in two. The neck separates from the body and turns completely around... the amps moan in pain...The exorcism is done. Father Karas lies dying on the street at the bottom of the stairs.

"I see you trembling, you look like shit!....I am the ultimate God, God is second to me!!...don't look back at me, mutherfukker!...don't even gaze upon me with your naked eye!!"

The players heave a few breaths and survey the debris field. They turn back to retrieve new instruments as the singer returns to his microphone...

"Ladies and Gentlemen, the most dedicated band in the history of Texas rock'n'roll: the goddamned Butthole Surfers!"

Surely none of the multitudes in the audience could argue with this declaration, even if it was self-professed. Nobody could look away, whether in awe of the beauty and audacity, or appalled by the grotesque noise. All eyes were fixed forward. But, even the most ardent supporters of the Butthole Surfers might have misconstrued Gibby's proclamation on that day.

After all, it certainly takes a band dedicated to entertaining to smash their instruments to pieces during their opening number. But, the Butthole Surfers were not just dedicated to entertaining the crowd at the Reading Festival on this particular day. This appearance was, in many ways, the culmination of the previous decade's worth of sweat and toil.

Through the better part of the 1980's, the Butthole Surfers were on the road, dropping acid to stay awake for marathon 3000-mile drives to gigs on opposite coasts. They lived out of a van for three solid years without homes, love interests, or money of which to speak. The road was where they made their living, and the foundation upon which they built their legendary reputation. The early part of the decade was spent meandering the streets and back alleys of towns to get themselves noticed, the latter part was spent flying to play one-off gigs at large theatres to satisfy the throngs of

Gibby at Reading, 8/27/89
© Ric Wallace

freaks, punks, art-fags and ne'er-do-wells who worshipped the ground upon which they walked.

When the decision was made that the Butthole Surfers would be their full-time jobs, there was no guarantee that their plan would work, or if there was a plan to begin with. It was a huge gamble on which to hedge their bets. But what began as a joke was cherished as if it was their one true calling. There was no "Plan B" in the minds of Gibby and Paul. If this endeavor failed, they would be jobless. Homeless. Dead.

Their ethos, if there was one, was to keep moving, keep playing, keep writing, and to record when the opportunity afforded itself. There was no stopping to rest. No luxury of settling down for any length of time to write songs before spending weeks in the studio practicing and polishing demos. Write songs in the RV, drive to the next gig and try them out in their set. The band's tour schedule became the stuff of legends. They settled down long enough in one city to play a dozen or so shows in the area, only to head back out onto the road again for months on end.

18

Since leaving the stability of San Antonio in the summer of 1984, they spent most of their lives touring. They bought a cheap trailer and gutted out (then bass player) Terence Smart's Chevy Nova and piled in, with their equipment in tow. Belched out from Texas and onto the highways of America.

Even that first makeshift tour of the United States seemed unlikely in the years leading up it. Most of their early existence was spent searching for people who were willing to join them. They would welcome anyone into the studio who could tolerate Paul's Stratocaster onslaught and Gibby's sardonic wit, regardless of their abilities or their punk rock credentials.

The band began in the living room of a house shared by Scott Mathews and mutual friend Cheryl Dawn Dyer on Woodlawn Avenue. It was just off campus from Trinity University, where they all attended. Scott took the throne behind the drum set and another Trinity pal, Scott Stevens, strapped on a bass guitar. Paul had taken the money he received as a refund from his student loans and bought some guitars and amps and they were instantly and irrevocably in the business of making music.

Within a few scant months of their first practices, they were playing parties at the Butthole Manor, as Scott referred to his humble rental estate. It was on or about May 17, 1981 when they scored their first public gig, at an exhibit opening featuring some of Cheryl's artwork at the Shawn-Davenport Art Gallery. The band had not actually settled upon a name at the time, as thoughts of playing out to people who weren't their closest friends had barely even crossed their minds. They only had a handful of songs written, but music was not their concern. This show was all about action and reaction.

Gibby had become a bit of a local celebrity himself some months earlier for his art piece entitled "Hold the Pickles at Auschwitz". The piece, which depicted dozens of 'chalk' outlines laid one on top of another on the floor, was startlingly original, and completely thought provoking, Cheryl recalls. Parents Weekend was coming, however, and the chair of the art department at Trinity was understandably squeamish about its display at the school, and the prospect of offending any potential alumni and donors. A censorship battle ensued between students and administration that made local papers, fueled by Cheryl more so than Gibby, she slyly confesses.

The owners of the Shawn-Davenport caught wind of the battle and offered up their space to display and perform without fear of reprisals from the Deans or the Cabinet at the prestigious, private institution. After only a couple of performances, however, even the liberal owners of the gallery were questioning their views on censorship, and kindly requested that they find a more suitable venue for their 'art'.

For the show, they had gone about cutting hundreds of sheets of paper into squares, each piece containing a photocopy of a photograph of a cockroach that Gibby had caught in his apartment, named Shiny, and claimed as his pet. One side of the paper had the top side of the creature, the other side had the bottom. They stuffed mannequins with the roach confetti, as well as with household appliances, food and utensils, and random found items.

Gibby roughed up the dummies and then passed them around for the blood-thirsty crowd to rip to shreds. An alarm clock inside one of the effigies was swung around like a rodeo lasso. It was a bacchanalia of free form expression, and the small crowd watched with glee. The shows at the Shawn-Davenport continued the tradition Cheryl started with her own solo exhibits at Trinity, where mixed-media pieces adorned the walls while lesbians on roller skates offered hors d'oeuvres to patrons.

If there was any motivation behind forming the band, aside from alleviating the boredom of watching other horrible bands while they stood around in frustration, it was to provoke a response. The music and performances, like the paintings and silkscreens they all created, were meant to elicit a visceral reaction. Their mission was accomplished on this occasion, and at the closing of the exhibit, as well.

❧

Scott Mathews:
"Paul used to go around San Antonio writing things on people's doors and stuff. He had little Xerox things with little phrases on them like "SELF-CONTAINED UNIT" that he used to paste on people's doors. He was into that whole guerilla art thing. We were sort of doing performance art. Gibby was one of the first guys on campus to jump into the whole punk rock thing."
[2001, Chris Smart interview]

❧

It would be a few more months before they would become the Butthole Surfers, but even as the Dick Gas Five, the name they opted for on that particular performance, the seeds were being tilled for a revolution of the mind.

The Five tore through their short set with a fervor and got a spirited response from the modest crowd. Songs like "Peggy on Mannix" and "Out of Control (Bodies)" were part comedy, part art damaged noise, and part sloppy\poppy British influenced punk rock. They were still better at printmaking than they were at playing their instruments, but music was more visceral and fun.

No one who witnessed the shows at the gallery would seemingly ever forget them. They had been left indelibly scarred, and it wasn't long before the Dick Gas Five began creating a buzz in the few local bars around campus that would have them play.

San Antonio is a college town, but it wasn't the hot spot for new music, and certainly not for punk rock. Most of the Trinity frat boys and preppies just didn't get it, and the art department, the one enclave of free thinkers, was only so big. Austin was the place to be if you were playing anything other than country-western or bad cover songs. So, the yet-to-be-dubbed Butthole Surfers decided to send a tape out to the Big Boys, who had become darlings of the local circuit in Austin, to see if they'd help get them some shows together in the capital region.

Upon hearing the cassette, the Big Boys, too, were impressed. Perhaps more at their audacity than the music they heard but upon meeting, the two bands hit it off almost immediately. Before long, the Big Boys and Butthole Surfers were playing together at clubs all around Austin. They'd pulled drives to Dallas and Houston as well, and even played back in San Antonio, where a show with the mighty Big Boys might actually draw a crowd.

Soon enough, the band that had been using a different name every show was gaining a small following of their own with their own brand of wild antics, something they would need if they were going to rival the larger-than-life Big Boys. By the time anyone had the chance to hear of them, however, they had become the Dick Clark Five.

The name of the band didn't matter much, getting people out to the shows did. Hence, the Dick Clark Five begat The Vodka Family Winstons. The Vodka Family Winstons begat The Ashtray Babyheads. The Ashtray Babyheads begat the Bleeding Skulls; the Bleeding Skulls begat the Secret Blood Nurses, or Scottish Donkey Logs, every day a different name. Ed Asner is Gay, The Right to Eat Fred Astaire's Asshole, Abe Lincoln's Bush. The list of potential names on any given day was endless.

During the early 1980's the Texas punk scene became notorious for what would be known as "poster bands", bands that existed in name only for the sole purpose of creating and promoting guerilla artwork. Posters would be hung up on any spare telephone pole announcing bands that never existed except on the art that advertised them. The band that eventually became the Butthole Surfers was real, but they obviously had this same mentality in mind.

Quinn Mathews:
"The big source of entertainment was to come up with the dumbest names, like Dick Gas Five, Dick Clark Five, Dick Christ Five, whatever had a 'Dick' in it. Later they had the Ashtray Babyheads and the Secret Blood Nurses. The early stuff was based on Gibby and Paul sitting around drinking beer and thinking up dumb stuff. Those guys were a great team together as far as creativity goes. They'd just bounce off each other."
[Chris Smart interview, 2001]

As one of the infinite number of legends that have been conjured up about the band over their long and enigmatic history, how the name Butthole Surfers was finally settled upon remains a mystery. Legend states that they were mistakenly introduced as such by the Big Boys' bass player Chris Gates, who confused their moniker du jour with the name of one of their latest songs. They played a good set, and even got paid $150 bucks, more money than they were probably worth at the time. It was their first paying gig and, believing it was a good omen, they ran with it.

Dick Gas 5 @ La Vallita Patio, San Antonio, 9/4/81
© Bill Daniel

Yet like most of the stories swirling around the band, it's hard to separate Butthole truth from actual truth. As early as their first known club gig, the name Butthole Surfers was being used on flyers, as was Dick Clark 5…sometimes for the same show. They used the Scottish Donkey Logs well into their career as Butthole Surfers as well. Whatever the reality may be, the name was one that everyone could agree would shock, bemuse, and offend, and so the Butthole Surfers was born.

The rest of 1981 was spent writing songs and booking shows, often with the Big Boys and equally iconic, Dicks. Randy 'Biscuit' Turner, singer of the Big Boys, was always one to promote how cool the Texas fringe was, and he was instrumental in getting touring punk bands from all across the U.S., Los Angeles, San Francisco, Washington DC, and everywhere in between to stop for a spell and play deep in the bowels of Texas.

While bands were in town, Biscuit, or fellow bandmates Tim Kerr and Chris Gates, would hook them up with good eats, a place to crash, and tapes of some of their favorite local bands to bring with them for the long drives to God knows where. As the
word began to get out that Dallas, Houston and Austin had vibrant underground scenes of their own, and weren't solely full of rednecks, Texas became a viable place for punk bands to play. No longer would the Circle Jerks, Black Flag, the Misfits or Minor Threat skip the Lone Star State when booking their tours across the USA.

Soon tapes of local bands, including the Butthole Surfers, were circulating far outside of the borders of Texas, thanks to the Big Boys endless promotion of the scene, and the open-minded punks who were listening.

The Big Boys seemingly looked at the Butthole Surfers as the band to carry the torch of they had set aflame several years prior. And like the Big Boys, the Butthole Surfers were a melding of punk and art that was as much about the art of performance (not necessarily performance art) as the art of music.

Clothespins, mousetraps, stuffed animals, fake blood capsules and an endless array of costume changes became as much a part of the show as the music itself. The MC5 once called The Stooges their little brothers, and the relationship between the Big Boys and the Butthole Surfers during their early days was nearly identical.
It was difficult to take your eyes off the Big Boys when they started their sets: with Biscuit donning dresses and costumes and commanding the stage with a larger-than-life presence to match his hulking mass. Along with the girth of Chris Gates and the spaced-out, alien locks of guitarist Tim Kerr, the Big Boys were a mighty force to behold and the Butthole Surfers had to come up with some tricks of their own if they were going to be noticed at all.

But not even the insane and hilarious antics of Biscuit, Gary Floyd, or even Gibby himself for that matter, could detract from the vast array of quality music being pumped out of Texas at the time. It was often as angry as any of the LA bands that were making headlines, but it showcased a much greater diversity and tongue-in-cheek humor. This gave many Texas punk bands more dimension than many of their LA counterparts.

The big 'Fuck You' spat out by LA bands like Black Flag, GERMS and FEAR was given a new spin by most of the bands from Texas, who didn't have a seemingly endless pool of punks to piss off. The Texas scene was, almost by necessity, more inclusive; inviting fans onstage and encouraging them form their own bands.

This aesthetic obviously had a huge influence on a band like the Butthole Surfers, who themselves would eventually become like a community of freaks operating completely separate from the rules which governed the society outside of their own insular world.

❧

Andrew Mullin:
"The show we played at La Villita in SA, around Labor Day of 81, was my first encounter with the Big Boys, and it was memorable, impactful, if also sort of shattering. Shattering in the sense that they were living, breathing exemplars of punk, on their way to being monsters of funk, as well, and endowed with ferocious energy and presence.
As things progressed, in terms of subsequent shows, I was never half clued-in to what was going on, in terms of who was deciding what or where we were headed next. Maybe on Wednesday I'd get it at practice that we were going Austin for a Friday show.
We'd piled in a pair of Toyotas and scream up to Austin to play with the Big Boys at the Klub Foot. I don't think I had a clue where we were going, or what that joint was about, but we walked in and it's like 'oh, shit, they got a sound system AND lights? What are we doing here?'" [via email 2024]

❧

And, like a kid in the corner with his back turned laughing to himself, more and more kids came over to see what all the fuss was all about. Soon, shows started to fill up, and the venues got larger. A bill of Big Boys, Butthole Surfers and the Offenders which once would be booked at small club like the Studio 29, would soon call for a theatre the size of the Ritz, to hold all the kids who were coming out.

Within a year of playing their first show, the Butthole Surfers had a small, but fervent following in and around Austin, Dallas, Houston, and San Antonio. After original bassist Scott Stevens left toward the end of August 1981 to focus on his own visual art, Paul, Gibby and Scott Mathews called upon Andrew Mullin to take over.

Andrew had a car, and Gibby had an old Dan Electro bass. They spent much of their time terrorizing the campus of Trinity; smoking weed, playing nude tennis, making their guerilla art projects. Silk screened pillowcases of Lee Harvey Oswald, mixed media collages on cardboard and, of course, the cacophony of sound.

At night, they'd jam or drive to Austin and catch local acts. Head over to Gibby's dorm room where he set up a massive stereo system featuring a Bang & Olufsen turntable that looked alien, and a very capable amp and set of perhaps Klipsch speakers. Rewards of being the son of Mr. Peppermint. Gibby knew what to look for and where to find it, Andrew recalls, and they'd blast Devo, Wire, the Ramones and Residents on Gib's state-of-the-art equipment. Andrew was more of a Doug Sahm afficionado at first but he quickly got schooled in some of the newer mavericks causing a stir in the scene.

Gibby, Andrew & Paul, 9/4/81 © Bill Daniel

Although a guitar player at heart, Andrew seemed a natural choice to take over the empty space as bassist. In no time a set developed with songs like, "British Accent" "Motorcycle Wreck", and "Negro Observer".

But, his demise was in motion from before he even joined the band. A relationship that blossomed into a marriage and a job delivering furniture forced him to move into a seedier section of town and made getting to practice a challenge. A violent robbery left him shaken, and a car accident with an expired license only caused more trauma and hardship. Drinking and the Rx drugs prescribed to deal with his injuries wreaked even more havoc on his emotional state. After a gig in Houston, in what seemed like a moment of clarity, he decided what he needed to do. Set himself on fire.

Studio 29, Dec 19. 1981
© Dixon Edge Coulbourn

Andrew:
"During one of those long, dark rides back from a weekend in Houston, I just sort of lapsed into this "I have a new vision" thing. A simple way to put it is that I decided to blow town. What's more complicated, and still confusing to me, is to say why, or what I planned to do. I had some money, incredibly, so

one evening, following a day of toxic-level alcohol intake, I got a cab to the airport and just booked a flight out to…Phoenix.
Why Phoenix? Why indeed, still don't recall. I did have this dimly formed idea to walk out of the airport and just wander off into the desert, sort of go hide under the rocks and evaporate. Somewhere along this phase, I did briefly consider the self-immolation option." [interview July 2024]

Mixed media on cardboard 1981 by Andrew Mullin

Quinn:
"They did a show at the Omni in Houston and Andrew Mullin took a bunch of acid and took all the band funds and hopped on a plane to L.A, so they decided to be a three-piece.
I was watching a show in Houston with Diana from the Mydolls and we both thought they sucked so I decided I would be their bass player.

I picked up their bass in the practice room and learned all the songs from a tape. They auditioned several people but, it didn't work out, so I played a set with them and became their bass player." [Chris Smart interview, 2001]

Paul & Gibby (hidden) watch the Big Boys, Texas Love In, January 16, 1982
© Dixon Edge Coulbourn

Andrew:

"I was somewhat non-plussed to learn that some versions of the departure story have me stealing band money. This is so far off, egregious, that I find it sort of amusing, as in, I was never aware that the band even had any money.   If they did, who was the treasurer? No idea. It's worth pointing out here that the pay I can recollect from the band's shows consisted of 1.5 cans of Schlitz from Phil at the Island in Houston, and some weed that the crew up in Dallas paid us with for a New Year's gig at Mohawk Mike's." [interview, 2024]

After a couple of shows as a trio, with Paul taking the role of bassist and Gibby on guitar, the band finally solidified a core lineup of Gibby and Paul, with Scott Mathews on drums and his younger brother Quinn on bass.

Quinn Mathews had been living with Scott and Cheryl Dyer after having recently dropped out of San Marcos Baptist Military Academy and picked up the bass that Andrew put down to go and die.

Once established, the new Butthole Surfers band spent most of its free time practicing at the Mathews' place, or at Bob O'Neil Sound Studios (nee: the BOSS) in San Antonio; writing songs and laying down demos. Much of the rest of the time was spent ping-ponging around the state; playing shows at the Omni or the Island in Houston, or at Studio D in Dallas, or Mulligan's and the Bonham Exchange in San Antonio, or the Club Foot and Studio 29 in Austin. With the number of shows increasing, Scott Mathews sold his car to buy a 1976 Chevy van to accommodate all the band's equipment on treks to and from gigs.

What began as a tongue-in-cheek joke between Gibby and Paul had turned into a true quest. How far could they take this thing called they called the Butthole Surfers? No doubt, by the time Gibby decided to leave his lucrative job as a staff auditor at Peat, Marwick and Mitchell in the spring of 1982 (hastened by some nasty pictures he left in the company photocopier), he already had his heart and mind set on being a Butthole Surfer.

He certainly felt as if he had a higher calling, and not just as publisher of 'Strange V.D.' Magazine, his own subversive, hand-distributed fanzine of all things communicable for which the photocopies were intended. No, the Butthole Surfers would become the vehicle of his subversion, and now with lots of free time on his hands, his band took center stage.

He had been jetting to practice after long hours in the office, stripping off his suit and tie down to his boxers in the oppressive heat of the studio; a tradition he kept when playing shows as well. Now, he donned torn jeans wrinkled t-shirt when showing up to practices, and the shedding of his suit and tie for good was like King Kong breaking free of his shackles.

After nearly a year and a half of playing late nights in seedy dives, dealing with the shriek of the all- too- early morning alarm clock's beckon, it had to be liberating to finally be able to sleep in and forsake the daywear and long shifts of the working week, even if it was for the filth and destitution of being in a punk rock band. It was as if the sky had opened and God himself had spoken to Gibby. That is perhaps the only explanation that could justify the insanity of leaving the safety and security of a well-paying job to join a punk rock band, well into his 20's and well on his way to becoming a financially secure accountant.

It was with his new epiphany and sense of purpose that the band finally decided it was time to see what else might be out there beyond the borders of Texas. They looked westward into the setting sun. It was, after all, the Golden State of California that had spawned some of the most infamous punk bands of the time, and there was a seemingly endless supply of venues to play. The punk rock scene in Los Angeles was massive, where 3500 capacity auditoriums would sell out with bills like Black Flag, DOA, and Minutemen.

The hardcore movement was in full swing in LA by the summer of 1982 and there was fear in the minds of parents and school administrators alike. Punk rock was being featured on national TV programs, with Tom Snyder and Rona Barrett asking parents if they knew what their kids were up to at the concerts they were attending. Parents were paranoid, kids were curious, and venues were packed. Money was there for the taking and ready to be plucked like the forbidden fruit.

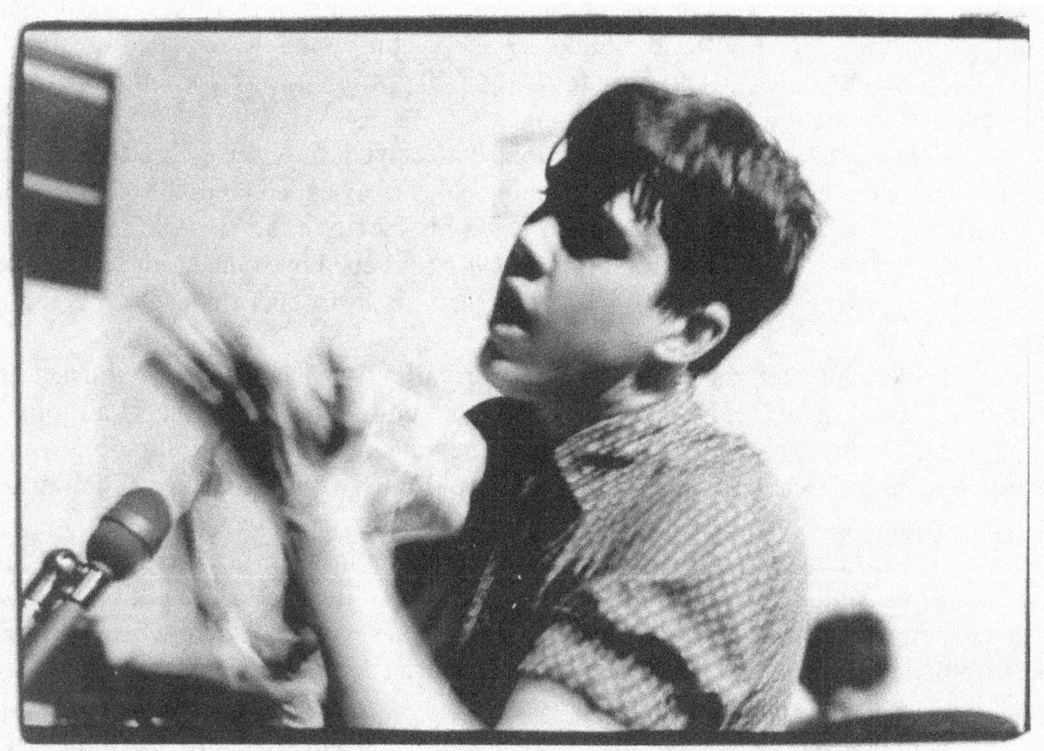

Gibby at Studio 29, Austin, TX, 12/19/81
© Bill Daniel

Well, that was the perception, at least. This group of young men from Texas were still a tad wet behind the ears when it came to the music business. While they may have been correct that Texas didn't have much to offer them in terms of success, they couldn't have possibly imagined the shitstorm they were about to endure once they hit the west coast.

They played a huge sold-out show with the Big Boys and Offenders at the Ritz in Austin on June 4, 1982, and said goodbye to Cheryl and to the few but faithful fans in Texas, then packed up their equipment and left to seek their fame and fortune under the bloody red sun of fantastic LA.

The show at the Ritz was a wonderful send-off for the band, and it gave them the justification and confidence they needed to on their way out west. They were excited and filled with the hubris of Odysseus as they set off on their journey. There was little doubt that after defeating the odds in Texas, they would prevail on their adventure to the bright lights and glamour of the City of Angels.

But Austin is a long way from Los Angeles, and even playing two sets a night to hoard as much cash as possible before the trip, the boys were living on a shoe-string budget.

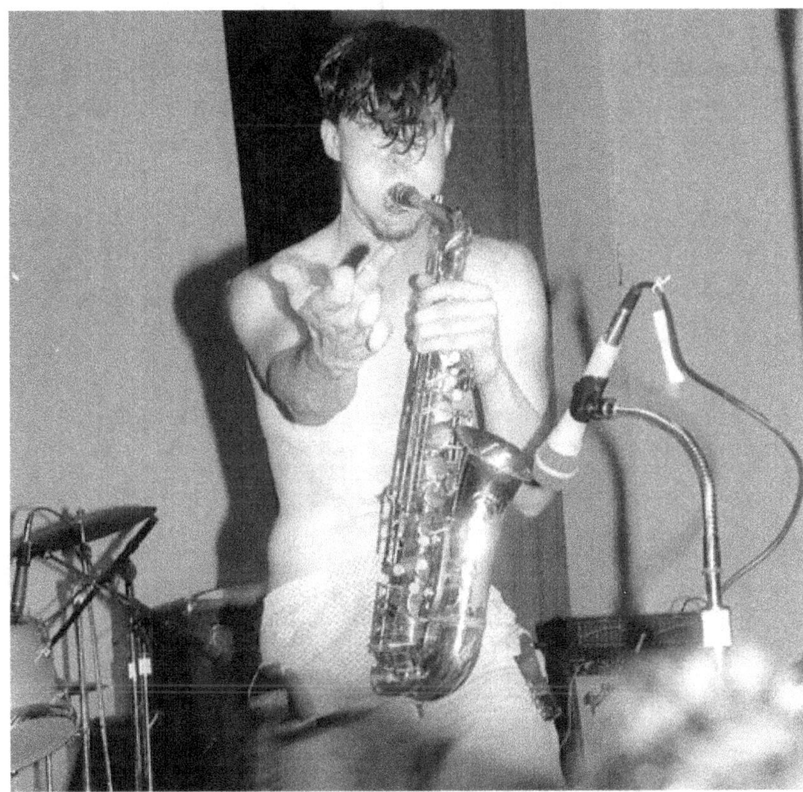

Gibby bids adieu at their goodbye show at the Ritz, June 4, 1982
© Dixon Edge Coulbourn

Their minds were filled with delusions of grandeur yet there was still a hole in their tender little hearts that couldn't be filled by merely playing punk rock in front of a handful of people for peanuts. It was a longing of sorts. The nagging need for companionship during their long drive into the sun. So, on their way out of town the boys stopped at an animal shelter to pick up a sad pooch that, like themselves, needed a home and the love of some newfound friends. A true loyal fan who wouldn't judge them on their crazy, naïve notions and that would love them unconditionally. They would all make it out to California together, with mouths agape and tongues wagging.

And so they adopted Brown Dog, a beautiful, stout, pit bull terrier. She instantly became the band's leader and biggest fan as she led them across the sands of New Mexico and into Arizona. Like Noah leading the Israelites across the Red Sea of destruction, she led her exiles out of the desert and toward their own personal New Jerusalem on their sweltering and cramped voyage westward.

Gibby had done a decent enough job planning the open-ended trip out west and had gotten the band a gig in Arizona on the way. He got on the horn with Tony Victor, the man responsible for booking just about every punk rock show in and around the Phoenix area and Tony was able to squeeze them onto a bill with local darlings JFA at Merlin's. Tony even hooked the boys up with a place to stay for the night.

Brown Dog stayed obediently tethered to a tree outside while the four Buttholes grabbed spots on Tony's floor. JFA had raged and the boys just knew they were in for a great trip: Killer bands, sweet, perfumed desert Indica and the promise of a new life away from Texas; what more could they ask for?

Gibby and Quinn, 6/4/82
© Bill Daniel

Tony Victor (promoter)
"I remember it well... It was a Tuesday evening at Merlin's in Tempe. I squeezed them into an already scheduled show. Don't know who was playing that night. They stayed at my house. They left Brown Dog's leash tied to my front yard tree." [email, 2005]

There was also a bit of a support network in California once they arrived. They had friends up in the San Francisco Bay area in MDC, who left Austin several months earlier to seek some relief from the blazing Texas heat and half empty clubs for the broader audiences and more accepting venues in the City by the Bay. MDC had become a model of success to the punk bands of TX, having formed their own record label, R Radical Records, and releasing their own blistering first album themselves, the now classic, 'Millions of Dead Cops'.

The Big Boys were also heading out to the big CA for a west coast jaunt and they lined up a gig for them both to play later that month with the Descendents at the Grandia Room. Despite the support network in San Francisco, there was no way of knowing when the Butthole Surfers would ever get settled in their new hometown. They had little money to spend on extravagances like hotels, had no leads on a pad, and no friends of which to speak down south in Los Angeles.

Gibby and Paul had visited LA before they started the band, selling some of the Lee Harvey Oswald silkscreens they had made on Venice Beach for some spare change, but they still were entering town as complete strangers. The little they did know about LA centered around the fact that it was the home of SST Records, which was releasing the albums of all their favorite bands at the time.

It was the first Meat Puppets LP on SST that inspired Paul to pick his guitar up again after it sat dormant in its case for nearly his entire four years at Trinity after his high school graduation. Gibby wanted to form a band, but Paul was reluctant. It was the fury of that first, eponymously named record, with its vague country twang veiled behind a shrieking blaze of hardcore fury that struck a nerve with Paul and gave him the courage and desire to give guitar playing one last try. Along with the Minutemen, Husker Du, and the legendary Black Flag, the stable of bands on SST records gave them the inspiration they needed to give punk rock a try. The label seemed to espouse to the DIY mentality of helping struggling bands in need and this gave them an idea. With no place else to go, they showed up on the doorstep of the SST offices in Long Beach, wide-eyed and looking for a handout.

SST was started in 1966 as Solid-State Transmitters, selling the electronic equipment of its 12-year-old founder and manufacturer, Greg Ginn. By 1978, SST was repurposed as a vehicle for Ginn's latest business venture as guitarist of Black Flag. At no point in SST's existence was it ever a hotel, yet there was an old, stinky mattress under the console desk they were told they could use. Black Flag's lead singer, Henry Rollins, used to sleep on it when practices ran into the wee hours. If they could stand the pungent smell of stale sweat, it was decided, the band could hunker down for the evening.

Beggars certainly couldn't be choosers about their sleeping accommodations and the Butthole Surfers were just a step above vagabonds at this point. They didn't even own a sleeping bag between the four of them. The space was cramped, and the mattress was filthy, but they were more than happy to be able to sleep anywhere outside of the sweatbox that was their van.

Strat-o-sphere 1982
© Edward Colver

The next day they hung around the SST offices, meeting staff and getting a feel for the inner workings at the label. Robo was there, a punk rock legend in his own right, splitting his time drumming with Black Flag and legendary horrorphiles, the Misfits. He was endeared to the Buttholes commitment to branching out from Texas, but mentioned he thought that they needed some product to get some cash in their pockets. Robo had never met the Butthole Surfers before, but this sage advice would loom over them like a dark cloud, long after Black Flag departed LA a couple of days later for their summer tour of the US.

With no product to sell, they had little prospect of making any real money aside from gigs. And while playing shows was a top priority in their minds, there was only one booked so far. It seemed as if they still had a lot to learn about the business of music, even though Paul was a mere semester shy of his MBA, and Gibby had been an accountant. The important thing was that they were out of Texas, and despite the oversight of not having any product to sell, they were ready to take California by storm.

As the afternoon waned and the summer's sun dipped low in the sky, the boys hopped into their van and headed over to the Grandia Room to get ready for their evening's performance with the Minutemen.

The Minutemen were one of Paul's favorite bands, and he was completely gobsmacked upon meeting the three troubadours. Only a day into their trip and he was already meeting some of his musical heroes. It was a dream come true. The two bands hit it off almost immediately and this introduction began a lifelong friendship.

Paul:
"We gave D Boon a ride in our van after that first show. And we had hung with Robo before the show. I was starstruck. We had come to town the day before the show and slept at SST. We just showed up and they let us crash. I slept on a mattress under a desk that supposedly belonged to Rollins when he wasn't on tour. It stank." [email, 2012]

When Paul's mom, Doris, grilled him about the ill-advised move to LA, he cited the vibrancy of the scene, pointing to the Minutemen specifically as his inspiration to leave Texas. *"There's a band out there that writes a 100 songs a week,"* he told her, repeating the folklore of the day. Paul's mom replied, *"That's because they can't stand the ones they've already written!"* A classic parental retort which really meant, "Get your head out of your ass, son."

But, Paul's head was firmly implanted up there and his heart was dead set on going to Los Angeles. His mom was forced to concede defeat as she waved goodbye and her son drove westward to pursue his new career. Now, here he was in LA only one day and already living his dream. D. Boon, George Hurley, and Mike Watt were talking to *him,* imparting their wisdom and well wishes. It was something he could have barely imagined while grinding out an existence in the clubs of Texas.

On June 10, 1982, a week after departing from San Antonio, the Butthole Surfers play their first gig as California state residents.

Your Pain Makes Me Hungry

The packed club was heaving in anticipation. The house lights dim on the tiny stage and an amplifier's buzz becomes audible as the kids in the crowd start to sway and jockey for position.

With the house music still pumping out of the speakers, the first strains of "Matchstick" lurch from Paul's guitar. The intro chugs and bubbles into a slow simmer as the soundman struggles to quell a nagging bit of mid-range feedback. After what seems like an eternity, Gibby staggers up to the microphone and spits out the first strains of the lyrics.

"Matchstick...Rolling down a 2x4....Tight fit...Nothing like I've seen before'.

The Mathews bros come crashing in, as Gibby pleads:

'...don't fuck me...in the ass this time...no shit, matchstick, I'm running outta time, I'm running outta words that will f-f-f-f-f-f-fucking rhyme...'

With mousetraps dangling from his nipples and shaggy hair, Gibby rolls around in his underwear and hurls venom and a bag full of photocopied cockroaches at the crowd:

...Hey! You! Get outta my life...I hate your guts, I fuck your wife...'

The kids thrash themselves around in time. The off-kilter music doesn't really lend itself to a typical slam dance, but that doesn't deter them from throwing themselves into each other anyway. Paul's face contorts as if he's choking the notes out of his guitar, plucking and bending the strings, before sliding the neck against his mic stand...

'Something she said to me last night...something she said to me...When I kicked her in the teeth she was out the door, I just know she'll be back for more...'

As the band crashes to a halt, the crowd gives them a smattering of applause and yells requests for songs they've already played.

The band is still bleary-eyed from doing little else other than driving, drinking and playing shows since leaving San Antonio, but they could still see a tidal change from the old dives they were restricted to while still in Texas. They blazed through their 40-minute set, and despite being relative unknowns to the crowd on hand, they receive a spirited response. The Minutemen play an equally inspired, or rather awe-inspiring, set.

At the Grandia, 6/10/82
© Edward Colver

Paul recalls the tiny plywood stage at the Grandia sagging, bulging, and bending under the massive weight of D. Boon bounding himself about the club.

In the nearly three years and four releases since the Minutemen had evolved, they themselves had just begun to reap the rewards of the vibrant LA scene. Though still far from having the star power of their fellow label mates Black Flag, the minutemen's infusion of manic jazz, funk, and punk rock was finally winning them over with crowds and critics alike. A good-sized cult following was beginning to develop around them despite their deviation from many of the already ingrained punk

D Boon (left) and Mike Watt from the Minutemen, Wilson Park, May 22, 1982
© Dirk Vandenberg

rituals. They didn't spike their hair, they didn't pose, and Mike Watt wore flannel in homage to some of his musical heroes, Creedence Clearwater Revival. They didn't even distort their guitars.

Like the Butthole Surfers, the Minutemen, and their compatriots and labelmates the Meat Puppets, congealed their influences, often originating far outside the genre of punk, and melded them all into an entirely new beast. Country, funk, and no-wave minimalism could all be deciphered through the blazing, blistering fast, punk rock they played.

Mike Watt, D. Boon and George Hurley built their modest career around playing shows. Even here in 1982, before their first official tour of the U.S., their name was nearly omnipresent on flyers in record shops and stapled on telephone poles from their hometown of San Pedro, at venues like Dancing Waters, all the way up the coast to the Mabuhay Gardens in San Francisco.

Upon branching out and across the United States for the first time in 1983, their tours became marathons; 50 gigs in 53 days were not unheard of, and that ethos would be the roadmap that the Butthole Surfers would follow.

'If you're not playing, you're paying'... Mike Watt

Quinn and Scott
© Edward Colver

The two bands smoked the mota, yucked it up, and compared band notes as friends, fans, and well-wishers meandered in and out of their conversation. At some point it was overheard that somehow these 4 guys from Texas who had blown into town just the day before had no place to stay. Paul still had the stink of Rollins' mattress etched into his nasal passages, and SST surely wasn't running a flophouse for wayward punk bands. The idea of returning to their offices for another night's sleep seemed a non-starter.

Thankfully an angel appeared over their shoulders and smiled down upon our heroes on their journey. The angel came in the form of a girl named Cari Faber, a stalwart in the LA scene who had some spare space at her pad on Formosa Blvd. She offered the band place to crash until they were able to set up camp on their own.

It seemed as if the stars had been in alignment since they left Texas. Their first night in town and they had met some of their biggest musical inspirations, put on a rousing show, and found a home base to begin their quest to win over west coast audiences. Once unpacked, they immediately got busy calling as many bands and venues as possible trying to weasel onto as many shows as they could.

Their second gig in LA was with Geza X at the Cathay De Grande, and according to legend, it was even better than the Grandia performance. However, with bills that often included four or five bands that were equally as desperate, and unknown, as the "Butthole Surfers from Texas," money was scarce.

Club owners and headlining acts took most of the money home with them and the rest was split between the remaining acts. With ticket prices generally in the range of around $5.00, and most clubs' capacities under a couple hundred patrons, it left the bands who were old enough to be out of their parent's houses with their bellies rumbling and their landlords pounding on their doors threatening eviction.

Paul:
"We only had one show set up in LA when we left Texas. That was it. A couple of days after that show, we were hanging at the beach, and some guys came up to us and said we were playing that night at Cathay de Grande. We had no idea. But we hauled ass to the club just in time to take the stage. We opened for Geza X. Backstage after the show, this big bald hairy guy came up to me where I was sitting and just started staring me down. I asked 'Are you gonna kick my ass?' And he said 'No, I'm El Duce of the Mentors!' Gibby immediately says 'Aren't all of your songs about anal sex?' El Duce said 'No! Well.............Yeah.'"
[email, 2013]

Paul and Gibby and Scott and Quinn had amassed a catalogue of dozens of songs by this point and had even done some professional sounding recordings at the BOSS prior to leaving San Antonio, but they still had nothing to sell at shows.

After a couple of weeks crashing at Cari's pad, the band stumbled across a small apartment for rent they could almost afford, above a carpet store on Pico Blvd down the block from the Santa Monica Civic Center. The landlord seemingly could tolerate 4 young punk rockers and their strange hours, so they blew most of what they had left in the band fund on the month's rent and frantically tried to set up some gigs to try to make enough money to cover the next rent payment.

The fact that they were getting positive reviews from the bands that inspired them to start the Dick Gas Five in the first place gave them an even greater sense of purpose. But accolades couldn't put food on the table, or gas in the van, or do much to quell an angry landlord, so they called as many promoters as they could in hopes of landing themselves onto a bill, any bill, and the small pittance of revenue that playing a show brought with it.

❧

Paul:
"We didn't even have T-shirts in California. Gibby and I had sold Lee Harvey Oswald T-shirts on the boardwalk in Venice a couple of years before that; before there was a band. It just took us a while to figure out to sell T-shirts at shows. We had no idea what we were doing." [email 2013]

❧

While they didn't make much cash from the first two gigs they played, they still viewed them as modest successes and were full of youthful exuberance about their stay. They were more ready than ever to play their next gig. But with nothing lined up in LA until later that month, they figured the time was right for a little road trip. They caught wind of the free food kitchens up north, and the prospect of seeing some old friends and getting a hot meal was just too good to pass up. So, with no area shows booked, they headed up the Pacific Coast Highway to the more temperate climate of San Francisco to meet up with some of their old pals from Austin.

From the time the band left LA, things began to go awry. Shortly into the journey, the van began to belch and sputter. The temperature gauge crept up and the van bucked harder than the mechanical bull at Gilley's Bar. The smell of gas permeated the interior of the vehicle leaving these urban cowboys feeling green and nauseous. It was a tug-of-war between Man and Machine the rest of the way up the coast. They all coughed and choked, and pressed on, white- knuckled and fingers crossed, until their van could finally press no more.

The city was in sight, but as they approached the top of the Bay Bridge arch, there was a loud "Bang!". The engine seized and smoke began to billow from the undercarriage. They held their breath and prayed to the Gods of Physics. By sheer grace, and gravity, the van made it over the hump, and rattled down the rest of the span, coasting through a fortunate green light at the bottom, and onto Valencia before grinding to a halt at the curb. The engine hissed like the snakes of St. Patrick as they drew a collective deep breath, blew a long exhale and gathered their wits about them. They made it into the City by the Bay by the skin of their teeth and now here they sat in a brief moment of contemplative silence.

They had absolutely no idea where they were. Daylight was waning in the dark cavernous city and they were stuck and broke. When they finally snapped back to reality, the boys noticed a commotion brewing outside their windows.

Degenerates, malcontents, and drunkards were milling about the sidewalk with intent. Some had guitar cases littered with stickers: Anarchy signs and the Black Flag

The Tool & Die show the Butthole Surfers crashed

Bars. Torn jeans and spiked hair…the van must have broken down and glided straight through the Pearly Gates.

Some of the freaks wheeled amplifiers and carried guitars toward the front of the building where their hobbled craft had finally sputtered and died. And there they sat, dumbfounded. Looking around they realized: it was a punk rock show! A punk rock show meant money: Money to eat. Money to buy parts for the van, money to pay the landlord, or buy some weed; MONEY! Their adrenaline skyrocketed. They got out, opened the back doors, and started unloading their equipment into the club.

The Tool and Die was a tiny venue in the Mission District that had no store front or signage and a ladder as the sole means of entering the basement room. They were completely frazzled from their harrowing journey, but they were here and it was now and a gig spelled C-A-S-H. They found the promoter outside, scurrying about between bands and punks loitering about out front. She stopped them as they passed an amp down into the chasm of the club.

'…wait…WHO??'…

'The Butthole Surfers?'

'No, Sorry, we don't have you on the bill tonight and there is no way we can squeeze you in…'

Their hearts sank deep into their chests, but Gibby was primed to use his gift of gab to get his band their first show in San Francisco. They would be playing and there was little anyone, even the promoter, could do to stop them. They hadn't been in town for more than 5 minutes, but they were determined to play this gig as if they were the headliners written on the crude flyers which advertised the gig.

Gibby worked the promoter over with Southern charm, peppered with a maniacal air of intimidation. She had little time, however, to concern herself with the woes of any Texans NOT on the show she had booked for this evening. Paul and Scott and Quinn stood to the side with their equipment, and bated breath, and let Gibby handle the negotiating.

It was a punk rock show in SF, and inevitably, Jello Biafra joined the ranks of the riffraff outside. Gibby continued to weave their tale of woe as the promoter's attention drifted and she toward the bass cabinet sitting by the side of their dilapidated van. Less out of sympathy of their plight than out of necessity for bass amplification, the Butthole Surfers were given the word that they could play a few songs to kick off the show providing they lent their cabinet to some of the other bands.

It wasn't quite the set they wanted, nor the infusion of money they needed, but they were thankful for even the meager stage time they were allotted. After all, Biafra was there and they planned to make the most of this most peculiar opportunity that somehow dropped out of the sky. They dragged the rest of their equipment out onto the curb, over to the opening of the club, and hoisted it down the ladder and into the depths of the basement below.

Of course, recollections of the show are incongruent. Paul has absolutely no recollection of MDC or the Big Boys playing. Jello got them on the bill? Bass amp woes? According to several sources, the show they crashed was on June 18, 1982. MDC's own tour states the Butthole Surfers played. It seems odd they couldn't get more than the three songs granted to them while the Big Boys and MDC were in the house, but, as was noted previously, Butthole reality and true reality are often in a tug of war…

Tom Flynn (guitarist of FANG):
"I also have to regrettably call bullshit on the story about coasting to a stop from the Bay Bridge to the Valencia Tool and Die. To get to the Tool and Die from the nearest freeway exit (which is also not the first exit after the bridge, but more like the fifth), it's about 3/4 of a mile, slightly uphill, through about 5 stoplights (including a left turn). Someone in that van must have known there was a show there and guided that van (smoking or not) to the location."
[email 12/20/2014]

Nevertheless, Jello Biafra was most *definitely* in attendance and was always one for checking out new bands. Legend of the Butthole Surfers would have certainly reached his ears before they arrived in SF and he made sure he was inside to see what they were all about.

Jello received tapes from all over the world of bands dying to get his seal of approval. Getting in with Jello Biafra could really provide a band with notoriety. Aside from the press that he had received as a mayoral candidate in San Francisco a few years prior, his band, Dead Kennedys, was one of the most infamous bands in the US punk movement. They were loved by kids, hated by parents, and vilified by politicians.

They epitomized everything punk rock was supposed to be; caustic, belligerent, intelligent, fun. They were also one of the few punk bands whose name was widely known outside of the world of punk rock, mostly due to the antics of the outspoken Biafra.

Jello loved the chance to clamor from his bully pulpit and was often heard on the local radio station KPFK during its *Maximum Rock'n'Roll Radio* show playing obscure bands from all over the world. Bands sent their demo tapes directly to Jello hoping for the opportunity to have him mention their name on air, or better yet, get a chance to release a record on the label which he co-owned, Alternative Tentacles.

A year prior to their chance meeting, Jello and Alternative Tentacles released the classic compilation LP, *Let Them Eat Jellybeans*. With international distribution, the LP offered kids all over the globe some of their first exposure to the US hardcore movement. Bands like the Bad Brains, Black Flag, DOA and the Circle Jerks all shot to international punk rock super stardom (perhaps, an oxymoron, but surely as close as any punk bands ever got) due to the record's release.

Before long US hardcore bands were booking tours across Europe and drawing large crowds. While Biscuit was acting locally at the grass roots level to promote the scene in Texas, Biafra was a global phenomenon.

And the tapes poured in from Finland, Denmark, Hungary and Italy; Japan, South America, and even Southern America. Punk rock spread like wildfire across the globe. Bands played punk rock even though critics were ignoring them, clubs wouldn't book them, and most kids of the day were listening to Journey.

Kids in Europe were on the front lines of the cold war and lived in fear every day. They lived separated by the Berlin Wall with nuclear missile silos peppering the landscape in their own backyards: pawns in the chess match between the two superpowers. The normal trials and tribulations of adolescence were compounded by the very real threat that the world could end on any given day. They were scared and pissed, and they formed bands, just like the kids in the U.S. did, and Jello listened to everything.

Hundreds of tapes per month would pour into his office. The odder the name, the more obscure the hometown, the lamer the artwork, the better the chance it would

June 28, 1982 @ the Grandia
© Bill Daniel

be interesting. So, when Jello got word that there was a band from Texas called the Butthole Surfers playing the Tool and Die that night, he was sure to be inside early to check them out.

Despite the short set, the Butthole Surfers left quite an impression on the few who happened to catch them. Jello was so impressed he decided to invite them to play a show he already had set up for the 4th of July in LA. They jumped at the opportunity but had no idea how they were going to make it there, with a broken fuel line in their van and limited funds to spend on its repair. The smile of promise gave way to the sight of crippled craft sitting at the curb, still emitting the nauseating odor of gas.

Paul:
"We left Los Angeles for San Francisco without a gig lined up. I think we were more interested in the free food kitchens so we could eat. We were in Scott Mathews van, and its fuel pump started to fail. It was sputtering pretty bad, and we were having to pull over a lot. We got to the Bay Bridge and started going uphill up the bridge. The van started sputtering really bad, and we barely made it to the high part of the bridge. Just as we made it to the top, the engine died. We barely had enough momentum to coast, and then we were coasting

downhill, with no engine power. We pulled off of the first exit and coasted to a stop. We were trying to figure out what to do next when we noticed some punks loading a drum kit into the building we were parked in front of. So we started loading our gear in, too. A woman stopped us and asked who we were, and then said we weren't on the bill. We somehow talked her into letting us play, she told us we could play three songs. That place was the Tool and Die. The show was in the basement, and you had to climb a ladder to get in and out of it. It was pretty packed, and the Dead Kennedys made a "surprise" appearance. Jello saw our three songs and liked us enough to put us on the bill for their 4th of July show at the Whisky-a-go-go in Los Angeles, and later to give us our first record deal. So a broken fuel pump led to our first record deal.

That night, after we played Tool and Die, the van started up and went three blocks before breaking down again, this time on railroad tracks. We sat there for a while, and eventually a cop car drove by. The cops shined a spotlight on us, and I waved at them and yelled that we were broken down and needed help. The cops told us to wait right there, that they'd be back for us in a little while. They never did, and we spent the night on the railroad tracks hoping a train wouldn't come." [email January, 2013]

They got through the night without being flattened, and the next day hooked up with Franco from MDC, who drove them to pick up to the auto parts store for a new fuel pump. After Paul got the van in working order, they decided to spend the day down at the ocean. A chance to relax before making the ride back to Los Angeles. It was here that the trip turned from bad to worse. While in the beach parking lot Brown Dog got away from Paul, ran straight out into the road, where she was hit by a car and killed. The look on her face still haunts Paul to this day, he laments. The band was devastated by the tragedy and they never fully recovered from the loss. With their biggest fan and supporter gone, the rest of their time in California would quickly deteriorate into a living nightmare.

The van ran, but it needed a new fuel filter every few miles to avoid breaking down. They bought a case and after an exhaustive trek down the PCH, they finally pulled in front of their apartment and dropped unconscious into a slumber.

They dreamed things would get better. Every show they had played since their arrival, there were more and more mutterings about the band with the funny name who were a strange combination of performance art and art-damaged punk rock. They had a wealth of material, and they had a stage show few could forget, with Gibby running around in his underwear and singing through his coveted toilet paper roll. They mangled mannequins and tossed confetti cockroaches into the crowd. Surely anyone who had accidentally wandered into the club during one of their performances was going to come early next time to catch their full set and was going to drag a friend or two with them as well.

At night, they were quickly becoming darlings of the LA art-punk scene, perhaps even closer to progenies, since there were so few punk bands in LA who were daring to break the deeply entrenched loud-fast rules of the time. The days were long, however, and spent rationing groceries and cigarettes and doling out change amongst the four of them so they could eat that day.

Perspectives of their brief stay in California vary. Scott Mathews remembered it with fondness; the many great responses they had at the gigs; the friends and musical heroes they met along the journey. He recalls it as the time each of them began to realize their dreams of having a viable band weren't as 'pipe' as they initially seemed.

Quinn the Eskimo tells a different story; a tale of the friction that began to develop within their ranks, as they dealt with the daily possibility of starving to death. A tale of blown opportunities, when the universal positive energy of the unit began to sour. They were ill-prepared, destitute, and bitter, and tempers flared.

Paul acquiesced and took a day job at lumber yard on the other side of town, having to transfer twice on his bus route to get there. After noticing several employees were missing digits, he figured the lumber business was not for him, despite Tony Iommi. Someone suggested Scott try to get himself into the studio audience of 'The Price is Right', in hopes of getting picked. The Joker's Wild was talked about too, as was Family Feud: Gibby and his three younger brothers. Perhaps Richard Dawson would plant a slobbering kiss right on their mouths before shouting up at the board…"Survey SAYS!"…

BUUUUZZZZZZ

'So sorry…,please tell the Haynes Family their consolation prizes.'

These dreams all led them down the dead end of reality. They were the mirage-like hallucinations brought on by their own growling bellies and they were becoming ever more frequent and bizarre.

The July 4th show with TSOL and the Dead Kennedys was the best show they ever played together, according to Scott. They played as if their lives depended on it, and essentially, they did. SPOT was running sound, and the band sounded tighter than ever.

Scott Mathews:
"We played with the Minutemen at the Grandia Room and word got around about us really quickly. We went up to San Francisco and played this gig and Jello Biafra saw us and freaked out. [About] a week later Jello had us open for the Dead Kennedys and TSOL at the Whisky. It was one of the best shows

we ever did. Gibby was doing his toilet paper thing and stripping down to his boxers. We had these huge bags of paper cockroaches that we were dumping on the audience. Gibby was into roaches...there were so many roaches in San Antonio that he decided to make it art. We'd take clothes and stuff them with cheeseburgers and mousetraps and condoms and tear them apart at shows and throw them at the crowd. We played like 2 or 3 encores and they were still yelling for us when the Dead Kennedys came onstage. That's when we knew we were like a national band...Everybody in LA was talking about us the next day." [Chris Smart interview, 2001]

Impressed, Spot agreed to let them come down after normal operating hours for a session he would produce at Total Access Studios, in nearby Redondo Beach, where he worked as an engineer.

From the darkest depths of despair to soaring, ethereal heights, California was a roller-coaster of emotions. Could this finally be the break they so sorely needed? Could this be the bright light of hope streaming down from the storm clouds; a life raft thrown in the sea of shit where they were adrift? Not only might they have product to sell, but Spot had recorded some of the most legendary punk records of all time. His resume was filled with classic albums by the likes of the Meat Puppets, Big Boys, and Husker Du, as well as the minutemen and Black Flag. With a real producer at the helm, they might be able to claim their own spot in that pantheon. Perhaps more importantly, they'd have something to peddle to buy some food.

They piled into the studio to record a couple of takes of about half a dozen songs. With Spot's expertise, the session captured the true essence of the band. They pulled out staples like "Radical West," White, Dumb, Ugly & Poor," and "BBQ Pope". They banged and screamed the songs out with a fire, and a buttload of cheap beer, in their bellies. A rousing success!

They finished; patting each other on the back for a job well done, They gathered their stuff and got ready to go. Spot then packed up the reel and asked them for the $300 dollars they owed him. Broke and embarrassed they weren't recording on credit, as they had done so often at the BOSS, they walked out emptyhanded.

The band never did pony up for the master reel and it remains lost to the annals of history. Without a recording or single gig lined up, somebody broached the topic of whether the trip to California may have been a wee bit premature. The Big Boys tour had ended a few weeks prior, Brown Dog was gone, and MDC and the Dead Kennedys were both heading out on their own respective summer tours. The Butthole Surfers were running out of friends, as well as money. With few options left, they agreed to collect their losses, get the van road-ready, and return to Texas.

Though always seemingly right on the verge of a big break, it never came to

Butthole Surfers in LA 1982
© Edward Colver

fruition, and the trip to California was regarded as a huge failure by the band. It was considered a bigger failure by the Stalwarts of Texas scene, who were now being asked to welcome them back.

Years later they would reap the rewards of the relationships they established during that expedition out West, but this time, there were no homecoming parades. They were back playing the same venues they had outgrown and were shamefully forced to confront the old friends they abandoned and to beg for forgiveness.

The California trip lasted a little over a month. A pitiful display by anyone's account. They blew into Los Angeles like a tornado and left just as quickly. Shortly after their departure, they learned the apartment they lived in on Pico Blvd had been destroyed by an actual freak tornado that had blown through the city in a particularly violent thunderstorm. One of the few strokes of good fortune was that they were well outside city limits when it touched down.

Holey Men 6/10/82
©Edward Colver

Texas Tornadoes

Back on the familiar scorched turf of Texas, the bruised and beaten Butthole Surfers were not content to just sit around and cry on anyone's shoulder. They had accomplished a lot in the month they were in the Golden State, and though they left town on the I-10 shaking their fists in defeat, they knew that someday they would return, armed with the lessons that had been bestowed upon them to conquer as warriors.

For now, however, they were steadfastly focused on winning back their old friends' favor. They booked themselves at Studio D in Gibby's hometown of Dallas and were able to squeeze themselves onto another a few weeks later at the same club, with none other than the Dead Kennedys and MDC who were both passing through the Lone Star state on their respective summer tours, as well as longtime pals and resident terrorists, Stick Men with Ray Guns, and Fort Worth's own Hugh Beaumont Experience.

The boys had been milling around a lot of late, with shows still at a minimum, and wounds still fresh from the trip to California. As it would with most bands, the step backwards began to cause irreparable rifts within their ranks. Tensions ran high this evening as each member began to stew upon why the band had been unable to capitalize upon their early triumphs out west. Why were the Dead Kennedys and MDC leaving town after the show while they were still stranded in Texas?

These brooding thoughts often manifest themselves into bad blood as each member starts to talk with friends, all of whom offer up their own opinions as to who is to blame for the bad karma. Though only back in Texas for a few short weeks, the band began to break into factions, with Gibby and Paul on one side, and the Mathews brothers on the other. At Studio D, things came to an inevitable inflection point.

As usual, Gibby collected the money from the promoter after the set and put it into his pocket. Then he and Paul went to go sleep at Gibby's parents' house, rather than making the trip back to San Antonio all loaded and high in the dead of a scorching August night. The Mathews brothers stayed behind at the club, and the revelry of early evening simmered and bubbled into the bitterness of late night. Soon Scott started questioning Quinn why they hadn't gotten their share of the payment for the gig they just played. Tempers began to seethe and pulsate, and Scott thought it was a good idea to show up at Gibby's parents' house with Quinn and some pals to demand their fair share of the door.

Although they all had been best of friends and spent the previous months together through hard times and destitution, this night Scott rang the doorbell of Gibby's childhood home at 3AM with a head full of beer and rage. Shouting and accusations ensued and inevitably, somebody threw a fist.

All hell broke loose in suburbia. Gibby's dad, famous as Mr. Peppermint, host

Quinn 1982
© *Edward Colver*

of a local children's television show, *Peppermint Place*, now had a warzone of drunken rage unfolding on his front lawn. Eventually cooler heads prevailed, the shouting subsided, and the crowd began to disburse, but once the dust had settled and the fighting was finally over, so too were the Butthole Surfers.

Scott Mathews:
"We played with the Dead Kennedys in Dallas and Paul and Gibby took all the money and went to Gibby's dad's house and they didn't want to pay me and Quinn, so I got into a fistfight with Gibby in Mr. Peppermint's front yard in the middle of the night. That was the last time I played with them. It's a shame because we were all such great friends before."
[Chris Smart Interview, 2001]

Paul:
"...we were going to divvy up the money the next day instead of trying to do it while we were drunk after the show. Gibby and I crashed at his parent's house. At 3 in the morning, Scott showed up drunk, beating on the front door of Gibby's parent's house, screaming at the top of his lungs about how Gibby was ripping him off. I went outside to talk to him and he punched me in the eye. He got whatever money he demanded and left. It was pretty retarded."
[email, Jan, 2013]

Scott Mathews, June 1982
© Edward Colver

After the shit storm of poverty and blown opportunities that was their move to California, things never looked bleaker than they did now. Gibby and Paul were unemployed punk rock musicians, alone without a rhythm section. Paul was 25 years old, and Gibby's 25th birthday was less than a month away and they both had some serious choices to make. For some odd reason, despite the dark shadow of reality looming over their shoulders, they never gave up on the dream of remaining Butthole Surfers and of eventually playing out again.

They had come so close to achieving their dreams and, in many respects, had already achieved much of what they set out to accomplish when they starting the band. They played with many of the groups they admired and had made tons of friends and supporters over the course of the previous year and a half. This setback was seemingly looked at as more an opportunity to regroup and get focused than it was as a rallying cry to grow up and face reality.

In retrospect, it was a blessing. The band with Scott and Quinn was not going to lead them to the promised land. Scott was a bit more worldly when they first started playing together, but his drumming abilities were limited at best. He was smart and funny and had some money in his pocket from his gig as a bartender in San Antonio, as well some inheritance money he received upon the passing of a relative, but without the resolute vision of the Butthole Surfers name in lights, none of it mattered.

Gibby and Paul had dreams of what the band should be, and those dreams did not include Scott and Quinn Mathews. As difficult as it may have been to admit when things were going well, perhaps this was in the stars. Perhaps it was for the best. As one door closed, another was opening. Perhaps this was not an end, but a new beginning.

Gibby had gone through the grind of utilizing his accounting degree from Trinity. He had seen the working world. He had seen the "bright future" that was most certainly his destiny were he to decide to walk away and get back to the life he was destined to live before his spark of an idea to start a band. It was scary. There was no fucking way was he ready to travel down that straight and narrow path.

So, he grabbed a bass guitar and began laying down some rudimentary demos to tape. Soon, those experimental recordings began circulating. Dubbed 'Gibby's Brown Circus', the same name that the Butthole Surfers had used to earn extra cash as an opening act for themselves. The songs were raw and bombastic, utilizing two boom boxes to multitrack, but in them, he pushed further the experimentative leanings of the band he was trying to salvage.

As for Paul; he was just 15 credits shy of his master's degree at Trinity, where his dad was the Director of Development, as well as the Dean of the School of Business and Management. A single semester could have provided him with the credentials he needed to get himself a lucrative job and a bright future as well. It was with a single-minded determination, however, that he too avoided the trappings of adulthood and continued writing songs for the non-existent Butthole Surfers band.

Soon, the collection of recordings began to accumulate and, using a small Peavey amplifier and some effects pedals and recording into a cheap Sony cassette recorder, the tapes began to fill up. It was the best they could muster up as a duo of punk rock musicians in San Antonio. There was little hope of finding new recruits to live in desperation and despair as Butthole Surfers. Punk rock was a young man's game and two guys flirting with 30 with little hope of earning any real money seemed to be the last thing even the most ardent punk kid was willing to step into. It looked as if the Butthole Surfers were finished.

A Brown Circus

With most people assuming the Butthole Surfers were gone for good, Gibby and Paul started quietly booking time at the BOSS one thought in mind: releasing an album. Jello Biafra had given them word that if they could get the songs recorded, he would release them on Alternative Tentacles. It seemed that this promise was good enough for Bob O'Neil to allow them to record on credit. Spot still had their demo session, but it never seemed to dawn on anyone to get an advance from Jello for the tape, so here we are.

Rehearsals were slow and tedious, and they got little accomplished in the way of real demos. Gibby played some bass and guitar and Paul could get the sounds committed to tape, but as just a two-piece band, they struggled to get things together.

Paul pulled in a stranger named Gene DiLibero, who wandered into the BOSS one day and coaxed him behind the drums for a session. Gene had no idea about punk rock, which was of little surprise being from San Antonio in the early 1980's, and his complete incomprehension of their quirky material left him floundering behind the set. They struggled through the practice trying to get something accomplished. Despite his complete ineptitude, Paul was able to cut and splice together the tape to complete his song, "Hey". He would let nothing stop the Butthole Surfers from achieving their mission, not even the woeful incompetence of a complete stranger.

Thanksgiving came and went, and Christmas stockings were hung then packed away, and the Butthole Surfers, or Gibby's Brown Circus, or whatever they wanted to call themselves, were no closer to achieving their goal of recording an album than they had been the night Scott punched Paul in the face.

Thankfully, they had become close with another punk band that had recently formed in San Antonio that called themselves the Marching Plague. Gibby and Paul helped them out with some backing vocals and support during the recording of their now cult classic 7" EP, *Rock'n'Roll Asshole*, and in a gesture of brotherhood and camaraderie The Plague's drummer, Brad Perkins, agreed to step in and lend his services to their cause.

Soon after, Gibby and Paul were introduced to a local jazz musician named Bill Jolly, who didn't have a steady gig at the moment but who might be interested in helping them out with recording their demos. Paul gave Bill a tape he had of an old Mathews brothers' practice through their mutual acquaintance and waited to hear what Bill thought about it. Surprisingly, he liked it enough to agree to come down to a rehearsal to see how things panned out.

Bill's musical journey couldn't have been more different than Gibby and Paul's. He had been a music major at UT Austin when, at the tender age of 19, he took a leave of absence to record with The Viola Crayola; a progressive jazz fusion outfit featuring guitar virtuoso, Tony Viola. The Viola Crayola recorded what would be their

Flynn & Keith and the Marching Plague, 9/16/83
© Suzanne Ferguson

only album, *Music: Breathing of Statues* in NYC in 1974. The record garnered critical praise and attention, and it seemed they were on their way to being mentioned in the same breath as Mahavishnu Orchestra or Weather Report. Once they finished recording, they began booking a tour across the USA.

Sadly, just a month after the record's release, the band's namesake was tragically killed in a train\car collision. With the Viola Crayola's premature demise, Bill, grieving and disheartened, returned to Texas to finish his degree at UT

Despite being an outsider to the whole punk rock scene, Bill was impressed by the tape of the Butthole Surfers. Gibby and Paul were also hilarious individuals who didn't take themselves too seriously, something that was as rare in the realm of punk rock as it was in the realm of prog-rock. One practice laid the groundwork for another, and after spending some time together, Bill agreed to help out, not only with the recording process, but join the band full-time.

Bill Jolly:
"I thought I was about to hit the "big time" with the Viola Crayola after we recorded an album in NYC in 1974 when I was all of 19, having taken time off from being a music major at UT Austin. Tony Viola was one of the most

incredible guitar players I had ever seen. He played a right-handed guitar left-handed, i.e., the strings were "upside down", but he was killed in a car/train collision the month after we recorded the album. At that time, we were getting a lot of national bookings lined up, but his death ended that venture." [email: 2010]

Bill had received many offers to gig with cover bands after his return to Texas, but he remained resolutely out of the music business for the next several years until Gibby and Paul inspired him out of his self-imposed exile. Despite their very different backgrounds, their outlook and approach seemed to be completely in sync. Bill hadn't been looking to be in a band, but this band was actually fun, irreverent, and oddly original. He quickly learned the cache of songs from an old ¼" reel Paul gave to him and immediately got started laying down basic tracks at the BOSS.

Bill:

"I was amazed at how prolific and creative Paul and Gibby were (still am) and that sold me on working with them, and I had an absolute blast working with them. Touring was an experience like no other, even when my bed was a sleeping bag. I could not even begin to tell you all of the places I slept, but seem to recall Jello Biafra's floor/couch when in San Francisco…Gibby, at the time, even though somewhat clumsy with bass and guitar, really came up with some great bass riffs." [email 2010]

Bill's virtuosity and Brad's thundering drums infused the band's older songs with a new vehemence. They gelled instantly and sounded tighter than ever. Without a full-time drummer they were still 3/4th a band, but with a classically trained musician on bass, and a highly proficient drummer lending his time behind the kit, they sailed through practices without the labor-intensive process that was necessary to teach Scott and Quinn the material.

This quasi-Butthole Surfers band still held onto many of their older punk staples, but newer material began to veer into entirely novel directions. Still goofy, sloppy and snotty, they began incorporating influences of the classic psych-garage rock bands they had grown up listening to. They had always been known within the scene as the punk band that played a Bloodrock cover, but they expanded on that tradition with their newest batch of original songs.

They persevered through the limitations of recording the first EP while not being a band by grabbing any friends they could find to support their cause. Keith Rumbo, singer of the Marching Plague added the voice of "Anus Presley", and when Brad couldn't make it down the studio because of prior drum commitments with the Plague, they would grab any drummer that was available.

Then Bill had an idea. He would call up an old college roommate from UT named Kevin Leman to see if he would be willing to help. Bill told Kevin about this odd punk band he just joined that was making a record and needed some help to that end. Kevin was as skeptical as Bill had been, as he too was an accomplished musician who found little redeeming in the incompetence of most punk bands. It was his friend Bill, though, and if Bill was able to be persuaded out of retirement to join a punk rock band, then Kevin figured he'd come down to check out what the Butthole Surfers were all about.

They got some practices in and were able to lay down drum tracks to a newer song they'd written: a barnburner called "Suicide". Kevin, too, was impressed by the material, or at least intrigued enough to stick around for a while to see what might become of this odd union of punks and jazz heads.

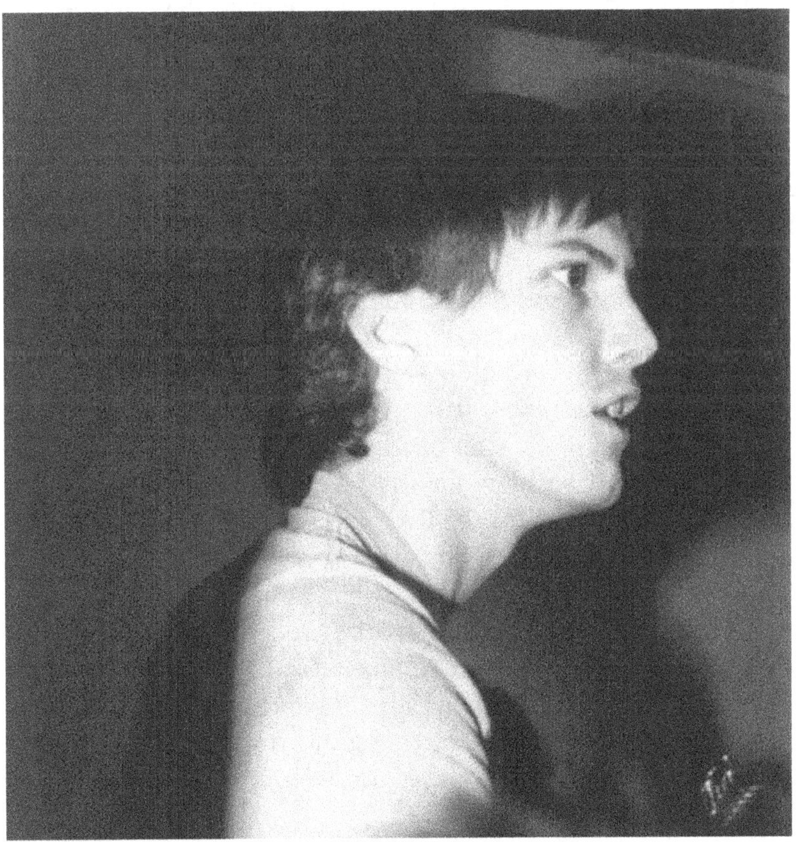

Paul at Studio 29, 2/4/83 © Suzanne Ferguson

Bill Jolly:
"The first time I got together and played with them was at BOSS so they were already well into recording Brown Reason to Live, though I never heard that title until after it was released. Their stuff was set up there and it was obvious they had already been recording. I know that is also where Kevin first played with us but I seem to also recall Brad playing there as well. As a matter of fact, I cannot recall practicing with them in San Antonio at any place other than BOSS, though we likely got together at Paul's parents' house in SA, but I don't recall it ever being a full-blown session, i.e., don't think we ever had drums set up there." [email, 10/2010]

So, after months of getting little to nothing accomplished the Butthole Surfers were a band again! They made their live debut in January 1983 opening for the Brains (whose "Money Changes Everything" would become a huge hit for Cyndi Lauper just a couple of years later) at the Bonham Exchange in San Antonio. With a full-time drummer and bassist in the band, they were ready to take Texas, and the rest of the world, by storm.

The next gig was February 4, at Studio 29 in Austin. Art-damaged punkers, Kamikaze Refrigerators, were on the bill, as was a brand-new band comprised of some old friends calling themselves Scratch Acid. The Butthole Surfers were no strangers to the Studio 29 stage and friends showed up in droves for their triumphant return to Austin. The boys from the Marching Plague were there as well, and pre-show revelry lead to the suggestion that Gibby tattoo himself up with a black Sharpie.

They drew a cock coming out of his boxer shorts that he inevitably stripped down to every show and, in large letters, scrawled "MARCHING PLAGUE SUCKS!" on his arm. Onstage, the band blew through some of their newer material like "Eat Shit and Die", as well as unleashing the live premier of "Suicide". They were so proud (and looped), they played the song twice.

The months locked away in the studio had done them well. They polished their sound and returned with a renewed sense of purpose. The tight, highly competent rhythm section gave Paul the ability to vamp, solo, and improvise on top of an steady backbeat. The songs exhibited much richer textures, off-kilter timings, and odd tunings. Bill and Kevin were proficient enough to run with Paul's ideas and the gig showcasing this new rhythm section was a great return for the band.

The excitement level in the crowd was palpable, with audience members chiding and ribbing the bands throughout their sets. As the night progressed, Gibby stripped down to reveal his latest creations. Bounding himself around the stage half-naked, belting out an old crowd favorite they had been playing since their earliest practices in Woodlawn Manor, "Mexican Caravan".

…Take me, Mexican caravan, south of…south of the Rio Grande, take me to that Miguel town, where I can score some of that heroin brown….

The enthusiastic crowd reveled in it until someone noticed Gibby's tattoos. One particular patron was not too amused by the Marching Plague reference Gibby so proudly boasted. The joke flew right over the head of the ignorant attendee and, shortly thereafter, a bottle whizzed right over the heads of the other fans in the crowd. Aimed directly at Gibby, he exhibited the lightning-fast reflexes he learned as a star basketball player in high school and ducked out of the way just in time.

Kevin, trapped behind his drum set, was not so lucky. The bottle smashed a direct hit into his face, spraying blood and beer against the wall behind him. He slumped off his stool onto the ground and moaned into his hands as the music stopped abruptly. After a minute spent examining the mess that was Kevin's face, Gibby spat out into the crowd…

'Yeah, Fuck you….

Fucking dick!....

You're as stupid as you look'…

The drunken perpetrator yells back something to the effect of…

'yeah he's on the floor and I don't care…'.

Brad Perkins recalls:
"Kevin played a few shows with them. One was at Studio 29 in Austin. Before the show, Keith Rumbo and I gave Gibby a bunch of magic marker tattoos. One prominently said "Marching Plague Sucks" Some punker kid took offense to that and heaved a beer bottle at Gibby. It missed and hit Kevin in the face. That was Kevin's last BHS show." [email, 2010]

Kevin Leman:
"I think there were 2 gigs, and I'm not sure how many studio songs-I think three or four…" [email 11/2/10]

Paul, Gibby, Kevin, and Bill at Studio 29, 2/4/83
© Suzanne Ferguson

The house lights come up and the DJ puts on a record in hopes of quelling the rising tensions in the room. The night ends with fights breaking out in the parking lot outside and people disbursing out into the chilly, winter air. So ends the show, so ends Kevin Leman's tenure as a Butthole Surfer.

As hopeful as they were that this new line-up was going to help them fulfill their destiny of finishing their album, those dreams were now bloodied with a pair of black eyes and slumped on the floor behind a drum kit.

Sadly, it was an all-too-common occurrence at punk shows. The few poseurs who used punk rock music as an excuse to get drunk and violent often won in the battle against themselves, as venues systematically shut down or else refused to book punk bands ever again due to the self-defeating behavior of these denizens of 'the scene'. It was generally just a few bad apples, but they were there at most every show. The next day, Kevin let Bill know that his days of playing punk rock were numbered.

And as quickly as that, the Buttholes were, again, reduced to a trio. Without a drummer they really aren't a band, so they go back to practicing at Brad's place when they can and recording at the BOSS as songs fall together. Brad, again, becomes a substitute Butthole Surfer; called off the bench to pinch hit in a jam. His team is still the Marching Plague, though, and they have a full schedule themselves, even considering most of their shows are local. Playing with the Buttholes meant his main meal ticket, the Plague, weren't on the bill, or else he had to pull two sets with two different bands. It was not the best situation for anyone, but Gibby and Paul were in true desperation mode to get back out into circulation.

Yet another month goes by and the future of the band was as uncertain as when the Mathews brothers quit that night back in Dallas. They mustered up 3 or 4 shows with a couple of different drummers and were able to scrape together some drum tracks over which they could continue recording the project they hoped to release, but they were more or less shackled to the studio through the first half of 1983, unable to play live, make money, or find a steady drummer to join their ranks.

Bill was on call whenever they needed a bass player, but through much of the recording process that led to the eventual release of *Brown Reason to Live*, it was often just Paul and Gibby laying down all the tracks themselves. They laid down their vocal bass and guitar parts over whichever drummer friend had the night off from the other bands to which they were committed.

Winter passed as silently as freshly fallen snow, and as spring began to blossom it was time for the band to awaken and flex the muscles that were stiff with the atrophy of hibernation. What was left of the Butthole Surfers was still reeling in confusion and disarray, but when they received word that their pals in TSOL were heading to Texas to play a trifecta of gigs in Dallas, Houston, and Austin, they immediately knew what they had to do.

Gibby and Paul were able to rally the troops together for a show at the Skyline in Austin with little problem, and the show was guaranteed to be packed. With a line-up set to include themselves and TSOL, the Big Boys, and Scratch Acid, it was bound to be a great night. There was excitement in the air to debut the new songs they had been working on, and to squash the memories of the Studio 29 debacle.

The boys in TSOL were almost as excited as the Buttholes were to be playing together again. TSOL had become huge fans of the Butthole Surfers after the show at The Whisky on July 4th alongside the Dead Kennedys. Being on the same bill in Austin was great, but they wanted more than just one show together.

They had a gig lined up for the night before in Houston and it would be perfect for the Buttholes to join them as well. So TSOL had their manager get in touch with the promoter, Tom Bunch, prior to arriving in Texas. They told Tom, in no uncertain terms, to get the Butthole Surfers on the bill.

But, again, the Butthole Surfers weren't really a band, despite Gibby and Paul's willingness to make the 3-hour drive on a Wednesday night to play the Houston gig as well. Bill and Brad's schedules prevented it; Brad had an early morning class the next day and Bill can't recall any reason why he would not have been able to make it, but he couldn't because he didn't

So when Gibby took the call from Tom Bunch, who had just started booking shows in Houston under the name 'TAB Productions', it was with a heavy heart that Gibby declined the invitation. Bunch had done his part and figured the case was closed, but when he returned with the news, the TSOL boys scoffed and were insistent that the Butthole Surfers were on the bill. They told Tom to call back and offer them more money.

'Hey that's really great, but tell them we can't do it...we really don't have a band right now...'

Gibby hung up the phone, perhaps in slight disbelief he had actually admitted that fact out loud. When Tom relayed the news to TSOL that the Butthole Surfers said 'no', they were not having it...

"Offer them more cash...tell them we'll give them $200."

Bunch was perplexed. He had never even heard of the Butthole Surfers. They hadn't played a show in Houston since before the move to California, nearly a full year prior. In fact, they had only mustered up a smattering of shows anywhere at all since returning from California in embarrassment and shame. '

"Why was TSOL so fixated on the Butthole Surfers, and not the Big Boys or local giants Really Red?" He shrugged, picked up the phone, and called Gibby.

"Really, man, that's great, but we don't have a band...."

The banter carried on as the pot got sweeter. At some point in the proceedings, the offer became one they couldn't refuse. Even though he had no idea how they could possibly pull it off, Gibby agreed.

They were now committed to play the show as a duo, so after some deliberation, they thought up a brilliant idea. Why not lay down some drum loops to tape? They could play the songs along with the taped drum track. Genius! It might just work! They went about recording the drums for the backing track onto a cassette. They wouldn't have to cancel the gig after all. Problem solved!

When they got to the Lawndale Art Annex and met up with TSOL the two bands started yucking it up almost immediately. TSOL had been out on the road for a couple of weeks, touring with Spot engineering their shows, and they were sounding great. They had a stop in Phoenix on their way to Texas, and the tour had been a blast so far. They were on fire, and were partying like rock stars, and were even able to heist a case of whiskey from the club they played at the night before, thanks to some careless bar back.

Celebrating the reunion with his old pals in TSOL, Gibby commandeered a bottle for himself, and by the time the Gibby and Paul Butthole Experience hit the stage, its contents were but a spit puddle.

There the two Buttholes stand awkwardly in front of TSOL's equipment which was already set up behind them. A tape hiss sounds as if there is a rainstorm inside the club. Gibby slurs and stumbles around to 'Sinister Crayon', a lumbering dirge they had often played with the Mathews brothers, but which was a bit of an odd inclusion in the sets these days. Here, the song works well, with Gibby's sinister swagger and visceral growl adding to the sense of foreboding and minimalist skronk.

'Sinister Crayon…Totally played…Lack of Confusion…Totally played…'

They get through the song with fans hopping up on stage screaming into Paul's live mic. They manage to pummel through their one of their newest creations, "The Shah Sleep's in Lee Harvey's Grave" without much trouble, as Gibby straps on the bass and belches out as much noise as his trembling hands can muster. It works, but the crowd starts getting restless. The whiskey is beginning to cloud Gibby's peripheral vision and his knees are beginning to buckle under his lanky torso. He takes off his bass and begins to strip down to his boxers, trying to remember the theatrics he was able to pull off at most every show when they had been playing all around Texas with clockwork regularity.

The few who showed up early jumped around mockingly. The ones looking to start a slam pit were left holding their cocks in futile, testosterone-fueled angst. Instead of a hardcore band there stumbled a demented duo devoid of drums, and an incapacitated bass player plucking along to a cassette tape piped through the club's shitty sound system. The drums are barely audible and Gibby's woeful drunkenness leaves him in a near vegetative state.

Being denied even the remotest excuse to slam dance, the crowd begins to play catch among themselves with Gibby's shed garments. A shirt lands on his bass guitar and gets caught in the tuning keys as they break into "BBQ Pope". Paul is resigned to tapping and stomping his feet to keep some semblance of timing, but it's of little help to the cross-eyed and painless Gibby. A guy in the crowd hops behind TSOLs drum kit, and another, who apparently had thrown the last sock he could find, stands at the lip of the stage and tears off Gibby's boxers. Jerked around from the violent debriefing, he now stands completely exposed to the crowd, unfazed in his sorry condition.

The bass emits a few fart notes, as "BBQ Pope" is far beyond what our bassist can comprehend. Paul tried to cue Gibby, whose eyes are transfixed on the floor. He tries to remind him: your name is Gibby Haynes, you are onstage in the city of Houston, TX, in the year of our Lord 1983.

The soundman gives up on trying to mix the cacophony and steps out from behind his board. He mercifully tries to cover Gibby's privates with some clothes that found their way back onto the stage due to some errant throw.

Tom Bunch:
"I booked TSOL, and TSOL's manager, Mike Vraney, also managed the Dead Kennedys. The Butthole Surfers had done a record on the Dead Kennedys' label, and TSOL requested [them] as their opening act.

I called Mike Vraney, and he gave me a phone number in San Antonio for Gibby and Paul. I called them and said, 'Hey, TSOL wants you to open up for 'em in Houston.' They said, 'That's be great – we'd love to do it, but we don't have a band. There's just Paul and me, and the people who were in our band are no longer in our band anymore, so we're not capable of playing a show in six weeks.'

So I called Mike back and said, 'Well, they'd like to do it but they have no band.' Mike just kept calling me back, saying, 'Tell 'em we'll give 'em 200 bucks.' I called Gibby and said, 'They'll give you 200 bucks.' At that point in time that was really good money. He goes, 'Well, I've got me and my guitar player; we don't have a bass player, we don't have a drummer, we haven't practiced, we're not capable of doing the show.'

So I called Mike Vraney back and told him that, and he said, 'Tell 'em we'll give 'em 300 bucks.' So I called them back. I think when it got up to 350 bucks they agreed to do it, under the contingency that only two of 'em were going to do it, that they had no bass player and no drummer, and that we had to understand that that was going to be the case.

So I called TSOL's manager back and said, 'Well, they said they'd show up and play the show, but only two of them.' He said, 'I don't care, we want 'em to play. They're great.' So they agreed to play the show, and they showed up late....

... They showed up just high as shit on acid. Two guys with a reel-to-reel tape player that they had programmed some drum loops and stuff. They plugged in the tape player and attempted to play along with the tape, with Paul playing guitar and Gibby playing bass. Gibby can't play bass – he can't keep a beat, so he's up there trying to play bass, Paul's trying to play guitar. Paul played guitar great, and they're both high as shit and the tape player's going. It was a huge fucking mess....People started yelling and screaming and flicking cigarettes and throwing stuff at 'em, and they started yelling back at the audience, and then it kind of degenerated into a show. People had never really seen them before, so they didn't know that this wasn't what they were supposed to be doing. It went on for 30 or 35 minutes, and that was my first Butthole Surfers experience." [email, 2008]

A film crew Bunch commissioned in hopes of promoting his new company and documenting the Houston scene truly got a clear picture of the underbelly of Texas punk that night. Memories of the worst show ever played by any band in history would only add to the legend of the Butthole Surfers in later years.

But Gibby and Paul didn't have the luxury hindsight. They were living this nightmare every day. When they woke up the following morning and swept together the scattered memories of the previous year, they had to realize their plight was dour. A bottle to the face of the only potential steady drummer they had been able to find, and now this drunken nightmare. Perhaps punk rock was a game for the young, for those whose parents could support and fund such endeavors. Gibby and Paul were destitute and sleeping on couches and making a record which few people might even care about.

Maximum Rock'n'Roll, April 1983:
"The Butthole Surfers have reformed and are hanging out around somewhere around Texas. I have nothing to say about the recent TSOL show, but the MDC show was great. It was held at the Soap Street Saloon, an R&B hippie hangout. Everything went ok!" – [Duck Butter]

They rode the waves of success and failure with intestinal fortitude. They returned home from Houston alive, but they needed to face the stinging rays of reality; Something had to be done about their lack of a drummer. They had barely played a cohesive show since the Mathews brothers quit, and despite their success in getting tracks laid down on tape, it would all be for naught if they couldn't promote it on the road.

Perhaps the biggest irony came the next night in Austin when they played what was perhaps the best show they ever had to this juncture. It turned out, with a proper rhythm section, they were bawdy, tight, confident, and surprisingly adept. Brad and Bill laid down a concrete foundation as Paul scratched sonic hieroglyphics against the rocks. Houston was a glimpse of Gibby and Paul amidst the turmoil of not having a full-time band to count on, Austin was a glimpse of the band on the precipice of greatness. No one knew which band, or whether half of the band, would show up on any given night.

For the Austin gig, most people in attendance had seen the Butthole Surfers before, but they never saw this Butthole Surfers before. Among those at the venue was one Jeffrey 'King Vitamin' Coffey, who had been drinking all day in anticipation. By the time the Buttholes hit the stage, he was passed out in his own puke in the parking lot of the club. His friends told him glorious tales of the show he missed; of the quality of their new material, how tight they sounded; and about Keith Rumbo in a lycra, wrestling mask playing the role of Anus Presley. Anus stumbles about the stage and challenges any and all in the audience to take him on in a true Texas death match…:

'You will die, you will all die, because it is my time…God is second to me…you suck, you all suck…'

King could barely forgive himself for his over-indulgence.

King:
"…at the Skyline show with TSOL. Anus Presley himself [Keith Rumbo in a wresting mask] sang "Revenge…". Everybody said it was fantastic. Myself, I was passed out and vomiting in my friend's car. I drank too much that evening in excited anticipation for the show. The only thing I remember is waking up the next day on the sofa, smelling terrible. Still, people tell me the Butts (and Anus Presley) were incredible."
[email 2005]

But, what may have eluded King this night, through the infinite darkness of an alcohol-induced coma, would not elude him much longer. Though he was not in attendance at this show on this particular night, there were many more nights to come where King would be a fixture.

Gibby and Paul had met King in the past and had seen him drumming with his band, the Hugh Beaumont Experience several times. They did some pondering and knew he would fit in perfectly. So, they went to Bill to tell him the news that they wanted King Coffey to play drums for the Butthole Surfers.

Bill may not have met King before, but once he did, he was dubious that this scrawny kid with his mohawk and torn jeans was the right man for the job. How could he fill the void? Brad and Kevin were solid workhorse drummers. King didn't even have a kick drum.

King was also still drumming for the Hugh Beaumont Experience, but that fact was of little concern to Gibby and Paul. They had seen him play and had been impressed with his unorthodox style of playing while standing up. They invited him down to the studio to help them get some tracks laid down, and once the recording session was finished, they were convinced he was the right man for the job.

King gave the old Mathews bros era song, "BBQ Pope" a new pep with his cymbal accents, and blazed through a full throttle Texas rockabilly romp entitled "Wichita Cathedral". Paul traded bass and guitar duties with Bill on the song, and Gibby sang like a weathered, cotton-mouthed bluesman. It was unlike anything they had done prior and showed how quickly they were advancing into the stratosphere since the days of struggling to progress with Scott & Quinn.

Before becoming a Butthole Surfer, King had forged his own reputation in the Texas punk rock scene. He produced five issues of a photocopied fanzine called 'Throbbing Cattle'; an assemblage of "cultural musings for mammals", and he was a fixture at gigs in the DFW area by such local bands as Stick Men with Ray Guns and Tex & the Saddletramps. Being a punk from Dallas was hard enough, but living on the Fort Worth side of the metroplex was downright impossible. So after the Hugh Beaumont Experience recorded a couple of tracks for a local compilation, they picked up and moved to Austin to glom onto, in hopes of assimilating into, its vibrant scene.

King had great friends in the Experience, and he had no intention of leaving them just as they were finally finding their niche musically. Like the Butthole Surfers, the Hugh Beaumont Experience started as a snotty, British- influenced punk rock band, but they began to stretch out on their latest recordings. Like the Butthole Surfers, they too were getting off on alienating punkers whose narrow view of punk was limited to the loud fast rules principle so rampant in the US hardcore movement.

The Hugh Beaumont Experience's latest offerings, "Fred" and "Purple Things", found them branching out into new and more psychedelic territory. "Fred" even incorporated some hip-hop flavoring. They were by far the most professional songs the band had recorded, and their release on 'Steel Rok Presents', a cassette compilation showcasing the Dallas \ Fort Worth scene, meant that they might finally have a product to help showcase their new direction, even if they weren't in the scene to witness it.

The two bands seemed to mirror each other: Punk bands whose off-kilter styles left them alienated even among those who were seemingly most alienated. A series of bad breaks had almost destroyed HBE, like the Buttholes, but their perseverance through adversity kept them together even in the face of the fact that few people really cared whether they stayed together or not.

A falling out with the girl who funded their first record, prior to King joining the band, caused the owner to destroy not only the remaining unsold records, but legend has it, the master plates as well, virtually wiping it out of existence. 'The Cone Johnson EP' remains one of the most elusive and most sought-after records in the annals of Texas punk rock history.

Local punk bands were often pressing up their own records and tapes to sell at shows or on consignment to the few brave record stores that would stock them. Even among these privately pressed records, *The Cone Johnson EP* retains its title as one of the rarest, and sought after, TX punk records of all time, with a mere 50 copies rumored to still exist.

An early live cassette they released entitled *Virgin Killers*, was the first recording to feature King, but it did little to promote the band or raise an eyebrow,

Anus Presley, and his security detail, at the Skyline, 3/10/83
© Bill Daniel

even among the local stalwarts in Dallas. Of late, though, they had been trying to get the money together to release a session they recorded with Husker Du's co-frontman Bob Mould working the desk. This recording would most certainly catch the ear of die-hard Huskers fans, or perhaps even catch on at SST: the BIG TIME!

The band had been having some difficulties getting cash together, however, and hoped the move to Austin would enable them to earn the money to get it released. They were able to book a few shows as Austin residents but were still wallowing in destitution.

Without much prospect of being able to release the sessions legally, a couple of members of the band got hold of a checkbook and started writing bad checks around town. If not their intent when finding the lost checkbook, the result would still be the same; perhaps they could save enough of their own cash to release their LP.

They tried to remain active in the scene, playing as many shows as they could get themselves on to, and even did a professional recording at the BOSS, which found them covering Cream's "Sunshine of Your Love", but the song, if it had been released, was bound to only alienate them even further from the punk rock kids they needed to buy their merchandise. A stolen checkbook was probably a more potentially lucrative endeavor.

The band's guitarist returned home with word that the police had been to the house asking his whereabouts, and so rather than face the other, less palatable, music of reckoning, he and the band's vocalist, took off and fled Austin heading toward

Spot helping to BBQ the Pope at the Skyline in Austin, 3/10/83 © Bill Daniel

Louisiana. Mirroring the events in Billy Wilder's classic 1944 film noir 'Double Indemnity': Hugh Beaumont was on the lam.

King was left holding his sticks dumb-founded, and decided to take the call from Gibby and Paul and go jam with the Butthole Surfers, while letting the Texas legal system decide the future of the Hugh Beaumont Experience. It was just the odd piece of karma Gibby and Paul needed to get things going again on a steady basis.

When King walked into the first session with his wiry frame, barefoot, and sporting a bushy, blonde mohawk, Bill was immediately suspect. A scrawny punk kid was not what the band needed to complete their rhythm section. As the night progressed, however, and things started to mellow out, they found themselves getting along rather well. When King started busting out drum parts from Blue Cheer's *Vincebus Eruptum* LP on just a couple of toms and a snare drum, Bill's view softened even more.

There are rumors of an ultimatum that if King was in, Bill was out, but as practice stretched into the wee hours, Bill conceded that he may have been a bit premature in his judgment, and that perhaps they should give King a chance after all. With little prospect that the Hugh Beaumont Experience would ever get back together again, King shrugged and agreed to join the Butthole Surfers as their full-time drummer.

King:

"[Bill] was a bad ass player, but sort of a serious musician type (which I clearly wasn't)...he really didn't want me around at first. I remember him saying to Paul, "either he goes, or I go." Paul said (without missing a beat), "Well, I really enjoyed having you around. King's our drummer."

...I remember seeing them at Studio 29, where the drummer got hit on the head with a beer bottle. You could tell he wasn't a punk (when Gibby came out with 4 asparagus stalks drawn on his chest in a Black Flag logo, you could tell it was completely above the drummer's head) . He was just a solid drummer who was probably a bit intrigued by this interesting scene. He just wasn't willing to get hit by beer bottles. Understandably, he quit.

Shortly thereafter, I let it be known to Gibby and Paul that I was quite willing to be hit on the head with beer bottles." [email, 2009]

With King now officially a Butthole Surfer, and the Butthole Surfers finally a quartet again, they were ready to play some real shows and started booking them like madmen. With Jello promising he'd release their record if they were able to get it recorded, they culled together 7 of their favorite tunes from the last few months of sessions and shipped them off to Biafra and packaged them as a self-titled EP. Biafra loved it and almost immediately pressed it up and, started shipping it out to record stores across the country.

It was the first bit of good news the band had gotten in nearly a year and it left them completely ecstatic. They could now boast a solid line-up, a record with their name on it, and a distribution network both here in states, and abroad through Alternative Tentacles' international distributor, Subterranean. They also had the backing of Biafra himself with his expert hawking abilities. He touted their moniker in interviews and professed his love for them as the newest and greatest band on earth. Yes, things were finally starting to look positive. The Butthole Surfers had been reborn.

So, in July of 1983, in what can only be viewed as an unparalleled demonstration of determination and perseverance, the *BUTTHOLE SURFERS* eponymously named first platter was unleashed. With its artwork culled from the same Strange VD magazine that caused Gibby's hasty departure from Peat Marwick, it was a big fat 'fuck you' to his former bosses there: surely another level of accomplishment in which he relished.

The 'Chub-Rak' image of the lower torso of Ethiopian kids standing on scales repeated across the cover obviously appealed to the DK's lead singer as well. Even in a genre whose propensity to offend was strikingly common, the Butthole Surfers managed to reach new depths of depravity. And once the needle hit the grooves, they didn't disappoint either.

By beginning the record with "The Shah Sleeps in Lee Harvey's Grave", they immediately demanded a reaction. This was not a band that wanted to be liked. No melody, no structure, and no message of which to speak, other than perhaps the utter breakdown of any sort of law and order. They screamed out "Fuck" by the fifth word. They taunted the listener as the voice of Anus Presley proclaimed his rightful place as the 'ultimate God'. The whole thing ends with our narrator screaming at the top of his lungs for us to "Shut Up!" and listen.

And when the song is over, and we assume that we are in for another voyage to back to hell, a single bass note lightly floats effortlessly in air, giving way to a gentle strum of a guitar. Ethereal and dreamlike, a more friendly and welcoming voice calls to us like an old friend… *"Hey...Hey, Hey..."*

What we thought this band was suddenly gives way to something completely different. By the time we get to the third song, "Something", we're hearing saxophones and bottleneck guitar. When we flip the record over for "BBQ Pope", we're treated to a blasphemous, sea-shanty about bed- wetting, and the misfortunes of the high holy leader of the Roman Catholic church.

What ranks amongst the oddest punk records ever released, can, to this day, leave a listener perplexed. It is amazingly cohesive, notwithstanding the fact that no less than four drummers were utilized over the various sessions, which themselves stretched on for nearly a year. The album goes from screaming ferocity to rapturous beauty and still manages to maintain a thread.

The novelty of the lack of any sort of credits anywhere on the jacket would become a fixture for the band's later records as well. But, the tradition that began with this first release was probably initiated due to the fact that they couldn't remember who played on what song, nor the name of the guy they pulled off the street that day to help lay down the drums for "Hey".

It had been a long slog, and drummers came, and drummers went. Bill hadn't joined the band until after they had already begun recording, and with Paul and Gibby often recording songs late at night by themselves, any semblance of who played what instruments on which tracks was a big blur. All that mattered was that they had dodged the many thunderbolts thrown at them by some vengeful God and managed to get their record out to the public.

The Butthole Surfers quickly became one of Jello's pet projects. He gleefully mentioned them in Dead Kennedys interviews and hung out with them when passing through Texas, and most importantly, added them onto the bill of countless DKs shows. Biafra dubbed the record, *Brown Reason to Live* and it became its new moniker, despite the fact the record was actually eponymously titled, further proof of his influence over the scene. It wasn't long before the name "Butthole Surfers" was being uttered by punks across the country.

The band was thrilled to have their name on their own record, but they were already lightyears away from where were while recording it, and by the time the EP was hitting stores, they were already practicing with a second drummer they met while working in the kitchen of an Austin restaurant, the Pecan Street Café.

San Antonio was losing its luster for the boys. The scene in Austin was weird and exciting, so they often shacked up with friends and girlfriends to remain within its city limits. Eventually, they got jobs to help with the bills.

It was while she was washing dishes at the cafe that Teresa Taylor first met Gibby and Paul. While smoking a joint in the loft above the kitchen at the café, Teresa mentioned that she had a practice space in her living room, where she was cohabitating with members of another Austin-based band, the Buffalo Gals. When the subject was broached if the Butthole Surfers could make arrangements to practice there as well, she couldn't find much of a reason to say no.

Teresa was just 21 years old, and though she had tinkered around with Buffalo Gals and local artist collective, Meat Joy, she was never officially in a band. the Butthole Surfers were *famous*. They had toured California. They knew Jello Biafra personally and had a record out on Alternative Tentacles! To her, she was washing dishes alongside the biggest band in the world, and in her world, they were.

It was during some downtime during a practice at the loft that Gibby picked up a guitar to jam upon. Teresa joined in on drums. Gibby almost immediately realized that something special was happening between them. After a short deliberation, he brought forth the proposition that she join the band full-time. After the struggle to find one drummer, they now had two. This irony was only outshone by the oddball idea that a punk band would have two drummers: like the Grateful Dead, the Allman Bros, or the JB's.

But as they practiced more, they knew that Teresa was the perfect fit for the band. Not even Bill was in denial about it. Being asked to join, for Teresa, was like a dream come true: a touring band with a record out on Alternative Tentacles was like joining ABBA. Now she was going to be a part of it. Her days working at the Pecan Street Café seemed to be numbered.

Bill:
"I think she was playing with the Buffalo Gals in Austin and I think a couple of "The Gals" had rented the second floor of a warehouse space on 5th Street in Austin right off IH 35 (some of them were actually living there) and they had

Gibby at the Club Foot 5/13/83
© Suzanne Ferguson

a permanent setup there and we would use that space sometimes to practice in and that is how, I think, I first met Teresa and think that she probably started to jam with us and that is likely how she ended up playing with us."
[email 2010]

With King playing his skeleton drum kit, Teresa began filling in the sparse beats he laid down with a dazzling array of tom-work and cymbal smashes. She meticulously tuned her drums until each was a musical instrument unto itself and worked tirelessly to learn the band's vast repertoire as quickly as possible When the loft was unavailable, they would practice at the Big Boys practice pad in Chris Gates' garage, and soon, the songs took on a new vibrancy and vitality.

Teresa was a frail waif of a girl but threw all of her weight behind her thunderous beats, catapulting herself off the ground with each bash of the floor tom. She stood beside King and they traded places behind each other's kits, sometimes mid-song. Between the two of them the rhythm section became like a steam roller. They took Killing Joke, the Velvet Underground, Wire and the Jimi Hendrix Experience together and intertwined them like the roots of a banyan tree. Crushing them like roadkill into hot asphalt. All the boys were impressed with the new possibilities Teresa offered their sound, and without dissention, Teresa 'Nervosa' Taylor was welcomed into the band.

Teresa remembers:
"They said they had just gotten their new drummer, King, and he stood up, and they needed a place to practice, so they started coming over there and practicing...Pecan Street was just walking distance over to the warehouse on 5th Street in downtown Austin... we rented a warehouse for $40 a month...One afternoon, Gibby was in the rehearsal room, just fooling around with the guitar, and I came in and I sat behind Jaime Spidle's, of the Buffalo Gals, drum set. I just started playing a little drums to what he was playing on guitar and we just jammed for like five minutes, it was really stupid, but like two days later he said, 'Do you want to join our band and come to California, and I was like, "SURE!!'"...[phone interview, 7/26/14]

9/16/83, Austin
© Suzanne Ferguson

Onstage, trading places behind the drum kits, it was difficult to tell them apart from each other. Perhaps at some point someone used the term "twin drummers" to describe them, and they ran with it. King and Teresa began referring to themselves in interviews as 'brother and sister' or 'womblings'.

Even now, someone may be reading this and learning for the first time that King and Teresa *aren't* actually related. The myths the band created around itself had the propensity to snowball into brand new truths. These new truths would soon be perpetuated in magazine articles, third party recollections, and when speaking to the band members themselves: who loved to make themselves laugh way more than they liked to give a proper interview about the band. Even as they gained an ardent fan base, few had any idea that the brother-sister drum combo in the Butthole Surfers was a fairytale concocted for their own bemusement.

Teresa:
"I feel bad because people like the girls in Frightwig...I heard later that someone would say that Teresa and King really aren't brother and sister, they had like tears in their eyes and they're like 'yes they ARE, I know them and

*they wouldn't LIE...', and I started to feel bad. Later when I would meet
someone in my personal life, and I'd be like yeah me and King are brother
and sister.. and they'd be like, 'tell me about your childhood,. and I'd be like
oh it's a big lie."* [phone interview, 7/26/14]

Watching them thrash behind their kits in perfect unison, one could easily
make the mistake of believing King and Teresa were incubated in the same embryonic
fluid. The drums that were once shambolic and disjointed under Scott Mathews, and
nearly non-existent after him, were now a sonic barrage, as Teresa frantically danced
around the solid and steady beats that King laid down.

One only needed to listen to the new tribal introduction to "Something" to hear
how far the band had progressed since Teresa's arrival from far beyond the stars. By
the time Gibby and Paul had time to exalt the release of *Brown Reason to Live*, the
Butthole Surfers were already shifting and forging further into new dimensions.

With their record in stores and a brand-new rhythm section behind them, it was
time to get back to California for a visit. They had unfinished business to attend to. As
the hot summer breezes blew into autumn, they borrowed a van from Bob O'Neil and
headed out west once again. With the record out, and a tour of the West coast set up,
Bob was hoping to finally see some return on his investment as well.

The tour began in November with a stop in Phoenix at Mad Gardens, a former
wrestling rink that still had ropes and turnbuckles for the bands to play inside. As one
photographer took pictures of the band for a local fanzine, Gibby grabbed his head and
crammed it into his crotch. The photographer, caught completely unaware, flailed and
waved to escape, to no use. Finally, Gibby let go and the photographer stumbled
blindly away from the stage. This tour, no one would be spared from the madness, nor
forget what band they were witnessing onstage.

From Phoenix to Pasadena, to play a massive show at Perkins Palace with their
pals the minutemen and TSOL all oddly opening for make-up clad Brits; the Sex Gang
Children. Then it was up to the Bay Area, and back into their element, with a couple
of shows with Jello and the Dead Kennedys, as well as their brethren the Dicks, who
like MDC, had recently reformed in San Francisco with an updated line-up. They then
headed up to Seattle for an extended visit, including a Christmas night show at the
Graven Image Club.

The persistent van troubles that plagued the first trip to California popped up
again, but this time, things got sorted out quickly and the trip flowed along without
much of a hassle. They ventured back down the coast, and even had some promotion
and support preceding their visits to each city. It was amazing what could be
accomplished when people believed in you and were on your side, and especially
people like Jello Biafra and Alternative Tentacles.

With the punks finally knowing some of the songs in their set, they began getting some decent support from the crowds as well. They had some of the first gigs as headliners outside of Texas and were even co-billed for a New Year's Eve gig with DKs, proving in just a few short months that they could be placed alongside even the premier punk acts in the country.

And let's face the facts for a moment: punk was where it was at, musically, in the Reagan era. You certainly couldn't find commercial radio breaking new ground in the 1980s. 80's pop rock was earning big money for major labels and in this pre-Nirvana world, there was little room for punk bands on their rosters, nor on the turntables of any of the commercial radio stations around the country.

Neither were they fed through the cables at MTV. The suits at MTV seemed content to play John Cougar Mellencamp's "Jack and Diane" 20 times a day; or Billy Joel's "Uptown Girl". Content with the same cash cows the industry had been milking for years, driving kids into the same mindless complacence they had in the 1970's. Now with music videos, it was even easier to herd the sheep into their tiny pens.

And yet, all the while, as the U.S. economy wallowed, and our Big Stick foreign policy bred fear into the hearts of children around the globe, there was an underground movement that spoke out against the self-centered egotism of the Me Generation. Our president, the former governor of the fine state of California, had once sent National Guard troops onto the campus of Berkeley College to break up Vietnam war protestors, calling them 'communists' and 'anti-American'.

Now, at the helm of the country, he built up a military industrial complex that stretched around the globe. Ronald Reagan ran the Cold War, as well as his new war on drugs, as if America was in the throes of battle. He had the hubris of the former Hollywood icon he was, and touted how Russia should be outlawed and that bombing would begin in five minutes. The government began enforcing property seizures and mandatory minimum sentences for repeat drug offenders and boasted a 43% increase in defense spending since taking the helm from the Carter administration in 1981, including serious plans for an ICBM missile defense shield in space, dubbed "Star Wars". Suddenly, American's paranoia against the counter- culture was amped up, and the threat of Communist infiltrators and a nuclear holocaust seemed quite real.

Air raid drills began being practiced in elementary schools again and a seemingly endless tide of conflicts sprang up in the Banana Republics of Central America between forces backed by both of the reigning Superpowers. TV movies about 'The Day After' garnered huge ratings as people sat back to find out what would actually happen should our President or the General Secretary of the Soviet Union at the time, Yuri Andropov, were to have a particularly shitty morning and make one hasty decision

It seemed as if these power mongers in charge dealt with the threat of nuclear holocaust as a by-product of having the finer things in life. They strapped on their Walkman and went jogging to forget about the "world outside." Don't Worry, Be Happy.

But the kids who were forming punk bands were truly frightened, hurt, paranoid and pissed. They were left feeling betrayed by their parents, whose 60's ideals had been beaten out of them through endless evenings of frozen dinners and disco dancing. This wasn't just something happening on the TV news for the kids. They couldn't tune out or turn off until the next conflict broke out, like their parents had done. This was too real and too scary. The underground scene began to flourish because the residents who resided there felt called into some kind of action.

Teresa & King, Seattle Dec 16, 1983
© Carlene Heitman

As punk rock gained headlines for its "violent nature", authorities wondered what the root cause of America's troubled youth could be. The feminist revolution of the '70's, and a desire to attain a piece of the ever more expensive American Dream meant more and more housewives were entering the workforce. Their own desire for the finer things had created a generation of latch key kids and bored teenagers. The best the president's First Lady could offer to the youth was a "Just Say No" anti-drug campaign.

Punk rock was viewed by its critics as trying to destroy society, most kids, however, saw it as their call to arms in the war to save it. Punk, at its best, offered a vision, focus, drive, and purpose for these kids. Art, music, and literature offered higher levels of thought. But above all, punks admired those willing to act.

As many of the punk bands of the 70's slowly began to dissolve, the new hardcore movement that took hold in the U.S. had an agenda, or at least a motive, to act up and speak out. There was a unifying notion that the vapid and insipid bands who were ignoring the impending mushroom clouds on the horizon were accomplices to those who were attempting to create them.

The Dead Kennedys were a lightning rod for the idea of music as a political force. Biafra's run for mayor of San Francisco in 1978, though unsuccessful, gave the band mountains of mainstream press. His street corner buffoonery openly mocked the campaign process, as he grinned maniacally and kissed baby dolls before throwing them over his shoulder. He set up a political platform of banning cars from downtown San Francisco and requiring all businessmen to dress in clown suits as they rode their bikes to work.

However ridiculous, his message managed to strike a chord with those "average" city dwellers who were tired of losing their city to the big money power brokers setting the agenda. He came in fourth out of 10 candidates, a respectable showing that forced a runoff election between the front-runners that eventually led to a Diane Feinstein victory. She remained mayor until 1992, when she left for DC to become the state's senator until her death in 2024, so he was beaten by an institution.

Jello ran with the press he received and his knack for drumming up controversy and penchant for hyperbolic, absurdist wit carried on in the finest tradition of Abby Hoffman, H.L. Mencken and George Carlin. He put the fear of God into the Christian Conservative Right and their loudest mouthpiece, then known as the Moral Majority. You could bet that, when the Southern Baptist churches held their Saturday night record burnings, you would find a copy of "Fresh Fruit for Rotting Vegetables' or 'In God We Trust, Inc.' in smoldering pile of melted plastic.

Gibby and Bill at Metropolis, Seattle 12/16/83
© Carlene Heitman

And with the influence the Dead Kennedys had globally, hardcore bands began to spring up everywhere, not just in the USA, but in the countries of Eastern Europe torn in half by the cold war, and the third world countries used as pawns in the chess battle between the ruling Superpowers. They began to aspire to be able to make a difference, and, perhaps more idealistically, dream of earning a living wage as a member of a punk band. Of course, this had its unintended negative consequences as well.

More and more hardcore bands were faster, rawer, and angrier than the British punk bands who helped cleave the path before them, yet few were much more than that. Punks became suspicious if a band didn't fit into a precise formula, and often turned on each other with cries of "poseur" or "trust-fund punk" to make sure bands followed the rules as they saw them. The prospect of "selling out" became the sword of Damocles to bands, who had to make sure not to stray too far from what narrow-minded punks thought they should sound, or act or believe.

This made the Butthole Surfers an even stranger anomaly for the time. By not being quite 'punk rock' there was always a bit of suspicion of where they stood. By liking them, you were opening yourself up to ridicule. Of course, the band's name became the focus of so much publicity, as most people passed them off as a campy joke, or gay. "The Shah Sleeps in Lee Harvey' Grave" was almost as offensive to punks as it was to mainstream folks, for it seemed to mock the stupidity of punk rock as much as it did the insanity of straight society.

But as the band played out more and more, and often in the context of a Dead Kennedys bill, the more it was that open-minded punks began getting the joke. There was something more to the Butthole Surfers, something real. And while the Butthole Surfers could make you piss your pants with laughter at any given moment, there was nothing that seemed contrived about them. If Biafra was the man running the anti-establishment rally, the Butthole Surfers were the ones who were showing up trying to score some weed. They were the Dead Kennedys comic relief. Flava Flav to Jello's Chuck D.

They returned from California with their heads held high. The tour gave the band a whole new outlook on the profession they had chosen. Having returned with their first real taste of success on the road, they began to realize exactly what they needed to do to create a successful band. They needed to get out of Texas.

But, as 1983's sunset dawned into 1984's dystopia, the band remained firmly rooted in the Lone Star State. They managed to make a few short excursions back to the West Coast, to New Orleans, and even pulled a trip up to NYC to visit Cheryl, who had been attending the Pratt Art Institute, as well as to purchase some cheap equipment they found. They played a couple of 'one off' shows while in NYC, but most of their time was spent back in Texas, recording songs that would hopefully comprise their next release, and playing the same old venues where they had become mainstays.

They were still splitting their time between Austin and San Antonio, playing gigs in Austin at night, and practically living at Bob O'Neil's studio the rest of the time, locking themselves inside for days on end. Recording and mixing was going particularly well and tapes were beginning to pile up in the corner of the room. Bob O'Neil was brave enough to let the band use the room and record on credit, a risky venture, especially since the band was more or less broke all the time and had little hope of being able to pay him back.

The idea that Bob play piano on some tracks they hoped to release someday helped knock the bill down a bit, but with the endless hours spent recording, splicing

Paul in Seattle, December 16, 1983
© Carlene Heitman

and mixing, they were in way over their heads.

As word of 'A Brown Reason's' mixture of comedy and art-punk was spreading around the country, the band was near penniless, and in relative seclusion caused part by necessity, but also by the nagging feeling that they needed to reproduce their new sound on vinyl.

With the prospects of heading out on the road always lingering, but never seeming to come to fruition, Bill took a job as a landscaper, Teresa continued to wash dishes long after she thought she would have to, and they took on any odd jobs they could to earn some extra cash, yet which wouldn't hinder them from leaving should the opportunity present itself. Still, it was a full half-year now since the EP had been released and they remained languishing in their home state.

When the band was onstage, they were on fire. A couple of shows with New York's Shockabilly, in Austin and Houston were great, and then Shockabilly left to head back on the road. The Dead Kennedys, too, came and went, as did Articles of Faith, Minor Threat and Black Flag. Gibby and Paul and Bill, and King and Teresa watched bands come and then they watched them go. All the while they stayed behind to play yet another show at Voltaire's or Raw Power & Light Co. or the Continental Club. These tiny dives were practically bursting at the seams when the Buttholes played, but still they remained.

After the hope and anticipation of a proper U.S. tour only led to frustration, the drudgery of being cash poor began to wear on Bill's nerves. The cache of songs in the can was vast, and recording became less of a priority, and the idea of continuing to play around Texas got stale to him. There was little incentive to keep playing in a band that was going nowhere. Totally ready to commit, but frustrated, he sat back and waited for a call telling him when the tour would begin.

In his waiting, Bill stopped going to practice. His bass was at the studio, but he was never there to play it. Despite having enough material to fill two LPs recorded and ready to be released, it seemed like Alternative Tentacles, too, had taken a vacation from the band.

They began putting together a new full-length album that was driving them back into the dark recesses of the studio, instead of out onto the road, on those warm and sunny days. The music they were making sat on reels in canisters at the BOSS as Alternative Tentacles spent its time focusing on the band that kept them in the black: the Dead Kennedys. Word from the Butthole Surfers camp that they were ready to release their follow up record did little to peak any interest at Alternative Tentacles, nor with Bill Jolly. Bill was growing weary.

Bill Jolly:
"Part of problem for me was that when we got 'back' from the road, everyone had a place to stay in Austin except me and I had to resort to living out of my sister's house in San Antonio with no money. I would sleep on the floor at various places, I think partly with the bass player from Big Boys [Chris Gates] and Paul's girlfriend's house. If we would have had even some type of communal place to stay that might have changed things for me a lot. But being broke was no fun and with the prospect of heading out to tour, it was not very practical to get a 'job.' I remember working landscaping in San Antonio for a while just to scrape up some money, with the added benefit that I could just leave anytime." [email, 2010]

It is a bit unclear as to what might have been holding the band back. Perhaps it was the lack of a proper vehicle. Perhaps they were still sore from the wounds of the last failed attempt to leave, and still needed time to heal.   The band had tried to branch out of their home state before, prematurely. It was not only a financial failure, but it had literally torn the band apart. Long-time friendships were left strewn in its wake. It took Gibby and Paul nearly a year of struggling to piece together a 7 song EP out of the wreckage, and even longer to muster up a proper fulltime band.

Bill, Paul & Teresa, Voltaire's Basement closing, Austin, 5/19/84
© Dixon Edge Coulbourn

They had finally hit their stride again as a five piece. If they were to crash and burn now, it would have surely meant the demise of the Butthole Surfers. It would have been nearly impossible to tail drag themselves back to Texas to assemble yet another group of freaks to fill vacated roles a second or third time. But, with Bill not showing up for practice, it seemed as though their calculated and methodical approach was betraying them.

A huge show was being planned that was to feature 20 or so bands playing outside in a shady grove in the sleepy, rural town of Driftwood. The 'Woodshock Festival' would bring together almost all of the punk bands operating out of Austin and San Antonio at the time. Bill hadn't been heard from for weeks, and with the festival drawing near, they decided to play the show without him.

Again, left without a bass player, Paul filled the vacant slot and Gibby took on guitar duties. Bill watched from the crowd as they managed to pull a rag tag set out of their asses, switching bass and guitar, and even calling up King's former Hugh Beaumont Experience bandmate, David McCreath up for a song. With David on bass, it at least allowed Gibby to play sax on the newer crowd favorite, "BBQ Pope".

The 20-minute performance was almost a microcosm of the band the year after Mathews Brothers had quit, switching instruments and recruiting friends to get the job done. It was a difficult year and one which they had hoped was behind them, but the struggles were not over yet, it seemed.

When the performance was done, Bill hopped up on stage, grabbed the bass guitar, and pulled out a solo to put the icing on their set, and the nail in the coffin. Gibby, who had been forced into playing this gig as a guitarist, bassist, singer and sax player due to Bill's absence, sounds a bit flustered, as he tries to find the words to say…:

'That was….that was…Bill… our old…our old bass player, saying goodbye' …

Paul seems slightly more put off by Bill's appearance that night, and retorts something resembling…

'He forgot he was in the band…'

With Bill, backstage at Voltaire's Basement, 5/19/84
© Dixon Edge Coulbourn

There was a smattering of applause after Bill's final strum of the old bass he used while he was in the band. King and Teresa start breaking down their drums and Paul walked away to start breaking down his rig, avoiding any further mention of Bill and his bass playing. And just like that, Bill Jolly was no longer a Butthole Surfer.

During Bill's tenure, the band's reputation had grown to legendary proportions within the confines of Texas. He had been instrumental to the band in nearly every sense of the word. Without his input, they might not have ever completed *Brown Reason to Live*. Their entire existence after that late night fist fight in Dallas might have been in question had he not stepped up and offered his help. With his jazz fusion roots and agility on bass, they blossomed into the band most people think of when mentioning the Butthole Surfers, even today.

Newer songs like "Whirling Hall of Knives," "Lady Sniff," and "Dum Dum" featured odder, more complex structures and themes than their old cache of punk rock tunes. "Peggy on Mannix" gave way to "Cherub the Angel". They became a more cerebral band, without losing their sense of humor or visceral, punk rock foundation.

Though Bill Jolly's impact goes largely unrecognized, he was an integral part of the development of the new band's most notable feature: their rhythm section. The indelible mark he left on the band would leave a shadow far longer than his tenure, and though Bill's life span as a member, more than a solid year, was one of the longest in the laundry list of Butthole Surfers bass players, he often remains one of the forgotten names of their past.

Bill helped build the engine that propelled the band out of Texas, and propel they did, as shortly after he disappeared, they skidded away from the curb. He sat alone in the dust cloud as the Butthole Surfers headed out of Texas and across the United States of America. Just a mere few weeks after their shambolic appearance at Woodshock, they were gone.

Shortly after their performance, the Butthole Surfers were practicing with a new bass player named Terence Smart. Terence had bummed around the local music scene for a while as a member of the band Part White but was just about ready to give up on music entirely. As another Trinity alum, Terence and Gibby had crossed paths a few times in other capacities over the years: when Gibby had been president of his fraternity, and captain of Trinity's Varsity basketball team. Now the two would be bumping into each other on a stage, instead of in the halls of the college, and with Gibby in his underwear, rather than a suit and tie.

It was while heading into a local music store in San Antonio that the two formally met, while Terence was tacking his resume to a bulletin board. They got to chatting, which quickly led to jamming. Despite not quite having the chops that Bill had on the instrument, Terence had much more in common with the rest of the band than Bill did, plus, he had a car. They all soon became fast friends, quickly forgetting about Bill, the guy who had forgotten he was in the band.   So, with the band getting tired of Texas, and now having a vehicle to do something about it, they decided to give

Terence tapes of the vast catalogue of songs they had collecting dust, in hopes he was a fast learner. After all of Bill's waiting, it was not until his departure from the group that a large enough fire was ignited under their proverbial asses to make them realize they needed to strike out and venture out onto the road and out of Texas, even if they had nothing new to tour behind.

Enter Terence, July 1984, San Antonio
© Pat Blashill

King:
"...Bill stopped showing up for gigs. It was about this time that we made a pact with the devil that we would hit the road and leave Texas for good. It turned out the vehicle we would pack it all into was Terence's Nova. Besides being a cool guy, and cool bass player, his chief qualification, much like mine, was that he was willing to do it." [email, 2001]

They made plans to head back to New York City and to stay there long enough this time to book some shows down the east coast to cities they had not yet visited.

Aside from Cheryl, they had some other old Trinity friends in the area who were willing to help them out. They had some new friends too in their burgeoning, but avid, fanbase. New York seemed the ideal place to set up shop for an extended visit. With or without a new release to push, they knew that waiting around in Texas for Alternative Tentacles' interest to peak could spell ruin for the band.

The relationship between band and label had further deteriorated when royalties from *Brown Reason to Live* had all but ceased. When they finally got a hold of the DKs manager Mike Vraney, he told the band that all of the money Alternative Tentacles was bringing in was being used to subsidize a new Dead Kennedys record. A new Butthole Surfers album was not even on AT's radar. Now, there was a lack of wages in addition to a lack of interest. The Butthole Surfers had been Jello's pet project, but with his time being dedicated more and more to the Dead Kennedys, the Buttholes were left to fend for themselves.

Word that the Butthole Surfers had become disenchanted with their label made few waves, but it did pique the interest of one person: Corey Rusk. Rusk was once the bass player for seminal Mid-West hardcore band, the Necros, but since their demise had been focused on running his own record label, Touch & Go, out of his home in Dearborn, Michigan. The label was a hardcore label, used as a vehicle for releasing Necros material, along with that of his fellow co-founder Tesco Vee, and his band, the Meatmen, but Corey had been looking for new bands to add to the label's small roster in order to expand its horizons.

Touch & Go Records was born out of a fanzine of the same name that Corey started with Tesco several years prior in hopes of documenting the fledgling Mid-West punk scene, as well luring national bands to the play in the area. After releasing a handful of records by their own bands, they put out a couple of records by their friends Negative Approach and The Fix. In 1984, however, Tesco decided to relocate to Washington DC and in doing so, handed his half of the operation over to Corey Rusk and his wife Lisa. Now as sole proprietors, the Rusks were working hard to expand the label's limited cache of bands.

Even before *Brown Reason to Live* had been released, Corey was a huge Butthole Surfers fan. First, when his band the Necros played with the Dead Kennedys. Jello dropped Corey a tape, which he claims was quickly stolen, and apparently pretty much forgotten about. His friend in NYC, Terry Tolkin, also sung their praises while the Necros were playing some shows in the area that Terry had booked for them.

But, it wasn't until a year or so later that Corey began to honestly take notice of the band. Corey's long-time friend, Ian McKaye, gave him a cassette of some old demos he had gotten when his band Minor Threat had passed through Texas early in 1983, and Corey was finally hooked.

Minor Threat had been treated to some of Biscuit's Southern hospitality, setting up a show with Minor Threat and the Big Boys, giving them a place to crash, and, in departing, with some tapes of local bands to check out while on the road;

including a demo tape of the latest Butthole Surfers recordings.

Ian was floored. The godfather of Straight Edge philosophy didn't need to be high to know that this band had something to them. Upon Minor Threat's next stop in Michigan, he threw the tape at Rusk, touting his praises of the Lone Star State; the Big Boys; and the Butthole Surfers.

Corey agreed with Ian's assessment and began listening to the tape constantly; at first laughing at its crudeness, and then enamored by the infectious melding of Black Flag and the 13th Floor Elevators. If there was any chance that the Butthole Surfers were going to be without a label, then he was more than willing to provide them a proper home, and he made it his mission to procure them.

When Corey called the band at their home in Texas and was told they were heading to NYC toward the end of August, he decided to invite them to stop off in Detroit on the way, to stay with him and to play a gig at Paycheck's Lounge, a small dive bar in the Detroit suburb of Hamtramck. With no real agenda set in NYC, they accepted his offer. They were still a band very committed to remaining in the Alternative Tentacles stable, but a gig in Detroit with the promise of a place to crash was too tempting for the band to resist.

Only a scant couple of weeks after studiously learning the massive cache of songs the band had compiled onto a few cassettes, Terence gutted out his 1976 Chevy Nova, crammed in all 5 members of the band, and their unofficial sixth member, a new dog named Mark Farner (after the legendary singer/guitarist of rock power trio, Grand Funk Railroad), and pulled away from the curb of his house in San Antonio. A few hours later, they crossed the state line and headed out of Texas.

Teresa & Mark Farner
© Pat Blashill

Take me back to Detroit, Paul

The band arrived in Detroit to open arms. It must have been strange to meet somebody who was enthusiastic about seeing them. They had spent so many nights in Texas as just another band on the bill. But in Detroit, Corey made up flyers and promoted the show like a man possessed. The club was tiny, but it was packed and primed for a Saturday night fiasco, with the jubilant crowd anxious to finally witness the band that Corey had been gushing over for the previous year. They would not leave disappointed.

They Butthole's set opened as it often did back in Texas, with "Mexican Caravan", which despite being unreleased, always managed to whip the crowd into a frenzy. Its screaming guitar solo and guitarist shrieking about his penchant for the white devil kicked things off with a bang:

Take Me, Mexican Caravan, Let's score some of that heroin, you know the way to make the white boy sin, take me, Mexican...

The next song "Cherub", however, showcased a new direction for the band. A simmering, tribal brew bubbling to a boil; hypnotic and foreboding, Cherub is a tale of rubbernecking past a fatal car wreck that is every bit as creepy as Jim Morrison's vision of Indians strewn upon dawn's highway bleeding.

Paul eerily manipulated his feedback into a swirl of red and blue lights while Gibby, who by this point had traded in his used-up toilet paper roll for an actual megaphone, directed traffic passed the carnage. The Angel of Mercy struggles with the mangled vessel for the soul inside. The mood changes as she confronts the victims with a scream:

"They walk right past you, they stop and stare, your body is lying all over there..."

Sirens wail and horns honk before the mayhem subsides as time seems to stand still. The fleeting lives of the onlookers pass, trapped inside their own personal Hells. The song clocks in at over 5 minutes, an eternity in the world of punk rock, but the crowd was totally entranced the whole time.

The remainder of the set was mixed with staples both released and still unheard by fans outside of Texas. The two newest songs brought in with Terence's arrival were "Tornadoes" and "To Parter". The former harkens back to the band's earliest punk days, bashing away on a single note before a crescendo leads to a chorus about a twister blowing through their hair, while the second is a rollicking adventure about sailors, monkeys, Quaaludes, and our own failed public education system.

Gibby had taken to adding a second guitar for these songs, adding yet another element to the band's cacophony, which was now peppered with the nuances of everything from the Birthday Party in a "Big Jesus Trash Can", Chrome dropping a 'Cold and Clamy Bombing', and even Kaptain Kopter viewing the "Things Yet to Come". It was Flipper's minimalist aural assault with a distinctly Southern drawl.

Lyrically, Gibby ripped a page out of Faulkner and folded it into origami, twisting and bending reality onto an entirely new animal. Marcel Duchamp donning a dress and exposing his female alter-ego, Rrose Selavy. Strange meanderings interweave the beautiful and the grotesque. He pays homage to the best in Southern Gothic, while still pissing in 'The Fountain' of the high-brow art elitists.

This particular night ended with the droning 'Whirling Hall of Knives' trailing off into space until it was drowned out by the sound of applause and cat calls. Some bass amp troubles that plagued the band's set early on go largely unnoticed by anyone else other than the band themselves, and Corey, who had not been privy to the band's new direction, was left as stunned as anyone in the crowd, drenched in a daze of weed smoke and strobe lights.

After the gig, the band hung around Detroit for a little while, taking in the sights and forging the foundations of a friendship, while Corey tried to coax the band into releasing a record with Touch & Go. It was certainly a tempting offer considering the current state of affairs, but the band packed up their meager belongings, squeezed back into the Nova, and headed off to NYC, still very much Alternative Tentacles recording artists.

Summer in the City

The long drive from Detroit to New York was tight and uncomfortable, with each of them taking turns lying down in the gutted trunk of the Nova and Mark Farner the dog stepping over them. It finally ended at Cheryl Dyer's apartment on Mott Street, in the Little Italy section of Manhattan. Within days of arriving, they started playing shows, booked by Terry Tolkin, who Gibby had contacted just prior to leaving Texas.

Terry was pulling a part time shift at "99" Records [pronounced "Nine-Nine"] in Greenwich Village. From 99 records came the 99 Record label, instrumental in bringing many of NY's next wave of no-wave dance music out from the underground and into the vibrant clubs of Manhattan. 99 Records would go on to become iconic for releasing records by Liquid Liquid, Glenn Branca, ESG, and the Bush Tetras, but at the time it was a fledgling label garnering little attention outside of the SoHo area dance crowd. So, Terry took on an second job working nights in the offices of the Danceteria club to earn some extra cash, and to promote his gift of recognizing talent.

Danceteria was always hopping, whether a band was playing or not. The four-story building in Chelsea brought in celebrities, artists, and filmmakers, as well as students from NYU and the Cooper Union art school crowd. They would all mingle with the seedier Lower East Side punks looking to go uptown, get drunk, and coalesce with some rich, suburban new wave chicks.

After a while working in the office there, Terry was able to score a DJing gig on Tuesdays and Wednesdays, the slower nights at the club. He was able to play his own stable of bands, as well as pull records from his own stash, drawing from his vast knowledge of the underground scene from the US and abroad.

When he took Gibby's call, Terry was totally taken aback. He had been playing the Butthole Surfers EP in the record store ad nauseum and though perplexed, he was psyched to hear from the lead singer of his newest favorite band. Gibby told Tery the band was on their way to New York and wanted to book some shows. Although Terry had never booked a gig in his life, the phone call became an alarm whistle and gave Terry a flash of brilliance. He immediately went and asked the management of the club if he could indeed do some booking and promoting for the nights he worked. They not only agreed, but they gave him an allowance of $2000 to get it done.

The burst of inspiration got Terry booking them some other shows around the area as well, so when the Buttholes arrived in NYC they already had an itinerary. With some shows lined-up, it was the perfect inspiration to pack up and get out of Texas. It may have been a bit too late for Bill Jolly but, the rest of the band, with Terence, were ready to take on the challenge of winning over the fickle New York City audiences.

Terry Tolkin recounts:
"...Gibby just called me up at the store I was working at (99 Records) and said he heard that I booked shows. I never had but I was working in the office at Danceteria and DJ'ing there on their off nights, Tuesday and Wednesday. I asked the owners if I could book some shows on those days too and they gave me $2K each week to do it! I called Gibby back right away and they were on their way in a week." [email, Sept 2012]

Once they arrived in NY, Cheryl, ever the artist, got to work on helping them pimp their ride. This car was not fitting of a band as noble as the Butthole Surfers. She and the band took to their new art project: Terence's gutted Nova. It was spray-painted, and the number "69" was scrawled onto the trunk. The words "Lady Killer" adorned the hood, and rolls of barbed wire, rags of tattered clothes, and a dismembered baby doll were enmeshed into the front grill.

The band would cram into the 'Lady Killer' and terrorize the streets of New York City, or rattle across the Hudson into Hoboken. They even pulled a commando drive down to DC for a gig. The members not lucky enough to call shotgun were forced to lie in back on a bed of plywood, their elbows bruised and splintered from being bashed around the potholed streets.

A crazed cabbie in who cut them off bore the full brunt of the Lady Killer's wrath, getting caught in the barbed steel mesh, and taking the entire front end of the car with him, dragging it down the city streets spraying a trail of sparks in his wake.

Butthole Surfers shows began not when they hit the stage, but as they pulled up to the curb. The electricity snowballed from there, culminating when the lights dimmed and the band would pick up their instruments, seemingly as an after-thought to hanging out, getting loaded, and causing a ruckus.

Paul:
"That Nova was the coolest. Poor Terence let us "customize" it by sawing the trunk out so three people and Mark Farner could fit in the trunk on pieces of plywood, while towing the equipment in a U-Haul. We added rolls of barbed wire to the front grill, and spray-painted "69" on both doors, and "Lady Killer" on the hood. There was even a plastic baby doll and some clothes stuck in the barbed wire. One day a New York cab came too close to the front of us, and its

bumper snagged the barbed wire, pulling off the grill and front bumper."
[posted Jan 2011]

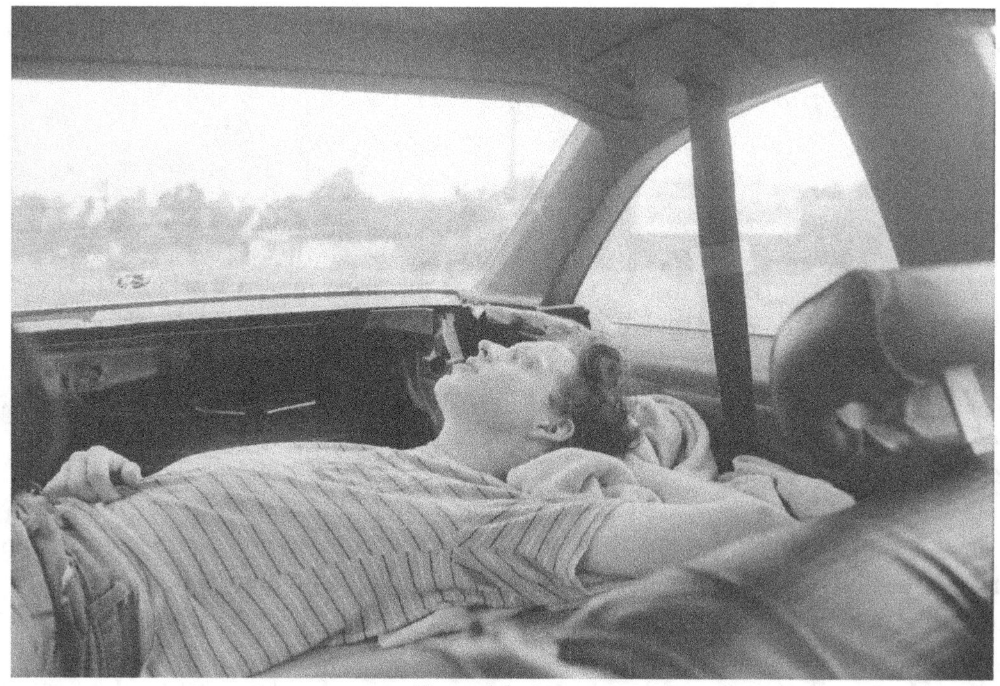

King of the Nova
© Pat Blashill

There was little pretention with the Butthole Surfers. They weren't trying to fit into the NYC art scene. They were in New York what they had been in California: Texans exiled from their home state due to their inability to make a living there. They'd walk into a club barefoot, with their faithful pooch Mark Farner meandering around amongst them, and at times, even with them onstage.

Their Texas drawls and dirty jeans made them look as if they were Wild West gunslingers walking into a saloon after a dust storm. This was not how NYC artists looked or behaved. It was probably a large part of what drew so many artists to them, as there is little that NYC artists love as much as irony.

Money was tight and their stay in the Big Apple was open ended. They'd scrounge enough to buy some meager groceries or toss a carton of cigarettes to their hosts before outstaying their welcome and moving on to the next hostel, cheap hotel, or apartment of some kind soul they had met the previous night.

Their new pal Terry helped them with a place to crash too. When Cheryl needed a break from the madness, they'd all go crash at his apartment on Bond Street, located in the Bowery just across from CBGBs. Cheryl's pad in Little Italy provided them free grub from the Italian restaurants discarding their unsold meals into the dumpsters out back. It was the desperation of survival mode that they adopted to stay alive. This trip would not end in failure, and if they needed to eat out of dumpsters to ensure its success then that was what they would do.

After a couple of weeks ping-ponging between Terry and Cheryl's, they headed across the East River into Brooklyn, to the apartment of long-time friends Alan Tubbs and his wife, Mary Hestand. Mary had attended Trinity with the boys and was now enrolled in grad school at Columbia University, studying drama. Alan had known Gibby since Junior high school back in Dallas and had been roommates with Paul while at Trinity as well. He had gotten his bachelor's degree in English but had now taken to sound recording, engineering, and editing. His affinity for sound manipulation and composition was put to good use by Mary in her performance pieces and 8mm art films. Once the Buttholes arrived, they not only had a decent place to crash, but a pretty nice studio in which to practice, as well.

Between Alan and Mary's apartment in Brooklyn, Cheryl's place in Little Italy, and Terry's pad in the Bowery, their new adoptive home was brimming with friends both new and old, as well as musicians, artists and filmmakers from NYC, and old Trinity pals visiting up from Texas. Their drama club and art school friends used the band as if they were dime store mannequins, trying out their props and costume creations, primping and blowing drying Paul's hair into a quaff like George Washington, or teasing up Gibby's locks into a huge, disheveled beehive. Never ones to shy away from shocking audiences with their audacity, they'd smoke some weed and try to sit still while being made over and experimented upon.

Paul decided that mere hair gel wasn't quite expressive enough, so he shaved his head into a sideways mohawk and dyed it pink. He then performed an operation on Terence's head, shaving peace signs and swirling spiral designs into his hair. It was a lot more acceptable in NYC than in Texas, and Terence recalls the odd feeling of not even getting gawked at while sporting the most ridiculous hairdos and outfits through the streets of Manhattan.

While their oddball appearance may not have gotten much notice from the passersby on the street, it wasn't long before the band was noticed by the local press. Soon, their faces were popping up in local fanzines; Gibby's hair filled with clothespins, his boxer shorts stained with fake blood.

They gave interviews to magazine writers as if they were yucking it up with their friends back at the apartment. Any talk relating to the band was purely coincidental. The enigma led to intrigue and within a few short weeks they were already playing to packed houses at venues like Tin Pan Alley, the Pyramid, and the Peppermint Lounge.

Often, like Danceteria, these clubs were packed every night regardless of whether a band was playing or not, and Gibby's bloodstained boxer shorts were exposed to throngs of kids in the depths of the NYC club culture scene, apart from the punks who filled venues like CBGB's and Trenton's City Gardens. The money was still non-existent, but the little money they did make from shows was immediately put into a communal band fund, which Gibby took tight control over.

They had a support network during their stay in NYC, at least, for as long as Cheryl or Alan and Mary or Terry could tolerate their carcasses cluttering up their apartment floors, or cooking for an army of hungry freaks, but any venture outside of the area needed to be paid and accounted for.

Things on the Alternative Tentacles front had quieted, and with the Dead Kennedys record produced, AT seemed now able to at least entertain Gibby and Paul's pleas to help them release a new record. There was still very little money to advance, however, and certainly not the kind of money they owed Bob O'Neil to get out of hock the hours-upon-hours of tapes he was holding as collateral for all the unpaid studio time.   They had slept in his tool shed out back, when they actually slept. Most nights were spent in the studio, and those often bled into sunup, when they'd stumble out to the shed for a few hours' sleep. Get up, buy a case of beer, steal a few eggrolls left outside to dry from the local Chinese restaurant, and hang out until the staff went home to record some more.

Bob O'Neil seemed to tolerate Gibby and Paul living on his property, using his van to tour, and filling canisters upon canisters of his tapes with their recordings, believing that Jello would bankroll it all. When AT seemed disinterested, there were thoughts of releasing the Butthole Surfers next effort on his own Ward 9 Records, Bob's newly formed label. At least, in Bob's mind there were. Should AT have second thoughts about another Butthole Surfers release, WARD 9 might be the band's new home.

It is unclear the method in which Bob O'Neil expected to get paid for all the studio time he fronted them, but he expected to get paid, no doubt, and Alternative Tentacles did not have its tendrils reaching into its pocketbook to do it.

So, with all their recordings held hostage at the BOSS, and with no money available for funding more studio time for a proper recording session, the band decided to throw AT an old live recording they had recorded the previous spring, back in San Antonio when Bill was still in the band. The recording, along with some crude clown renderings Paul scrawled on a piece of paper would comprise the next record. The recording had already been cleaned up by Paul and Mike 'Trombone' Taylor, engineer at the BOSS, and was mixed, mastered and released within a few weeks' time.

The resulting *Live PCPPEP* was basically an updating of the band's *Brown Reason to Live* record with the two drum line-up. Though it did feature an old unreleased set staple in "Cowboy Bob" and an odd sound experiment entitled "Dance of the Cobras" (later released in undoctored form as "Woly Boly"), it was not quite the new record they had in mind. While they got new product to help them pad their

Tools in the shed: at the BOSS, July 1984
© Pat Blashill

petty band fund, they themselves were left with a somewhat more empty feeling; slighted they didn't get the opportunity to give Alternative Tentacle a proper follow up to their debut outing. They knew they were capable of more, much more, and they wanted to give Alternative Tentacles a real studio LP to prove it. Instead, their entire recorded output on Alternative Tentacles featured two EPs that were filled with many of the same songs.

King:
"I barely remember what went down, but I do seem to recall that 'Psychic...' took a long time to finish, in both recording and figuring out what label would put it out. 'PCPPEP' was kind of a stop gap effort to put a record out in the interim and put some money in our hands.
I think initially 'Psychic...' was intended to be on Ward 9 (the label that put out 'Cottage Cheese from the Lips of Death' and the label side of the BOSS studio where 'Psychic...' was recorded). When it became clear that Ward 9 just really couldn't release an album properly, the band tried to steer it to

Alternative Tentacles. By that point, though, we had a big studio bill that AT couldn't afford to pay. The project was on hold until AT had some money themselves." [King, 2007]

Teresa

*"We hadn't even written any new songs, and it was like 'We'll just record the same songs live! That'll work!' It wasn't so much Alternative Tentacles that [wasn't paying us], I mean they were our label but, when we weren't selling records we went to Subterranean distribution, and the guy was like 'uhhh whatever, I'll **try** to get the records into stores, but you know how it goes,' and Gibby and Paul were like 'you gotta fuckin' get our records into STORES!' We had to threaten the guy."* [phone 7/26/14]

Oddly though, some people actually bought *Live PCPPEP*. They recognized the reworked arrangement in "Hey". They dug the new, lumbering, tribal intro to "Something", and the hilarious golf scores read during the rendition of "BBQ Pope". They also relished the prelude of the mayhem yet to come in "Cowboy Bob", which featured blood-curdling screams of another old Trinity pal, Michiko Sakai.

Michiko was the daughter of legendary World War II, Japanese fighter pilot, Saburo Sakai. He sent her to the United States "to learn English and democracy", and wound up at Trinity. She had been a fixture at Butthole Surfers shows whenever they played San Antonio, even before she took the stage to unleash the unholy shriek of her banshee calls. She had even been coaxed into joining the band for a short tour up the West Coast back when Bill was in the band.

But Bill was no longer in the band and Michiko was back in San Antonio and the Butthole Surfers were in NYC. And while the new EP with the old line-up was nice to have, their satisfaction with it, and with Alternative Tentacles, was dwindling. They put on their game faces, though. At the very least, they now had something new to tour behind.

Not that touring behind any particular record mattered much to the Butthole Surfers. Playing live was where they made their money, and they had been bouncing from club to club while in New York earning as much of it as they could scrounge. Tin Pan Alley, 8BC, to New Jersey and New York South and Maxwell's, there was seemingly a bottomless pit of shitholes and dive bars to play in the area, though it didn't take long before they were playing some of the bigger venues as well.

Danceteria, NYC, 9/8/1984
© Greg Fasolino

Terry's birthday party toward the end of summer meant a loft party at his place, with music provided by his friends, Frightwig, and much to his elation, the Butthole Surfers. This would have been a solid Saturday night line-up at CBGB's, a stone's throw away from his pad, but he held the bash in his tiny apartment instead. People were packed in like sardines, and stood out in the hall, and down the stairs out onto Bond Street.

When the cops inevitably showed up around 1AM, the Buttholes were thrashing away on a free form jam. Strobe lights were pulsating inside and flashing out onto the streets down below. There was little activity that was legal taking place, and when the cops finally arrived upstairs to the door of the apartment and saw the band, they immediately took notice…:

'Oh wow, it's the Butthole Surfers!'

Terry shook his head; all he could muster in the confusion through the haze of beer and LSD. The music crashed to a halt, and Terry called Gibby over to the door…

Once he arrived, it was like a family reunion. Gibby immediately recognized the cops. He had been wearing the same blood-stained dress from previous night's gig, when he had been taken in, detained, and begrudgingly released due to lack of evidence earlier that morning.

'No really, I'm IN A BAND, THE BLOODY DRESS I'M WEARING IS JUST A

STAGE PROP,' Gibby would plead.

It was a ridiculous story but with no evidence to detain him, they let him go, surely expecting the decapitated corpse of some prostitute to be found within days; washed up on the shores of the East River. Now here they were to find the same gigantic, cross-dressing Texan bashing away, not on some poor prostitute's skull, but on some real secondhand instruments. Vindication was finally his! The cops looked around at the crowd, swinging from the rafters…

'There have been complaints from the neighbors'…(no shit?)… *'wrap it up soon.'*

Terry told them 'no problem', that they'd be off within the hour. The cops shook their heads and walked downstairs to their car and drove off into the night. The Buttholes picked up where they left off, and the party raged on into the wee hours of the morning.

Terry Tolkin recalls:
"The cops showed up the night of the birthday party. They were so loud that Frightwig heard them from their car while looking for my place. They followed the sound and then the crowd.

People were strung down two long flights of stairs out into Bond St. The place was less than a hundred yards to the door of CBGB's. There wasn't enough power for Gibby to get anything outta his vocal amp. We were all tripping out on acid. So was everyone else who had started the festivities with us. A couple of strobe lights were pixilating everything. The cops showed up about 1am. Someone got me and I met them at the door. They wanted to know what was going on. I looked at them and then we stared at the crowd/lights/band.
One of them said to me 'That tall guy, he's from Texas, right?' I shook my head. 'We saw him yesterday on the Bowery,' the other cop told me.
I went and got Gibby and brought him over. When he recognized the cops it was like a family reunion. Gibby had been wearing the same blood-stained dress from last night's show when they "detained" and released him that morning. It was very, um, confirming to watch this re-match. Gibby was just basking in the substantiation he was getting. The very same cops who he told 'No really, I'm IN A BAND, THE BLOODY DRESS I'M WEARING IS JUST A STAGE PROP' were seeing him perform in that band They looked around some more, told us that of course the neighbors were complaining and to stop

soon. I spoke up and nailed them for another hour and they just shook their heads and left." [Sept, 2012]

It was great to have friends in New York, but with the drama of trying to get a new record out now behind them, it was time to start looking to branch out onto the road. Upon *Live PCPPEP's* release, Gibby immediately started booking shows, this time for a tour that would take them, not just down the east coast, but from one coast to another. It would be an ambitious undertaking that would find them stopping to visit Corey again in Detroit, as well as visiting just about every other market in between. They sold the "Lady Killer" to Alan in Brooklyn and used the more-than-gracious couple hundred bucks he gave them to buy a van so that anyone not sitting shotgun wouldn't need to lay down in back the whole way.

The increased space for the band was a welcome change from the cramped Nova, but the used van they bought from some gypsies in NYC was no less of a heap of shit. The gas gauge was broken, as was the speedometer, and it had little brakes of which to speak. It burned oil by the gallon, requiring 6 quarts nevery hour to keep it from overheating. A plume of dark, noxious smoke billowed from the tail pipe. It was risky at best to take this beast across the country, but it was a risk that they were going to take.

Paul:
"Besides having no brakes (or gas gauge or speedometer), it needed six quarts of motor oil added to the engine each and every hour we were in it. It looked like a comet coming down the street with massive smoke billowing out of the exhaust pipe. It was embarrassing to drive. After a couple of months, the engine caught fire from all the oil caked on it." [Jan, 2011]

There was one last thing they needed to do before departing NYC, however. They had surpassed the length of their move to California, and were about to embark on a coast-to-coast tour, there was reason to celebrate. They decided to throw themselves a surprise going away party, of sorts, in the studio of a local Public Access TV show they were invited to play called 'The Scott and Gary Show'.

The Scott & Gary Show, hosted by Gary Winter and Scott Lewis, was no *Uncle*

Floyd Show, neither in quality nor notoriety, but it was NYC's even lower-brow equivalent: slapstick comedy routines and gags, coupled with performances by some of the hosts favorite bands. While Uncle Floyd, based out of Hoboken, was able to score bands like the RAMONES, a burgeoning, young Madonna, and Bon Jovi, Scott and Gary's budget could only afford bands the likes of the Butthole Surfers.

It would take years before Scott & Gary's show was recognized at all, even amongst the most hardcore cult fanatics, and mostly due to the fact that the bands Scott and Gary could barely afford to coax down to the studio to play eventually became artists like the Beastie Boys, Jad Fair, and R. Stevie Moore.

The show would be a perfect bon voyage for the Butthole Surfers, so they dropped some acid and played a shambolic set, more due to the lack of monitors than to the copious amount of hallucinogens they had consumed. The complete and utter chaos and the ensuing cacophony they created, as well as the belligerent interview they conducted was brutal, and tasteless anarchy. In other words, brilliant!

To those who began to take notice of the band, the sense of danger was clearly palpable. It never really mattered if a show was disastrous. Fans seemed to understand that for them to transcend onto a new astral plane, they; the band, as well as the listener, would have to walk a tightrope and teeter on the brink of sanity. Like Phillipe Petit spanning the gap between the Twin Towers, the crowd watching with mouths agape below. All those watch in hopes that he succeeds, but knowing a 100-story plummet to the streets below would be almost as macabre and glorious.

Teresa:
"When I was in school, there would be 'opposite day', where you would say 'yes' when you meant 'no', and shit like that...years later when I was a punk rocker I'd say. 'every day is opposite day' 'whatever is really ugly, is really beautiful..." [phone: July, 2014]

Sometimes the music needed to be sacrificed for the sheer ritual. That thin tightrope could break at any time, or a sudden gust of wind could catch you off guard. This was the risk of striving for true enlightenment on that trip to the Holy Land of free thought and expression. Soon disciples start listening, and the congregation slowly increases. Day by arduous day, their numbers grew, and the flock joined them on their journey toward the New Jerusalem.

But this was NYC after all, and a band like the Butthole Surfers could be taken in and assimilated into the artist and underground community with relative ease here.

People had a frame of reference from which to draw. Most had witnessed the Punk and No Wave bands of the 70's; they had been exposed to Glenn Branca's symphonic guitar pieces, and Suicide's minimalist electronic violence. They had the Fluxus movement and the Theatre of Eternal Music with Terry Riley and La Monte Young as a frame of reference.

There were tribal-trance artists like Liquid Liquid, the psychedelic funk of Afrika Bambaataa, and the Avant-garde free jazz fusion of James Chance. The dissonant art-noise of DNA, Teenage Jesus & the Jerks, and John Zorn, as well as fan favorites Sonic Youth. The Butthole Surfers were not quite like any of these performers, but the artists themselves, as well as the crowds, embraced them in this spirit as one of their own. The southern fried spin the band added to their art only gave the Buttholes more kitsch appeal to the persnickety New York City art crowd.

A trip into the unchartered territory of the mid-west was a different story. There wasn't the same bastion of open-minded individuals supporting them in Kansas City, MO or Lawrence, Kansas for that matter. The long drives were punctuated by poorly attended shows in small towns. It was cold and grueling, and they lived out of a brown paper bag filled with their meager payments and the promoters' contact information.

The band had sharpened its fangs on the dark roads of Texas, on drunken drives returning from gigs, and though the crowds found in these small, rural markets are sparse, the few in attendance feel a kinship with a band that knows what a prairie dog is. And the Buttholes played small shows as if they were in a packed NYC nightclub in hopes that when they returned, more people would come out to witness them. They gathered enough money for gas, sleep on floors if they got really lucky, or just head back out onto the road for another late-night drive to the next town.

Chicago to Minneapolis, then a Halloween show in Kansas City with the gals from Frightwig. Up into the rarified air of Denver, and after two weeks of zigzagging through the heartland, they finally hit the warmer, more familiar territory of San Francisco, to reunite with their old pals the Dicks.

While in California, they booked some studio time to cut a track for an anti-nuke benefit LP their friend Dave Dictor was putting together. Dave Dictor's primary job was singing for MDC, but he had been spending most of his time of late putting together a compilation for the record label he ran, R Radical Records. The so-called 'P.E.A.C.E.' compilation was his most ambitious venture to date: a massive double LP undertaking featuring over 50 bands from around the world; including Japan, Argentina, Spain, and Holland.

The song the Butthole Surfers contributed to the comp, *100 Million People Dead*, is one of the only overtly political songs they ever recorded. Musically, it stretched the band in directions completely unexplored in punk music. With Gibby

Oakland 11/10/84
© Murray Bowles

singing through a new voice modulator box he purchased, and sounding as if he is broadcasting on a TV with a broken antenna, the song tumultuously thrashes and throbs as he reports the news:

> **'The sky blew up...there was nothing they could do...100 million people were dead..."**

Paul's guitar riff, filled with tremolo, wails like a siren over a persistent bass riff. Not one of the other bands on the compilation even remotely sounded like the Butthole Surfers. They poignantly summed up the horrors of a nuclear holocaust without preaching against anyone or anything. Here's what will happen. This is our fate should the button get pushed. Gibby's laugh, so darkly used on "Cherub", now laughed at all of us who were guilty of letting the world melt away to oblivion.

"100 Million" was the song that would not only foreshadow our fate if we were not careful, but also the forecast the emerging Butthole Surfer sound: improvised lyrics around a pounding bass, throbbing beats, and soaring, multi-layered and textured guitar solos. Buried in the middle of Side 4 and the 49th song of a 55 band compilation, it went largely unrecognized by anyone.

The fact that they didn't bother to contribute any information about the band at all in the compilation's bloated 72 page companion booklet meant that even the few who heard it and cared wouldn't have any inkling of who they were, what they looked like, or what their stance may have been, on the subject of war, or peace, or any other issue for that matter.

106

I see bodies...11/10/84
© *Murray Bowles*

There were more pressing obligations to which they needed to attend, and they set about fulfilling them. Shortly after they handed the tape over to Dave Dictor, they split the bay area and forged ahead. They ping-ponged up and down the Pacific Coast Highway for a week or two, then stopped in LA for the high point of the tour, a huge sold-out show opening for Public Image Limited at the Olympic Auditorium.

From there, they catapulted themselves back up the coast to Washington State, before turning around and heading back down the coast again and off to Phoenix. The tour culminated with a triumphant New Year's Eve homecoming: headlining the Twilite Room in Gibby's hometown of Dallas, with their old friends Stick Men with Ray Guns.

While in Texas, they took a couple of weeks off from travelling; tamed their hairstyles, played some local shows, and relaxed with friends and family for the Christmas holidays. They also shared a toast to celebrate the release of their new LP, which came out the first day of 1985. For this release, they finally succumbed to Corey Rusk's pleas and released it on Touch & Go Records.

The successful tour did little to win over Alternative Tentacles. Finally doing their part to promote themselves by getting out of Texas and criss- crossing the U.S, the band became totally frustrated with AT dragging their feet on financing a new album. They had spoken to Corey consistently since their last show in Detroit and told him about the tapes they had collecting dust with Bob O'Neil.

It was painfully clear that Bob O'Neil couldn't produce and distribute the LP in the same fashion as Alternative Tentacles could, and since AT was doing nothing toward that end band, nor paying any consistent royalties on the two EPs they had already released, Touch & Go seemed the only likely alternative to get the record out and have it distributed and heard by some folks.

With the would-be album still tied up at the BOSS, Corey decided to appeal to Bob O'Neil's kindness and make an offer to get the tapes out of storage. At first, it's told, Bob was pissed that the band had left him flat. He had always believed in them. He lent them his van to tour and had even included them on his recently released 'Cottage Cheese from the Lips of Death' compilation. He seemed to be expecting a call from Jello Biafra paying him for all the studio time, instead, he got a call from Corey Rusk, offering pennies on the dollar for the tapes.

As it became clear to Bob O'Neil that he wasn't getting a call from Jello Biafra, he finally succumbed to their persistence. Touch & Go was in its infancy as a label, and certainly did not have the purchasing power of an Alternative Tentacles, but Corey would not be deterred. He wanted to hear these tapes, and after some dickering, he finally offered the BOSS a sum which wasn't completely offensive. Realizing that he wasn't going to get any better offer from the band, nor anyone else for that matter, Bob O'Neil begrudgingly obliged. Once the tapes were securely in Corey's hands, the best of the massive cache of recordings were culled from the sessions and pressed up as the Butthole Surfers debut full length LP *Psychic, Powerless, Another Man's Sac.*

For the cover art, the band had rummaged through boxes of old photographs taken by Michael Macioce, an artist they were introduced to while hanging out in Greenwich Village. Macioce's photographs, often in black & white, were lush and dreamlike, heavy in contrast with wispy grey overtones.

One particular image he had taken was through a store window while walking down Mulberry Street. Atop a wedding cake, was the perfect depiction of a cherub dancing an eerie pirouette through the butter-creamed clouds of eternity. Paul grabbed the photo and showed it to Gibby and they both shouted simultaneously, "Cherub the Angel!" It was immediately swiped and used for the back cover of the record.

Macioce:
"I used to walk around the lower east side looking for window reflections to photograph for record covers for the bands I mostly met through Kramer.
The back cover [of Another Man's Sac] is a little Italy wedding cake from Mulberry street.... They came to the Cave (my studio on 10 St) a few times in this period and one time they went through my pictures found the wedding cake shot and Gibby and Paul announced it was "The Cherub"...People would

come over and look through (they still do sometimes) my boxes of prints for an image. ...Although it was not called 'DIY' back then, crudely assembling album covers was actively pursued. They were probably at my studio around 4 or 5 times. It was a good neighborhood for hot Chinese food which they liked to get from Tung Fu across the street."
[email 10/2011]

ℒ

The front cover was glommed from an old medical journal. A portrait of a man whose leprosy left his face disfigured with pox and lesions like a death mask or a crumbling statue. It was the worst image they could find, so Paul immediately went about drawing and defacing the image in neon orange and green like a child would an old newspaper; scratching out the eyes and putting glasses, a turtleneck sweater and a tongue licking at the already defaced old man: his final humiliation.

Another Man's Sac remains a masterpiece. From the defiled cover portrait to a defiling of every musical genre from punk rock to country, the album was everything they had promised to deliver Alternative Tentacles, and everything Corey was hoping they'd deliver to his label.

Although it was recorded over several months at the limited facilities at the BOSS, the record is amazingly cohesive, nearly to the point of being a concept album. The concept being the complete destruction of the concept of what punk rock was supposed to sound like. Without the speed, or the political posturing, the band released a record that was still undeniably punk rock.

And once it was finally released, Corey came through with a windfall of promotion. "Just When You Thought It Was Safe to Wipe" advertisements ran in every music magazine and fanzine around the country. Reviews were generally glowing, although most critics seemed to be in a competition to use the basest, most scatological language they could find in their pocket thesauruses when writing them. A review by their old friend Charles M Young probably best captured the feeling surrounding first hearing the record. In the August 1985 issue of Playboy magazine, he wrote:

"Like Vladimir Horowitz, The Butthole Surfers are virtuosos. Unlike Horowitz, they specialize in the domain of cheap special effects, free-associating over lots of drone and throb punctuated by strange noises. It used to be that you could understand a lot of what lyricist Gibby Haynes was free-associating, and that was the band's main appeal, because the most amazing stuff falls out of that boy's mouth. Now recording technique has improved to the point where you can't understand him most of the time--dementia unsullied by verbalization--and guitarist Paul Leary has developed a highly original style mingling psychedelic groove and feedback with a touch of thrash. The drum

section, King and his sister Teresa (no last name), consists of floor toms and cymbals and is guaranteed to induce undulations in your orgones. In concert, The Buttholes have always delivered on their name, and now they're preserved for the ages."

Terence & Gibby at Fiji, 11/10/84
© Murray Bowles

I would be remiss if I didn't state that Chuck Young had the idea for a book similar to this since the late 80's, such was his love for the band. Comparing the Butthole Surfers to one of the greatest pianists Hf the 20th century is some indication of his devotion, even in these early, lean years. Chuck was never able to pull it off, a fact that only adds to my presumption writing this tome. It has taken over 25 years to cull together, so there is much to be said for perseverance winning over talent, as the Butthole Surfers themselves might humbly admit.

And so 'Psychic…Powerless…Another Man's Sac' was released, and the Butthole Surfers finally had a full-length album all their own. Although the songs were still compiled from tapes they made back when Bill was on bass, or Paul subbing in on bass himself, *Another Man's Sac* finally cleaned out some of the warehouse full of tunes they had been playing regularly since they were still the Dick Clark 5.

The unveiling of "Lady Sniff", "Gary Floyd", "Negro Observer" and "Mexican Caravan" finally gave fans the live staples they had been longing to hear on vinyl. The record was a true skid mark left on the underwear of punk. It became a notorious piece of punk rock history and Touch'n'Go was ready to expend its full energies on its distribution and promotion. The band left Texas with high hopes, and now, with the sweet smells of a new love blossoming around them.

Terence Smart and Michiko Sakai had met as students at Trinity, and they kept in touch even after she returned home to her native Japan. Her stint back in Texas for the holidays coincided with the band's brief return to the state, and upon their reunion, the two fell hopelessly in love almost instantaneously. Future plans between the two were made, but the road beckoned and their time together was short.

To get a couple extra days together, Michiko decided to join them on their trip to New Orleans, to stay on Lake Pontchartrain at their mutual pal Mary's house. Michiko even found her way back onto the stage to recreate her infamous shriek in "Cowboy Bob" at the show, just like the old days when the band was stationed in San Antonio.

After her short trip to New Orleans, Michiko departed back to her native Japan but not before broaching the subject of marriage with Terence. His heart was with her, but he remained with the band as they continued to a scheduled stop in Birmingham, AL to play at Vic and Bill's club. Their next show at the Metroplex in Atlanta, (billed with none other than Jim "Dandy" Mangrum of Black Oak Arkansas), wasn't scheduled to take place until a couple of weeks later, but, with no real home to call their own, they headed to Georgia anyway to hang out for a while and check out the local scene.

A year earlier, while Bill was still in the band, they all had pondered a move out of Texas, and a random finger point on a large map of the United States landed right onto Athens, GA. The idea obviously stuck in their head, and now it seemed the time was right to go for an extended visit to see if prospects in Georgia held any more promise than a return to Texas might hold.

The band had enjoyed their stay with their pals in NY just fine, but they had always felt more comfortable south of the Mason\Dixon Line. Without any home of which to speak they decided to keep their southern roots firmly intact and sought to lay some new ones in the fertile soils of Georgia; the land of R.E.M.

R.E.M. seemed to leave a strange impression on the Butthole Surfers, perhaps even fanning the fires of hope within their ranks. While REM's music was certainly more accessible than the Butthole Surfers', and infinitely more commercially

King & Michiko on Lake Pontchartrain, January 1985
© Terence Smart

successful, R.E.M. hadn't forsaken their particular southern twang to achieve their success, which by this time had grown to near epic proportions thanks to college radio praising them for years as the Second Coming.

There was a feeling of REM like kindred spirits. Brethren of sorts. Like the Big Boys and Dicks before them, the Butthole Surfers were proud of their Texan roots, and Southern heritage. In the wake of the ultra-conservative, Southern Baptist tidal wave, there was a small atoll of vibrant and passionate outlaws and freaks, dating back before the days of Bonnie and Clyde. From the rhythm and blues artists like Blind Lemon Jefferson, Lightning Hopkins, and Freddie King, to ragtime composer Scott Joplin, and Janis Joplin for that matter.

The rich soils of Texas fertilized the seeds of artists who broke against traditions. The seeds grew into a newer crop of garage bands and artists who inspired the punks that would come later. And while REM wasn't from Texas, they too, like the Buttholes, saw no reason to forsake their own state's rich history: From Blind Willie McTell to the Allman Brothers, their folksy musical roots were solidly underfoot, and they branched out into many different styles and directions from that point of reference

And with the ever-piling dung heap of hair metal bands being shat out of Los Angeles, the proud southern gentlemen of REM offered the plume of a fragrant Cherokee Rose to freshen the stench. Without copping a British accent or donning

112

make-up or following any musical trend du jour, they cultivated their own, organic, home-grown success.

Regardless, Atlanta's scene, as was that of nearby Athens, was pretty hip, and was gaining national exposure from bands like the B-52's, Let's Active, Pylon, and Love Tractor. And while the Butthole Surfers weren't nearly as listener friendly as any of these bands, moving to Georgia might put them on Michael Stipe's radar, if nothing else. And after getting a taste of the underground club scene, as crazy and intense as it was, Georgia was looking like a great place for their finger, and van, to point toward.

But all this renewed enthusiasm to settle down in a new locale was not shared by all the members of the band, namely Terence, who had recently fallen in love with a girl who was far from the band's desired relocation. He could have only looked at the band's decision to stay in Georgia as a plot to deny him of any ray of sunshine through the crossfire hurricane that was traveling the country in a van that not even gypsies could tolerate for peanuts.

Terence had gotten a nasty stomach virus enroute from New Orleans as well and was now looking frail and emaciated from a nasty bout of vomiting and diarrhea, undoubtedly feeling the strain of living the last 4 months on fast food and cheap, lukewarm beer. Now lovesick, on top of being physically ill, the prospect of making a new home in the Peach State didn't quite give him a warm and fuzzy feeling. His ass was sore, his mood was vile, and the living conditions were cruel and inhumane.

Two weeks before their scheduled gig at the Metroplex, they showed up at the club's doorstep, as they had at the offices of SST. Somehow, they coaxed the owner to let them in and stay there until they could find a more permanent place to settle down. The gig they eventually did play, according to reports, was tortuous. A grand total of 17 people braved the awful weather to attend. Terence spent most of the set backstage on the shitter, and afterwards, he spent puking and shitting his guts out, convulsing with chills on the floor of the club. It was cold and dark and miserable, and he was ready to leave. It was hellacious for everyone.

Teresa recalls:
"I woke up one morning at the Metroplex and there was this giant fucking rat right in front of my face. I opened up my eyes and I was in contact with this big fat rat." [phone interview, 7/26/14]

According to a couple of accounts, the fateful day came about when a grocery run was made and Terence requested a carton of milk to quell his aching belly. When the shopper returned without the milk, it was the final straw. Terence became unglued. He screamed and shouted and hurled a beer bottle across the dark, cavernous hall. The sound of smashing glass echoed through the room and beer sprayed everywhere. He grabbed the piece of foam he called his bed and called his dad, who rented him a truck to get out of town.

He finally snapped. The only bassist to ever quit a band over a carton of milk, Paul laments. Shortly after his meltdown, Terence shipped back to San Antonio; to nurse himself back to health, eat a real meal, and settle into a job at the Majestic Theatre to earn enough cash he needed for a plane ticket to Tokyo, and to his new love.

Few sane people could look at his decision to leave as a hasty one. The Metroplex was dark, dirty, and freezing cold: a great place to quit a band, King recalls.

Terence states:
"[Conditions were] horrible. All I had was a piece of foam I had to fight over, and I slept in a corner of the balcony after the club closed every night... I don't remember throwing anything, (that was) more of a Paul Leary behavior trait. My father rented a U-Haul truck for me, and I drove it from Atlanta through Louisiana to pick up my sister's furniture from an ex-boyfriend's place in Slidell, then I drove into San Antonio, where I remained for a few months, working as a stagehand at the Majestic...until I had enough money for a ticket to Tokyo. 90 days later, in March of 1985, I flew to Tokyo; where we stayed, and where our son was born. Then I went back into the US Army."
[email, August 2014]

The club's soundman at the time, Jimbo Yongue, remembers showing up early for work one morning to find what appeared to be some wayward campers sprawled out in blankets on the stage of the club. A stirring suddenly revealed a giant, tattered soul, who, upon awaking, immediately grabbed a pre-rolled joint out of his satchel and lit it up.

The curiosity of how these people got into the club and why they were sleeping on the stage became less important than glomming a few tokes, Jimbo recounts. Without a word, he made his way over to the lip of the stage, gave an approving nod, and took the pass from Gibby. The two burly men spoke not a word, until the hunger pangs began to set in. They then began to contemplate getting a nice, hot breakfast for themselves.

Jimbo never got around to asking how they got into the club, nor why they were using the Metroplex as their own personal flophouse fraternity. It was time to

114

eat, so Jimbo filled Gibby in on his favorite diner, when he finally mustered up enough gumption to speak.

The Lucky Street Grill was just down the street, and Jimbo was a regular. They all spent the next couple of weeks getting breakfasts there, sharing war stories, touting the wonders of the Ibanez DM1100 digital delay, and jamming back at the club. The band had made their first friend in their new adopted home state.

Jimbo Yongue:
"I went to work one day when I was running sound at local club, The Metroplex. The band had arrived 3 weeks early for a show and were asleep in sleeping bags on the stage. I began my workday and eventually Gibby awoke, rolled over and promptly picked up a pre-roll hooter and began to puff.
I sauntered over to the stage, we nodded and smoked in silence. Over the next week or two, and many breakfasts at The Lucky Street Grill, we shared many a laugh, and a few jams on the stage at the club where Paul introduced me to the Ibanez DM1100 digital delay. Right about then, then bass player Terence reached critical mass and threw a beer bottle deep into the club and quit in a rage." [email, Sept 2012]

A new friend in a strange new town is nice to have, but a new town with no bass player was not doable. No one in the band could blame Terence for hitting the road for the warmth of Texas, and Michiko's loving arms. He had less to show for himself now than he had upon joining the band 6 months earlier. He sacrificed his car, his home, and about 20 pounds, to the cause. There was little else to show for his tenure in the Butthole Surfers than his bass rig and the slab of foam he used for a mattress. There was no fame, no glory, and no money. Just a bad stomach virus and a U-Haul his dad rented to get him back to San Antonio. The band waved goodbye to another casualty of their lifestyle, shed a tear for an old friend, and closed the book on yet another chapter in their lives.

The Devils Went Down to Georgia

The Butthole Surfers were all well into their 20's, and many of their old college friends were settling down, starting careers, and forging professional lives of their own. The kind of lives each member had forsaken when boarding this ship. And still, without a bass player, settling down was the last thing on their minds.

After months of getting the run around from Subterranean and Alternative Tentacles, their LP, on Touch & Go, was in stores. Though the track list was comprised of material culled from sessions held nearly prior to its release, *Another Man's Sac* was a still a proud achievement for the band. Their tapes were finally out of hock from the BOSS, they had a label in their corner in Touch & Go, and even some spare change in their collective pocket. They were looking to capitalize on all of Corey's hard work behind getting the LP out to the public. All they needed was to find a bass player who was willing to help.

Though Corey was a bass player himself, he wasn't willing to throw away his marriage and record label to take Terence's place meandering the country without a dime to his name. What Corey could provide, however, was a ton of connections to potential applicants. He recommended they meet a guitarist who had recently migrated to Detroit from Windsor, Ontario, Canada: Trevor Malcolm.

Like the band, he too was basically homeless, and the prospect of joining a band of gypsies, with a van to prove it, didn't seem to faze him. He may have been one of the few who saw the prospect of joining the Butthole Surfers as an opportunity. Based on Corey's word, the band made plans to go meet him.

They were looking to settle down after spending way too long with the rats at the Metroplex. They certainly couldn't drag Trevor hundreds of miles from his home to live in the nightclub where they resided. Thankfully, they were offered a piece of Southern hospitality by some stalwarts of Atlanta's 'NOW! Explosion' scene, the BBQ Killers, while they searched for a new home.

The BBQ Killers were gaining quite a reputation around Athens, and later that same year were named 'Best New Band' in the local 'Red & Black' newspaper critic's poll.

After searching local listings, they found accommodations in a small rental property in the sleepy Athens suburb of Winterville. After four months of sleeping where people kindly let them, they finally had a place to lay down some roots.

With Trevor at Walter's BBQ in Athens, April, 1985
© The Red & Black' All Rights Reserved

The three-bedroom house was modest, to say the least. It was not quite big enough to fit even the four remaining members of the band, let alone the new bass player who would become their fifth housemate. Packed to the rafters with drums and amps and all the recording equipment they had amassed along the way (including an ancient second hand 8 track recorder Paul scored from a guy in Memphis), there was barely any room left for furniture. With the bedrooms full of equipment, and their would-be kitchen dedicated as a recording studio, members were found sleeping in closets, or, like King, in the unfinished attic, with exposed fiberglass insulation tickling the inside his nose and irritating his skin.

Teresa recounts:
"I remember we had to draw straws for who got a bedroom, because there were 5 of us, and I remember thinking 'if I don't draw a bedroom straw, I am going HOME!'... and I drew a straw and I got a bedroom, so the whole time we were in Winterville, I had a bedroom..." [phone: 7/26/14]

117

❧

The house wasn't much for square footage, but it was theirs, and it afforded them the luxury of having a home base from which to venture out on tour. With this piece of business out of the way, and their new hometown decided upon, they could get on with the last and most essential priority: meeting their new bass player.

So, with few friends or options, they went with Corey's suggestion. Corey's word was good enough for the band to accept, and despite having never heard his playing, they welcomed their newest recruit at the Athens bus station on a chilly February day.

Trevor had been estranged from his parents since the age of 13 and was probably one of the few people on earth who could have looked at moving into a 3-bedroom house with 4 insane Texans and their dog as something other than the last act of a desperate man.

❧

King:
"Trevor arrived at the Greyhound station in Athens, GA. after we got settled in Winterville. He came recommended by Corey (how they knew each other, I really don't know). We had never met Trevor before, but at that point I think we were willing to invite anyone to join the band if they really wanted to. We were unsavory people nobody liked, after all. We were kind of desperate for volunteers and Trevor came to the rescue." [Jan, 2011]

❧

Both he and the band were anxious to get started, and they began cementing their repertoire almost immediately. Trevor came equipped with not only his bass and cabinet, but also a massive, white sousaphone that he reportedly managed to clip from his high school band room. There was no room for it in the house, but the band was thrilled to see the massive instrument, and before long, began incorporating the thunderous horn into their live shows.

The addition of the sousaphone made Butthole Surfers performances legendary. If ever there was a band from which you never knew what to expect, it was this one. While that reputation had always preceded the band before entering a town, there was no one who could deny that fact now. They were still playing punk bills, with the likes of Naked Raygun, Scream, and even the Dead Kennedys (despite the troubles they had with AT, they were after all, still comrades), and in this context, the sighting of a sousaphone was as about as commonplace as sighting a Reagan Republican.

With Trevor now a Butthole Surfer, any thoughts of hanging around Winterville drove off in a shitty van. The band followed suit, and shortly thereafter hobbled the 13-hour drive back north up to Detroit, to visit Corey and to showcase their new bass player and added accoutrements.

Corey booked them a couple of gigs at Traxx within a week of each other: one an all-ages affair and one 21 and over show. In the down time in between, they booked themselves into a small studio called Multi Trac in the suburb of Renton to lay down some new demos, with Corey and his pal Butch Vig engineering.

Corey had some leftover time at the studio from a session that had obviously gone better than expected. He offered the time to the band to complete work on the LP they had begun while back in Texas while still living behind the BOSS. The band was happy with 'Psychic…Powerless…Another Man's Sac' and with all Corey had done to help them get it released, but any new material was recorded with hopes it would comprise their next full-length album on Alternative Tentacles, not Touch & Go.

Even with all the payment issues they experienced while dealing with Alternative Tentacles, they still felt an obligation to give them the full-length LP they hadn't provided AT while still in their stable of bands. Though Corey arranged the sessions, he was seemingly aware of their intentions and respected the feeling of obligation to Alternative Tentacles. He had, however, seen how little effort Alternative Tentacles had put forth on the band over the past months, and probably had a sneaking suspicion that the only ones concerned about the Butthole Surfers having an LP on Alternative Tentacles were the Butthole Surfers themselves. This acute awareness no doubt gave him the hope that they could be swayed over to him and onto Touch & Go yet again.

Corey knew that with his connections through the fanzine, the relationships he forged as bassist of the Necros, as well his stewardship of the Touch & Go, that he could get the word out on the band. He was also well aware that with AT's attention transfixed on the Dead Kennedys, and his own on the Butthole Surfers, that he would win them over with patience and time, as he had with the release of *Another Man's Sac*.

In addition to all the other promotional tools at his disposal, Corey became closely affiliated with some local filmmakers who produced a Public Access cable TV show called *Back Porch Video*, which was the product of the legendary Russ Gibb. Gibb had gained notoriety as the promoter who had booked all the shows at the Grande Ballroom, back in the late 60's, at a time when the Stooges and MC5 were wreaking havoc in the Motor City.

As a DJ on the local WKNR-FM radio station, Uncle Russ, as he was known on air, broke the story that 'Paul McCartney was dead'; a legend which began to spread like wildfire after an hour-long program he hosted pondered the validity of the subject. Soon teenagers around the globe were twirling their Beatles records in reverse on their turntables and pining through their covers of Sgt. Pepper's with magnifying glasses in hopes of finding clues of Sir Paul's demise and of his replacement with a look-alike imposter.

In the years subsequent, Gibb had become a multi-millionaire speculating on the future of cable television and buying the licenses for nearly every market in and around Michigan before selling them off to major communication companies just a few years later. His love of teaching led him to Dearborn High School, despite the fact he was rich enough from selling the cable licenses to retire and do nothing.

He was intent on running the school's media department and laying the groundwork in the newly established media of closed-circuit TV and public access programming. Some of his students formed Back Porch Video, which showcased punk videos and filmed local shows for broadcast, passing on Gibb's own legacy to a new generation of miscreants and malcontents.

The *Back Porch* kids filmed both Buttholes gigs at Traxx, and the footage was soon in heavy rotation on the program, although they weren't even allowed to mention the band by name on air. It was such a professional shoot, the band felt compelled to eventually release the footage themselves in the form of the 'Blind Eye Sees All' video cassette.

The shows and sessions in Detroit went surprisingly well, even though Trevor had only been a member for a mere few days. It seemed as if they converged at the right time, with both Trevor and the band being a stone's throw away from homelessness and destitution. They were able to congeal and change what was assumed would be their collective and inevitable fate to those outside of their own ranks and the few, yet fervent, disciples: their own collective demise.

Even with a roof over their heads, the grueling, meandering tours, the constant lack of food and money and the marathons of sleepless days and nights tended to weed out those who weren't completely committed, or committable. Butthole Surfers bass players fell in much the same way of Spinal Tap drummers: spontaneously combusting into a mass of goo, often, never being seen or heard from again.

The core of Gibby, Paul, Teresa and King all had a single-minded vision, and any new member was not only joining the band, but was boarding a Viking ship in search of new lands to conquer, new villages to pillage, and new gold to plunder. There was nothing or no one that could tether one to the safe shores of home. Trevor initially seemed up to the challenge and they quickly gelled into a solid unit. And then the torment began.

Winterville may have been the band's new home, but the house there was, more often than not, dark and abandoned. They stayed in town long enough to play a show or two, score some weed, service the vehicle, or perhaps sleep on a mattress for a couple nights before spending a week or two heading north to NYC, or west to Dallas, passing into some small towns in between. When they'd get back to Georgia, they'd all retreat to their small slice of heaven, in various closets, attics and spare bits of unused floor, before setting sail again.

The old disabled gypsy van they purchased in NYC became the band's garbage dump, after the oil that was caked on the engine finally ignited and enveloped it in flames. Its gutted and charred carcass was left sitting on the curb in front of the house for the disposal of refuse. Yet another van or RV would take its place, until it too was beaten into submission. Vehicles and brain cells were expendable commodities on this endless coast to coast quest to be heard.

You could find the band playing in NYC for two or three shows, and then back a few weeks later for a few more, then off to Washington DC, before returning to NYC again, to sleep on the floors of the apartment of any friend or acquaintance who was willing to risk a fight with their boyfriend or girlfriend to put them up for the night.

Any poor soul with family, friends, a love interest, a job, the need for a decent night's sleep, or desire to have any money in his pocket that wasn't allocated by permission from the band fund might buckle under the stress. And it was finally upon a random 9-hour drive to Columbus, OH to play a one-off gig at Staches that the stress cracks began to appear.

After returning to Winterville to catch a few days respite and some much-needed sleep, Gibby was immediately back on the phone with promoters, booking yet another tour. This one would take them through Madison, Milwaukee and Chicago, before yet another homecoming show in nearby Atlanta. It was a relatively modest venture by Butthole Surfers standards, but it was one that Trevor was ill-prepared to make.

According to Trevor, it was the night of an Einstürzende Neubauten show at the 688 in Atlanta in May of 1985 that he first expressed his waning interest in remaining a Butthole Surfer. Still, he soldiered on; making a trip to NYC for several gigs before the show in Columbus, Ohio. Finally, he states, he packed his bags and called a cab, not worrying about whether they had found a replacement for him or caring if they did.

As the short Midwest jaunt loomed on sweltering July night, he became unhinged. He packed up the few meager belongings he had to his name and left and before the band realized what had hit them. They were, again, left without a bassist, for the 6th time in five years. Somehow, no job, no money and no home seemed like the better option than the abuse it took to live as a member of the Butthole Surfers.

Trevor Malcolm::
"I did not leave in the middle of the night, I walked [out] in the morning with my sousaphone…after allowing 2 months for them to audition someone. Two weeks is standard professional courtesy where I come from, so I thought that was generous." [email: March 2014]

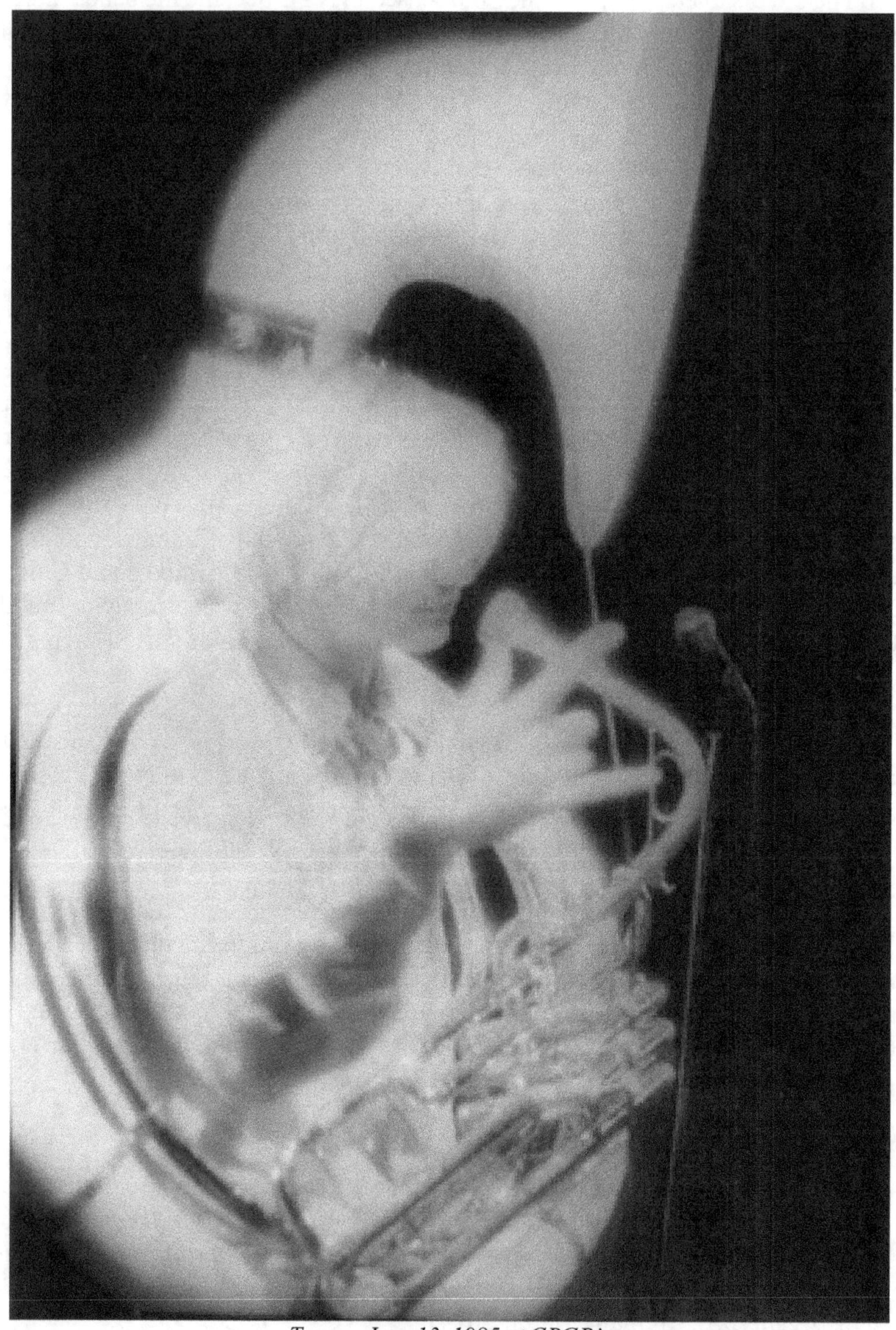

Trevor, June 13, 1985 at CBGB's
© Macioce

The band was used to having to find new bassists, but this tour was already booked and mere days away. They were left dumb-founded and fearful that they'd need to cancel the gigs or maybe perform as the rag-tag outfit they'd played as back in TX, the numerous times this fate had befallen on them in the past. Time was waning and choices needed to be made when a light bulb suddenly went on in their heads. Shortly thereafter, the lights flicked on outside on Juan Molina's front porch. It was the Butthole Surfers and, this time, they weren't looking to score a bag of weed.

Juan had tinkered around Athens in various bands, including the locally successful, and ironically named, Go! Van Go!. He'd sell weed to supplement the low pay of a life dedicated to the arts and he had enough chops on the bass to learn most of the material they had in a hurry.

It was a match made in heaven: the weed dealer and the Butthole Surfers. They told him of their plight and coaxed him into joining their traveling minstrel show of freaks for an impromptu summer vacation through America's breadbasket.

Juan Molina:
"I had gone to school in Athens in 1976 and ended up staying there for 14 years playing in several bands. By far the best one I had been involved in was called Go Van Go. I was involved in some projects there when I got to know Gibby and Paul. They weren't thrilled that Trevor had suddenly left when they had all these gigs lined up. It sounded like fun to me so I offered to play and they took me up on it." [email, Feb 3, 2007]

Juan didn't have a sousaphone, but he had talent and, more importantly, the ability to pick up and go on a moment's notice: pretty much the only thing they required at this point.
They would arrive early at the venues and iron out tunes during soundcheck for inclusion in the set the same night. Amazingly, the band sounded as good as ever. They had obviously become accustomed to flying by the seat of their pants and pulled off what had seemed like an impossible feat like complete professionals.

It was a hot night in early August at the Celebrity Club in Atlanta where the tour ended and they could finally exhale. Once again, the band of meddling kids had solved the case of the missing bass player, and they drove off in their own 'Mystery Machine' as an intact unit. They had gotten through the two-week tour without a hitch and they were ready to celebrate on their adoptive native soil.

Trevor had been in the band for less than six months and would be little more than a mere footnote in their history had he not been referred to as "The Most Hated Person in America" in an interview the band gave to the recently formed 'Spin' magazine soon after his departure.

Bob Guccioni Jr, the progeny of the editor of Penthouse Magazine, had followed in his dad's footsteps, but instead of smut, Jr. decided to peddle a magazine that would become the new generation's answer to Rolling Stone. SPIN Magazine finally put a national spotlight on the underground bands that its competition had all but ignored as it blossomed all around them.

The full-page feature on the band by Phyllis Heller ran with the headline "This Butt's for You". It pictured Gibby and Paul holding their dog Mark Farner over Teresa's head like Underdog in flight. The picture was a captivating sight, and the band was in the spotlight, as were Gibby's off-the-cuff statements.

In SPIN, the in-jokes and goofs the band often made in statements to the press were now being read by thousands, and not just confined to the dozens reading a local fanzine as they had been in the past. If Trevor hadn't been the most hated man before the Spin article, he soon became so, as the story of his departure became the more notable than his tenure with the band.

And though it may have been difficult to see at the time of him walking out, like Terence, he really couldn't be blamed for leaving. The band, after all, did not live like normal people. On the few, random days they were not on the road, they were all crammed into a house that was basically a storage shed for their equipment. They were perpetually drunk and high, often hungry, and barely had room to sleep. Aside from that, any thought of a life outside of the band, and from each other, was completely out of the question.

King:

"[Trevor] leaving in the middle of the night before an impending tour was a drag, but you couldn't really blame the guy. We were all living pretty miserably. The rest of us had kind acclimated to it in Texas, where he was thrown into our little dysfunctional world raw." [email 2003]

Trevor was forced to sleep on the floor of a closet, right next to a water heater that shot sparks out from its pilot light. His mattress, along with his person, had almost been set ablaze on several occasions, King recounts. Lawn maintenance was handled with a pair of scissors, and they lived hand to mouth every single day. Since spending money on garbage collection was not even in their consciousness, they used the gutted gypsy van as their own personal garbage dump. There were very few affordable expenses, aside from food, gas, and the rent, and all the money they earned was in a box that Gibby kept in his room. Luxuries were few, and all needed to be justified. Jeff recalls the band cringing when Teresa needed money to buy tampons as their bellies grumbled and the hunger pangs stabbed.

Members would quit every other day, King states, and prior to finding their newest wheels, and their old one nothing less a glorified garbage pail, they had only a communal bicycle for transportation. Combined with the fact that it was an 8-mile hike into to Athens, the closest civilization, they all abandoned the thought of leaving well before they had reached Winterville's city limits. Even after the gypsy van was replaced with the new one discarded by a local plumbing company (replete with logo and phone number on the side) it was the band's ride for touring, not for bailing. For better or for worse, they were stuck together.

So, when Trevor told everyone that he was done, it was probably taken with a grain of salt, that is until he finally grabbed his bass rig and massive sousaphone and started making trips back and forth to the curb. Only when the cab came to bring him to the bus station would it finally dawn on the rest of the band that another bassist had bitten the dust and his desire to quit was, indeed, for real.

Juan & Gibby at the Metro, Chicago, 7/25/85.
Courtesy of Ralph Pepper, All Rights Reserved

Trevor returned to the Great White North and to playing guitar for a locally popular band called Luxury Christ. He contemplated a lawsuit for all his uncredited work with the band, and even ran for mayor of Windsor, Ontario in 2000. But that was light years into the future. He was now just looking to get out of this scorching heat and back to more familiar environs on the northern side of the border, far away from these Texan lunatics.

And if the Butthole Surfers were going to survive to see the end of 1985, they needed a plan to get things rolling fast. So, they grabbed their weed dealer, strapped a bass around his neck, and brought him out on tour.

Trevor's tenure was short, but it was a prolific time for the band, and the itinerary during his 6 months tenure was constantly full. Though, it's sadly true that any fame he derived from being a Butthole was more from his likeness peppered throughout 'Blind Eye Sees All', his massive sousaphone, or the negative Spin article rather than for his talents as a multi-instrumentalist, as considerable as they were. He became yet another marcher in the parade of Butthole Surfers ex-bassists.

Gibby's 'Most Hated Man' joke to which Trevor became most associated was a bit of a shame, since so many others might not have even lasted as long as he had. Aside from Juan, who was only joining them for a quick stint, there were few others begging to cram themselves into a used plumbing van and meander state to state on an endless tour, nor many takers itching to set up their beds in the closet nearest the flame of the old water heater.

The Family style compound they set up outside of Athens was a more a commune than a home. A long-lost sect of voodoo hillbillies that somehow found its way out of the swampland and into a quaint suburban neighborhood. The Gein's next door. *'Never mind the overgrown weeds and strange smells emanating from the basement. 'Never mind the pitbull, she doesn't bite…most of the time.'*

Another drifter from Canada might have turned right around and ran straight to the authorities. Trevor laid down his bags and set up a place to sleep, a stranger in a house of brethren. Incestuous and inescapable, many didn't even bother taking their equipment with them upon leaving. They just left, indelibly scarred, to grow up and get real careers, or to light themselves on fire in the desert. Trevor merely fled across the border back home to Canada and never came back to the United States again.

And so, the Butthole Surfers made their way through the Midwest with Juan instead of Trevor and somehow pulled off a tour with a bassist who had mere minutes to practice their entire set, most of which was still unreleased on record. Finally, though, they arrived back in Atlanta and were ready to put the whole sordid affair of Trevor's daring escape behind them and to play the final show of the tour at the Celebrity Club.

The Celebrity Club had always been a favorite venue for the band. While CBGB's in NYC or The Whisky in LA may have had the most national notoriety, the Celebrity Club existed in the shadows, in its own world far from the prying eyes of the news media or the law. Drag Queens in leather chaps with tampon strings dangling from their asses, bull dykes who could take on the burliest of biker dudes, naked lady mud wrestling with nude girls peeing in large vats of homemade punch, all cavorting amongst the vast array of punks, artists and long-hairs simply there to see the band du jour. The Celebrity was at the heart of the Atlanta Now! Explosion; where Hieronymus Bosch and Charles Bukowski would meet to have a beer.

The oddball shows the Buttholes were playing didn't stop at the edge of the stage at the Celebrity Club, they spilled over the lip of the stage and onto the dance floor, over to the bar, and outside to the curb, like a thick, blinding carpet of fog. The band had experienced many other wild nights at the club by local bands such as Toast and the Easturn Stars, whose shows would turn into veritable orgies of sights and sounds, and they would assimilate this kind of bacchanalia into their own sets.

A night at the Celebrity guaranteed excitement: sometimes in the vein of Satyricon, sometimes Clockwork Orange. The fear that some butch with muscles twice your size in knee-high jack boots would give you a curb job in the back alley was not unwarranted. But that fear mostly set in on those nights that turned from the normal, casual weirdness to the truly violent and bizarre. This night was a joyous affair, and love and positive vibrations buzzed in the room like the low hum of an amplifier.

The celebration started early and continued through their set, and as the final strains of "Whirling Hall of Knives" became inaudible over the chatter, thoughts turned to who would be hosting the after party. Since a local suburb seemed a much better place to welcome the oncoming daylight than jail, or a ditch on the side of the road, they all packed up their gear and headed out to put the icing on an extraordinary night at a fan's house, who had invited them over, being her parents were out of town.

The scene at the club, as insane as it was, took a turn right into Dali-esque surrealism when they learned that Amy Carter, the niece of the inventor of *Billy Beer* and daughter of our 39th President, Jimmy, was also in the house. It seemed that Amy was planning to spend the night with the girl's younger brother and some other pals, at an innocent slumber party.

Each sibling had made plans for a sleepover that night, it seems, unwitting of the other's arrangements. While the teens stayed sheltered up in a bedroom, big sister brought home the Butthole Surfers home to play with, something the younger kids were surely not prepared for when setting up their sleeping bags earlier that evening.

Amy walked out of the bedroom and into a scene of general debauchery; drinking and smoking and cursing and the things in which the daughter of a president, current or former, cannot be associated. It was in the wee morning hours and the party, at least the one the Butthole Surfers were having, showed few signs it would be over before daybreak. So, the teens packed up Amy's clothes and toiletries into her overnight bag and headed out into garage to separate themselves from the criminal element that had taken over the house.

As hash smoke filled the living room with a hazy fog, Gibby got up to excuse himself to go to the bathroom. When he arrived back to the room a short time later, he was smiling coyly. Juan, who was sure the Secret Service would be busting in at any second, could tell that something was up. Gibby leaned over and, in a low voice chuckled, "I just dicked Amy Carter's suitcase…" As the band caught wind of what had happened, they could only try to hold back their laughter. A short time later, a black limousine pulled up to the residence and into the driveway.

Amy, who had probably gotten a bit nervous by now about the goings on at her friend's house, had decided to make that shameful late night phone call home to mom and dad to come and get her, rather than to risk rumors of the absence of forethought it took to remain in the same house as the Butthole Surfers.

Juan Molina:
"I remember spending the night at somebody's house and their daughter was friends with Amy Carter, who was there for a sleepover. She didn't hang out in the same room with us, I think she may have been scared. I don't blame her. I remember thinking that if Jimmy Carter knew his daughter was spending the night in the same house as the Butthole Surfers, we probably would have been hauled off by the Secret Service. She would have been 17 at the time. So, we're all hanging out in the living room when Gibby comes back from the bathroom with a shit eating grin. We know something just happened. He comes over and whispers, I just touched Amy Carter's shoe [sic] with my dick. He was really proud of that." [email, Feb 3, 2007]

In the final remaining hours of darkness, and clad in a lime-green, terry-cloth sport suit, stood the former First Lady of the United States, in the driveway. The band waived their arms about to clear the smoke away as they crowded at the front window for a better look. Roslyn escorted her young daughter into the back of the car, as an unsuspecting bleary-eyed former President snatched Amy's overnight bag by the handle and put it into the trunk; the same handle that had made scrotal contact with Gibson Jerome Haynes sweat laden nut sac mere moments earlier.

'EEEEEWWWW!!'…the band's collective faces pressed against the window grimaced before they fell about themselves uncontrollably…Molecular scrotal transfer! Who can count the number of foreign dignitaries that have since shaken that hand and have been scarred with the stigma of that night, The Nobel Peace Prize itself may even be tainted with that indelible disgrace.

Teresa:
"...all these Secret Service cars pulled up and we were so stoned on hash and watching Live Aid on TV, it was the day Live Aid aired, and there was all this hash smoke and we thought this girl was crazy talking about Amy Carter, then all of a sudden Amy Carter comes down the stairs, all these Secret Service pull up, and there's like a cloud of hash smoke, we open the door to the garage and all of the Butthole Surfers are standing there in a line and there's Jimmy and Rosalyn Carter. It was just bizarre." [phone, 7/26/14]

The dicking incident provided some much-needed comic relief, for although they had been able to pull off the tour that had been so perilously close to being canceled due to Trevor's hasty exit, the sunrise of the new day left them, not only with a nasty hangover, but also, an incomplete rhythm section. Thoughts began to scramble as to who they might be able to grab to fill the vacant slot. Then, it was decided they would make a long-distance call to the only person they could think of who might agree to help fill the position.

Paul reportedly made the call, which was answered by Mark Kramer, whose studio they had used to record several songs while Terence was still in the band; back when they were bouncing from apartment to apartment trying to settle into their newly adopted home of NYC.

Several months earlier, Kramer's band Shockabilly dissolved in a torrent of bad feelings and in-fighting and since then he had been focusing on running a rental studio in Manhattan he called 'Noise NY', located just across the street from Madison Square Garden.

Shockabilly had been at the height of their success prior to the final screaming match between Kramer and guitarist\lead vocalist Eugene Chadbourne that ended the band after a show in Lexington, KY. They had built a large cult following mangling classic rock staples and reshaping them into psychedelic, free- jazz experimentations. They had toured Europe 3 times and made enough money between touring and record sales to split their profits among each member of the trio and still live comfortably.

Along with Sonic Youth, Shockabilly was among the biggest bands in the New York scene, and had broken out globally into the European markets, as well. They could afford the finest hashish and to pay their separate rents months in advance before heading out on tour without having to hold down the side jobs waiting tables or working at record stores like many of those who chose the vocation of punk rock.

Kramer had built up quite a resume prior to joining Shockabilly as well. A multi-instrumentalist like Trevor, Kramer had been playing around the NYC area since the late 1970's, teaming with such luminaries as John Zorn, Daevid Allen and his NY incarnation of Gong; and the legendary reformed Fugs.

Chadbourne had run in many of the same circles as Kramer, both cultivated from John Zorn's fertile loins, and by the time Shockabilly became their primary vehicle in 1982 (along with drummer David Licht), they were already stalwarts of New York City's avant-garde music scene.

The continued success of the Shockabilly only fueled Chadbourne's ego, says Kramer, as well as his desire to do his own material without regard for the rest of the band's input. It began wearing on Kramer's patience and he became increasingly displeased with Chadborne's "rock star attitude".

He was an amazing talent, Kramer recollects, and even Bill Jolly remembers Chadbourne as a righteous guitarist from the times that Shockabilly played with the Butthole Surfers when Bill was in the band.

But after selling his own homemade cassettes from the stage after Shockabilly shows, many of which were duped on top of demo cassettes fans had given him of their own bands (which Kramer notes, he never bothered to listen to), Chadborne began charging people extra to sign his own autograph on them. Kramer finally lost it, and in a fit a rage, told Chadbourne to go fuck himself, leaving an entire double album's worth of material to remain unreleased.

Kramer:
"Eugene would take the cassette, say THANKS MAN, and within an hour or so he'd be on the floor in the corner of our little motel room with a dubbing cassette deck, taping one of his own solo releases over the cassette he just got from a fan, and slapping self-adhesive artwork onto it. The next night, he'd sell it for $5. That's how he kept his stock up during tours. He'd also start selling his "product" straight off the front of the stage the moment the show ended (which to me looked SO terrible), and charged extra for signing his name. He never looked into anyone's eyes. I mean, how COULD HE. All he cared about was $$$ and it was written all over his face. Finally, I couldn't take it anymore. he'd become a first class prick, and a completely fucking miserable human being,. so I bolted." [email Jan 2012]

Kramer had been a huge fan of the Buttholes for years and friends with them even before he had heard them. Befittingly, he hunted them down after reading their name on the wall of a Dallas restroom while taking a dump. "THE BUTTHOLE SURFERS – WE SHIT WHERE WE WANT". As his giggles echoed around the porcelain tiles, a voice beckoned from beyond the stall…'Do you always laugh when you're taking a shit?'

As luck would have it the voice beyond the stall was the club's promoter, who told him the Butthole Surfers were actually a band. *'I went to see them and they were fuckin' terrible…worst band I ever saw'.*

Kramer's first show with the Butthole Surfers, Danceteria, NYC 8/24/85
© Macioce

Of course, Kramer was even more intrigued and after he wiped and flushed, he headed to Austin for a scheduled gig and began asking around about them to folks in the bar. He was directed to Paul who Kramer states was hanging out nearby, and the two hit it off almost immediately. On Shockabilly's next tour through Texas a year later, the Butthole Surfers on the bill.

When Kramer took Paul's phone call and was made the offer to play bass, he was thrilled. 'I was joining the greatest band in the world,' he recalls. He had been through the rock star ego trip with Shockabilly, now he would be the grandfatherly elder statesman in a band that was barely scraping by. But he had a love for the music and shared the conviction that, together they could conquer the world. Kramer probably had more faith in the band than Paul did. He assured Paul he was ready, and that he already knew the material and didn't need to rehearse. He beckoned for them to just come up to NYC where he would get everything in order. Paul was a bit skeptical about not rehearsing, but upon their arrival in NY in mid-August of 1985, they all headed to the heart of midtown and into Noise NY, to hang out with their new bandmate and to mix a couple of tracks they had recorded a couple of years prior.

One, a version of the Guess Who classic "American Woman" was given a booming, acid house drum track before the genre was even known to exist. Kramer and Paul cut and spliced tape into the wee hours of the morning, transforming it, as well as another song, the ballad, "Creep in the Cellar" into a cacophonous array of guitar and vocal effects. They also gave more nuanced mixes to "Whirling Hall of Knives", "To Parter", and "Tornadoes", songs recorded for the record Alternative Tentacles seemingly cared nothing about.

The recordings Kramer produced were subtle and softly psychedelic, even ethereal and melancholic. Like the work of Macioce, whose photographs often graced the covers of his records, Kramer's production was rich in contrast and texture, almost as much of an instrument as the musical instruments themselves. Without forsaking their signature skronk, Kramer rounded off their edges and introduced some new elements for them to build upon.

And after utilizing Kramer's studio wizardry mixing their songs, the band utilized his bass skills and, after just one practice that Paul coaxed out of him, played their debut show together at Danceteria. A few days later they headed out on a short trip to Trenton, NJ, Washington D.C., and the college town of Morgantown, West Virginia. Kramer was right. He learned the songs in no time flat, and the news of the merging of Shockabilly and the Butthole Surfers quickly spread to fans eager to witness this new hydra.

After just these few shows, it became obvious to Kramer what needed to happen. They needed to get over to Europe. Paul liked the idea of getting out of the US for a few weeks but hadn't really thought about it was possible. They were barely scraping by in the US, how could they even think about Europe? He had no idea, but he told Kramer to make some calls to see if there was any interest in booking them. The impetuous trip to pick up Kramer left the band with some loose ends to tie up anyway, so they parted ways; Kramer back home to NY, the band back home to Winterville.

Kramer's loose ends included more aside from a tour to book. Unlike the rest of his new bandmates, he had a life, a wife, a studio, and a home. So, he got his domestic dealings in order and got ready to join the Butthole Surfers in a few weeks' time.

Not content to sit still, however, the band called on Juan to help them out with some shows that had been booked down prior to Kramer accepting the job. If Kramer was successful in getting them some shows overseas, they were going to need some money in their pockets to pull it off, and time was of the essence.

Gibby, Teresa & King at the Metro, 7/25/85,
courtesy of Ralph Pepper, All Rights Reserved

Kramer had toured Europe several times previously and had knowledge of the strange scene there. He had also made a whole lot of connections to boot. He made a call to his pal Rob at the Paperclip Agency in the Netherlands, who had booked the previous Shockabilly tour across the continent. It was a big success, and before departing home the two had already ironed out plans for Shockabilly's next trip abroad the following autumn. Now with Shockabilly dead, Kramer told him about his new band, and how they were interested in a tour all their own. Instead of cancelling the Shockabilly tour, Rob simply changed all the shows he previously booked to Butthole Surfers shows instead. With an entire European tour scheduled in a single phone call, Kramer had time to get his other business in order before embarking on a European tour with a band he joined just a few weeks ago.

Meanwhile, the southern Butthole Surfers contingent took their show on the road to the backwoods of the American bible belt. Gibby and Paul had been schooled to be businessmen and money was constantly an issue. They didn't have much, and didn't earn much, but they had always been able to survive on their limited means.

All the money they earned was put back into the band, either for general sustenance, or buying recording equipment, effects, stage props, as well as replacing stolen bullhorns. They also knew what they were worth to the club owner who was booking them, and made sure, if they were quoted a price, they were damn well going to collect every red cent of it.

With 5 mouths to feed, and the trip to Europe less than a month away, they had a scheduled stop in Birmingham, Alabama to play a show at a local dive called The Loft. They originally agreed to play the show for $450, but shortly before the gig, they called the promoter and told him things were tight and they wouldn't be able to play for less than $650.

Now, $650 was a whole lot of money for a punk rock band to ask, especially from a high school aged promoter in Birmingham, Alabama, but after much discussion and deliberation, the promoter reluctantly agreed to the new price, and the deal was done, or so it seemed.

Mike Portera (Birmingham punk stalwart):
"[They] booked the gig, at our tiny little local punk rat club, well in advance. At the time they were asking for a $450 guarantee, which was unheard of with the circle of punks on the road we were used to dealing with. However, the guy in charge of booking, Jimmy, went ahead and agreed. Well....2 weeks before the gig Gibby calls and says there is "no way" they would do the gig for $450. After all "they are going to Europe in 2 weeks and have a salaried bass player - so 450 is out of the question." Jimmy told Gibby to cool out and let him talk to "the money guy". Well, within a couple of days, Jimmy had gotten the

benefactor (such as he was (not)) to agree to 650 over 450. This was unheard of, but, it was the Buttholes. " [email, 2010]

The show was quickly sold out and the club was packed, according to all accounts. The bar sold drinks, and the money poured in even faster than the beer poured out. After the gig however, Gibby was handed a check for the original amount the band was offered as if the promoter and he had never spoken before. After Gibby was told they were only getting $450, he went ballistic. He began calling the teenager things the boy's virgin ears had never even imagined in his young life. Things got loud, and shouting filled the tiny backroom at the club.

Juan, Paul & Gibby at the Metro July, 1985.

Gibby ranted and raved, until finally he decided that if he wasn't going to get the money he was promised, he was going to destroy at least $200 worth of stuff. He grabbed a beer and dumped it down the back of a Sony Trinitron that sat in the tiny backstage office of the club. It fizzled and sparked and smoked, and the smell of burning plastic permeated the halls.

Gibby [Forced Exposure magazine, 4/18/86]:
"We got ripped off by a hick fairy high school punk rock promoter in Birmingham, Alabama, which is such a fucking drag. The only thing I could do when it was over was spit in his eye and pour a beer down the back of his Sony Trinitron"'

Punk bands were prone to getting ripped off by clubs and many just took it as a write off of the shitty life of being in a punk band. But, the Butthole Surfers weren't the average punk band. They didn't have day jobs. They didn't tour during a summer break from school or survive off their parents' allowance. The few dollars doled out each day for food, beer, or cigarettes was made from playing gigs. If the night didn't go well or money was tight, a choice had to be made as to which vice they felt they could do without that particular day. More often than not, it was eating.

But, the band had been steadily earning a reputation. Kids started to spread the word to their friends and clubs were starting to fill up. Club owners were often willing to book them, despite their reputation as being difficult, unruly, and demanding higher prices than the average punk band. The club owners knew the place would be hopping and bar cash registers would be ringing and buzzing like Tommy's pinball machine.

Most punk bands were paid based on ticket sales, where any shortage was taken out of their cut and livelihood. Most punk bands were lucky just to break even on the road. The Butthole Surfers was not one of those bands. They were getting to a point where they could assure the show would be a financial success for the club. They only requested their fair share when the profits were divvied up at the end of the night. They weren't living off any trust fund provided by Mr. Peppermint. Food, gas, and accommodations needed to be earned at the gigs and paid for by the band. And although they weren't greedy, you could bet if a club owner promised them an amount beforehand, it was going to be paid or there was going to be trouble.

The band soon gained a reputation with clubs, as well. A reputation of being surly, mean, or downright unreasonable for the amounts they asked, but the fact that promoters continued to book them meant that they were earning enough of a profit to put up with whatever shenanigans the band, or worse, their fans, doled out.

The band was wise to the racket of the promoters who often took away a healthy profit yet shorted the band at the end of the night. Punk rock bands were more prone to this than other, more professional bands that were older, wiser, and had a label and tour manager backing them up.

Paul recounts one fanzine interview in San Francisco where he was prodded endlessly whether he felt greedy for asking a $6.00 cover charge. He responded by asking her if she had a bed to sleep in that night with a roof over her head. *'I live in a van and don't have a bed or a home.'*

It was a losing battle in 'the scene'. Ticket prices over $5.00 could ruin your punk rock credibility. Holding fast to the "punk ethos" would wind up ruining the band. The Butthole Surfers didn't even have sleeping bags when they first hit the road. Gibby once contracted a flu which lasted a full six months, Paul remembers. The road was not a place for the weak and unprepared. Money, seemingly the root of all evil within the punk rock community, was the only way a band could survive. The Butthole Surfers realized this before many of their brethren had and consequently caught more shit for it than just about every other independent band at the time, nearly all of whom had day jobs and toured far less frequently. If the machine was going to have gas in it and band members were going to remain fed, money needed to be a priority.

Bands like Led Zeppelin had their Peter Grant's to keep their business dealings in order, the Butthole Surfers didn't even have a roadie. But Gibby knew accounting and stood at a menacing 6'5". He also had a vested interest, since he would be the one to starve if the promoters decided to renege on their guarantees. It became known that if some 16-year-old promoter would try to fuck the band out of $200, a Sony Trinitron, or worse, would meet its demise.

The band collected themselves and headed from Birmingham to Baton Rouge to spend another night at their friend Mary's house on Lake Pontchartrain, with yet another bass player in tow. Then they crossed the border back into their former home state of Texas for a short spell, where finally, Juan's services were rendered useless once and for all. Kramer showed up in Dallas to play his first official show at the Circle A Ranch on September 27, 1985. The band thanked Juan for his help and bought him a plane ticket from DFW back to Atlanta, GA while they prepared themselves for their flight to London \ Heathrow.

London: land of the Clash and the Jam and the Fall. Land where the Sex Pistols changed the topography of rock music forever. But the Sex Pistols were long gone, and there were certainly few bands that jumped at the chance of taking their place as the vilified monsters the press, club owners, and politicians loved to hate. Few bands wanted to be as stifled musically either.

The Sex Pistols became their own worst enemies by becoming exactly what everyone expected. The eventual arrest of Sid Vicious for murdering his girlfriend, Nancy Spungen, and his fatal overdose before standing trial was so sensational, not even the Daily Mirror could have made it up. There was no irony, only cliché: a bad cartoon.

The punk bands that formed in the wake of the Sex Pistols made great records by keeping punk's ideals yet incorporating more diverse styles. The Clash infused their punk rock attitude with Jamaican dub and reggae music; the Buzzcocks and the Jam with 60's pop and soul, and with solid songwriting. Even Public Image, Ltd, John Lydon's post-Sex Pistols band, quite intentionally strayed far away from the path cleaved by his former band and the strict conformist rules that the punk scene had followed in the UK.

Psychedelic Jamming 1985 © William McConnell

Most of the original cache of punk bands had already broken up by the time the Butthole Surfers booked their first tour of Europe. And while many of the next wave of US hardcore bands were still active, if not necessarily still going strong, many of the new wave of British bands had effectively abandoned guitars in favor of synthesizers. Rock music, as far as most British kids were concerned, had become passé, its creators, dinosaurs. Synthesizer-pop bands were all the rage now. But, like bringing a cooler full of steaks to a vegetarian BBQ, the Butthole Surfers took off from Dallas bringing guitars to Great Britain.

There was no telling how a band that had been playing Beatles and Donovan covers, as well as their own brand of psychedelic punk rock, would go over in a country where Wham! and Depeche Mode were ruling the charts and airwaves at the BBC, but they had driven down nearly every dirt road in the US they could drive and it was time to find out whether there was a collective open mind, or at least a sympathetic soul, on the other side of the Atlantic. It wasn't as if the U.S. was ready for the Butthole Surfers to be on the pop charts, after all. And it wasn't as if the Butthole Surfers really cared either way.

Kramer, Gibby, Paul in DC, 9/6/85
© William McConnell

139

A Royal Flush

The band had been trekking around the United States with tapes they made over the course of nearly the last two years, in Texas, Detroit, NYC and at their new home in Winterville. Tapes were cluttering up the tiny kitchen that doubled as their recording studio. The stockpile of canisters was accumulating faster than they could find a soul to release them, and with Alternative Tentacles consistently dragging their feet on when they might be able to afford their next project, the band seemed more stifled than nurtured.

A batch of songs liberated from the BOSS which hadn't made it onto *Another Man's Sac* was collectively referred to as 'Rembrandt Pussyhorse' A tape was passed on to Alternative Tentacles in hopes it might finally arouse some interest and allow the band to give AT the full-length LP they felt they owed them.

The tape was gladly accepted and was passed around like a bong at a keg party. Copies of copies were made for friends and for friends of friends, but while the tape was in heavy rotation on their tape decks at home, in their beat-up cars, and on their own portable Walkmans, there was still no word as to when, if ever, it might get heard by anyone else.

With Kramer, 9/6/85 © William McConnell

With a new bass player secured, and a trip to Europe in their crosshairs, their record languished. Still, it was about time for them to do something about updating their discography, regardless of Alternative Tentacles' whims or wants.

Setlists had been laden with songs that nobody could get their hands on, even the relative few who may have had the desire. And with release of *Another Man's Sac* nearly a year, and 4 bass players prior, it seemed it was about time to find another outlet for their art.

They had more songs collecting dust than they had committed to vinyl, enough to release several albums. They opted, instead, to press up a 4 song EP as a stop-gap effort. The EP would enable them to move forward quickly, without having to spend the time and money they didn't have to mix and master a full-length LP. They were still holding on to the notion that their next full-length would be on Alternative Tentacles, and this project wouldn't completely clean out the closet of songs they had while they waited for Alternative Tentacles to get their act together.

So, they culled a couple of songs they had laid down at a session in New York City, back when Terence was still in the band. Two of the songs they mixed with Kramer, now their bassist, at Noise, NY. Those songs, "To Parter" and "Tornadoes", were destined to be included on 'Rembrandt Pussyhorse', but with the project on indefinite hold the band figured they might as well get them out in some format that might actually see the light of day.

The other two songs on the EP were ones they recorded more recently in Winterville, on the second hand 8-track recorder they bought from a guy in Memphis. Those were recorded just after Trevor hit the road back to Canada. As was often the case, Paul stepped into the role of bassist for the recording process. Once mixed and mastered, the band got the tapes off to Corey before they had even settled on artwork for it.

"To Parter" and "Tornadoes" songs had been staples of the live set, and were fan favorites, despite having never been etched into vinyl. The two songs recorded in GA, "Moving to Florida" and "Comb" were newly written and were some of the most experimental material yet in their vast repertoire.

"Comb" is a feedback filled dirge about "America's favorite junkie", Lou Reed. The song sees Gibby's vocals drenched in effects as he moans, bellows and laments upon the name of the self-proclaimed Rock'n'Roll Animal. King and Teresa pound and flail away at regurgitated Mitch Mitchell fills. Paul squeezes his guitar into a chokehold. It squeals and gasps for air before he rakes his pick upward across the strings again and again:

Lou Reed!

"Moving to Florida" becomes the quintessential Butthole Surfers song. It was a song torn straight from the pages of Captain Beefheart's own journal. A diatribe in search of a melody about urban blight and dancing sausages that at once mixes humor with an odd sense of foreboding. This time, Gibby's drawl was guttural, with a mouth full of marbles and quivering with excitement, the same way a hobo's would telling a story beside a campfire…

Well…I be moving…down…to Florida*…*

His dog looks up to see what is stirring her master, then drops her head back down in the dirt, disinterested…:

And I'm gonna bowl me a perfect game…

A syncopated riff punctuates the night air and abruptly stops as we listen again to our wayward sage:

I'm gonna cut off my leg down in Florida, child…and I'm gonna dance one-legged off in the rain…

The guitar and bass blast out some quick riffs, but quickly stop as to not interrupt our orator…:

By this time I guess you all figured out about Florida…

the last quaff of whiskey finally rouses our narrator into hopeful elation, and he begins to dance around the fire:

…Just like Vince (Lombardi) I'm gonna win…

His excitement is palpable, but our protagonist never does arrive in the Sunshine State. His intoxicated visions of grandeur only live in his dreams. Like Ponce De Leon, he is sure of the fountain of treasures that await him. Ever elusive, he lives in hope and dies in despair.

Ironically, the anti-song entitled "Moving to Florida" would be the first Butthole Surfers tune to break on college radio in the United States and would become the first modicum of exposure the band would gain toward a larger college rock audience, not just the ones who had shown up early to a Dead Kennedys show and stumbled upon the band mid-set.

In "Moving to Florida" there was enough novelty for the new wavers to show the punkers they were hip, and enough sardonic wit and dissonance for the punks to crack a smile. The song would soon be heard on WNYU-FM in NYC, and KPFK in Los Angeles, as well as on listener sponsored and college rock stations throughout the United States: WUSC in Colombia, South Carolina, and WWVU in Morgantown; KEXP in Seattle and KJHK in Lawrence, Kansas and many more. The band was soon being played alongside the likes of Billy Bragg, Husker Du, the Replacements, and even their brethren, REM: the darlings of college radio, and pretty much the only place one could hear underground or independent music at the time.

The four song EP was dubbed 'Cream Corn from the Socket of Davis', even before they knew of the spoils it would give to them. The title itself came about after an image Paul had left indelibly scarred upon everyone's psyches. In response to the question of what he would he do if he and the band ever did become rich and famous, he replied, in effect…

"I would have Sammy Davis Jr. take out his glass eye, fill his socket with cream corn and have him dance for me…when he was done, I'd have him take out his eye again and have the cream corn drool down his face…"

Holy Mother of God! It seemed as if the band's purpose for being had been neatly tied up in a tight little nut sac. Their purpose for existing was secure. Perhaps with their continued focus and persistence they could achieve this, their ultimate goal. It gave them a new reason for enduring the endless maelstrom they in which they seemed endlessly embroiled. The music on their new EP could only hope to live up to that title and provide them with the wealth and opportunity of seeing Mr. Bojangles tapping his way toward this auspicious grand finale.

But, as of now, "Cream Corn from the Socket of Davis" was merely a record without any cover art, awaiting its unveiling. Terry Tolkin's roommate and business partner, Chris Gordon, made artwork befitting of the EP's title, but his all-too-lifelike depiction of Sammy Davis Jr. with cream corn dripping down his face was just too haunting and grotesque to actually use, even for the Butthole Surfers.

Sammy had friends in high places as well, let's not forget, and a defiled image of that beloved, one-eyed, one-legged troubadour on the cover of their record might lead to the band finding Mark Farner's severed head next to them when they awoke one morning like that horse in the Godfather. It seemed in everyone's best interest to leave that joke a private one.

Paul:
"I did come up with the title for 'Cream Corn From The Socket Of Davis'. We were spending a lot of time in NYC, staying at Chuck's [Charles M. Young] *place and Terry Tolkin's place. Terry's roommate was into the title, and he spent time putting together an altered photo that depicted actual cream corn coming from actual Sammy Davis' eye socket... We were scared to use it... didn't want to mess with Sammy when it got down to it."* [email, 9/13/13]

The record remained in a state of suspended animation awaiting its domestic release, but the band managed to slap some art together to have a release they could bring with them overseas. For that, they used a picture of the mom of an old high school friend, Scott Bevers.

The picture's seemingly random selection was perplexing to be sure, but her look of modest contempt seemed oddly fitting. She is the shining example of a middle-class American housewife of the 1960's, replete with horn-rimmed glasses. One nearly chokes in a cloud of Aquanet while frozen in her scornful gaze.

Scott Bevers:
"Gibby liked the picture. Chuck Young met my mother and witnessed her discovering that she was on the cover. Chuck had a great laugh over that experience. I am catching hell for it to this day from mom and my brother...it was all in the spirit of good fun."
[email, Sept 2014]

The look epitomizes the scorn the band received from the strait-laced, normal society at large. The release of 'Cream Corn' with this cover exclusively overseas would perhaps prevent Mrs. Bevers from ever seeing the record on the shelves, it was hoped. With any luck, and a little promotion, the kids of Europe wouldn't have such a difficult finding it.

The band had recently set up a new deal for distribution overseas, since Alternative Tentacles and the Subterranean were out to lunch. With this new deal, they were able to get *Another Man's Sac* released domestically for the kids in Europe, and with 'Cream Corn', had some new product available to release as well. They turned to an odd Atlanta based record label that dealt exclusively with import releases. During one of their all-too-brief respites in Georgia, they stopped off at the plantation style home of the label's founder, Richard Jordan, for some coffee, and to discuss band business.

Jordan had spent much of the 1970's picking around the United States, buying up used records and overstock collections and then selling them at flea markets and record fairs to earn his keep. He eventually went over to the UK and did the same there, creating a network of friends there who were into the same obscure music he was digging at the time.

By the early 1980's, he concluded that selling other people's used records was OK but selling records he himself might press up by the bands he loved would be even cooler. Out of this revelation came Fundamental Records.

Fundamental was based on U.S. soil, but distributed records abroad; often taking 'hot' underground American bands and showcasing them for the first time to European audiences. This idea was perfect for a band that had few contacts in Europe and was heading there in a mere few weeks' time. Fundamental had recently put out an import of *Another Man's Sac* with some alternate artwork, and 'Cream Corn' was now ready for an its import release as well.

So, Fundamental had its version of 'Cream Corn from the Socket of Davis' ready to roll, but Touch & Go didn't have artwork for the domestic release. To prevent the record from being leaked to the US market as a bloated-priced import, Touch & Go pressed up limited amounts in a green, die-cut 'Pre-Release' sleeve. The vast array of colored waxes they used was due to the pressing plant running out of black vinyl and not the band's desire to make it more collectable to record snobs, according to Terry Tolkin.

Upon their eventual return to the states in November, 1985, they would find the art they had been looking for, and the die-cut sleeve was replaced by some pictures they found while trolling through crates of a commercial photographer's studio.

They chose a picture they found in the archives of a professional photographer in San Antonio. Like the shot of Scott's mom, it had little to do with creamed corn, or the "Candy Man", but was just as elegantly twisted, revealing little of the horrors etched on the wax within. With everything in order, they could focus on what was important: the tour.

King:
"Once the title was settled on, the band then asked a friend in NYC to try to do a drawing of cream corn flowing out of Sammy's head, but it was just a little too real to be used for a cover... Gibby and/or Paul then came across someone in San Antonio who was a commercial photographer and he had photographs of what seemed like a debutante ball or something. In the foreground was a teen girl with a big flowing dress. In the background on some steps was the little girl who made the cover. The photographer had releases from all the models and he was delighted to make his subjects Butthole Surfers models." [post, Nov, 2005]

Europe had had very little exposure to the band at all, and they feared, perhaps justifiably, that the empty halls of their early days might have flown alongside them in some harrier jet to be transplanted on foreign soils for them to revisit once again. The food already sucked in England and the desire to eat out of garbage cans in the UK seemed entirely less palatable than the relative delicacies they pulled from the trash while at Cheryl's in Little Italy.

But Kramer reassured Gibby and Paul that he knew what he was doing, and the time was right for them to get overseas. Kramer promised they would win over the Euro kids, who loved anything from the American underground. He swore that they would, at the very least, break even on this venture. Despite their reservations, he recounts, they trusted his judgment and went along for the ride.

They played their first show in Wales, at the Stowhill Labor Club on October 3, 1985 and as Kramer predicted, the reviews were absolutely beaming. Somehow, the Brits were able to grasp what this undeniably American band brought to their uptight countryside. The Butthole Surfers seemed at once to verify their stereotypes of the crass, ugly American, yet somehow transcend them.

Gibby, who had taken to standing on a chair for many of the performances, became the 10-foot-tall ringleader, bellowing and beckoning on-lookers with his bullhorn. Paul tip-toed and swayed like a dancing bear at a circus, his eyes crossed as if engrossed in some religious rapture, the vehicle of some other-worldly force that spoke through his instrument.

Kramer chose to play his new purchase of a Hofner 500/1 violin bass without a strap. He crouched forward to prevent it from falling to the floor and twirled and swung it around in a manner that both sullied and paid homage to the ghost of Paul McCartney. Teresa and King had always been the wonder twins, but in the Motherland, where so many bands programmed their drumbeats into a robotic pitter-patter like so much rain on a tin roof, their barrel drums were like the organic rumble of galloping thunder; an old friend found through the London fog.

The Brits not only got the joke, but they also seemingly understood the power and the violence. They reveled in it as the perfect antidote to all the pomposity and stuffiness found in so many bands operating on their side of the pond. In an age when the UK was dancing to Boy George, and image conscious, gender bending pretty boys were programming their synthesizers and teasing their up their coiffures, the Butthole Surfers were a breath of stench-filled air. A reminder that rock music was not pretty or contrived. Their lack of any real style, be it punk, or metal, or hippie, meant they could be all those things or none of them at all. The Buttholes were hillbilly sheik.

But, no sooner had the rave reviews been inked onto the pages of Melody Maker and Sounds, than they were gone. off to the mainland to play the biggest show of their career: The Pandora's Music Box Festival in Rotterdam.

The Butthole Surfers were booked alongside some of the biggest new wave acts of the day. It was the biggest crowd they had ever seen. Well, maybe the crowd at Grand Funk Railroad with REO Speedwagon was bigger, Paul could say…maybe the Led Zeppelin show at Dallas Memorial Coliseum had more, Gibby might ponder, but they were merely in the audience at those shows, not scheduled to appear as one of the featured acts.

The Buttholes were given an ill-advised time slot of 1:40AM. It gave them lots of time to celebrate the fact that Kramer had bailed on Shockabilly and joined their ranks, leaving them with this huge festival gig as complete unknowns. It also gave Gibby lots of time to start some shit. By the time local radio station VPRO's festival coverage began, Gibby was already slurring and bleary-eyed. He was seen drinking whiskey out of his combat boot and running around lifting the dress he was wearing, exposing himself to any poor soul he happened upon.

Cheryl Dyer was in Europe at the time as well and made the trip to Rotterdam to hang out with her old friends. As was Richard Jordan, who came to promote his label and the newest Butthole Surfers releases.

In an interview with VPRO, Richard touted his recent exploits while Gibby, standing over his shoulder, touted his own. In his most professional manner, Jordan cited his humble beginnings while Gibby's draped his penis onto his shoulder. Once Jordan turned his head and saw the hideous beast staring back at him, he darted up out of his chair and scurried out of the room, completely mortified. Interview over. This was the way the Butthole Surfers got their press, not by talking about themselves, but by creating a spectacle of themselves.

Paul:
"Richard Jordan came to Holland to see a couple of his bands (including us) perform at a festival in Rotterdam. He was wearing a black suit and tie. A film crew asked him for an interview, and he talked on camera for several minutes about his bands before realizing that Gibby was standing behind him with his penis draped over his shoulder the entire time. He got mad. Maybe that's why he never paid us." [post, Oct 2011]

Later, Gibby swaggers and swings a bottle of Ballantine's Scotch around as the stage he commands is strewn with debris: torn dresses stained with fake blood, assorted bottles of alcohol, wooden clothespins, cigarette butts. They swim through the swirling fog the of Echo & the Bunnymen's smoke machine someone kicks on from the side of the stage. Gibby chugs directly from the bottle and nearly falls to his death frolicking around, not realizing the stage he is teetering upon is some 20 feet off the ground. During "The Shah Sleeps in Lee Harvey's Grave", he runs over and knocks the microphone stand to the floor as Paul tries to sing. Paul bends over to pick it up, so Gibby swings his guitar and it smashes to the floor again, chiding Paul to just give up the ghost of a song and watch him prance around like some giant, barefoot, prima ballerina on acid.

It was complete anarchy, and the awe-struck crowd immediately fell in love with them. Being so engaged in their revelries, they had no idea how the show had gone at all. They only knew there was a bevy of bands and bouncers they had pissed off with their antics, and they would need to do something to avoid them after their set. Perhaps, with luck, they would all be asleep at this late hour.

In an odd coincidence, Gibby was nearly accosted by five huge security guards. He had finally pissed off the wrong group of people. But, who? There had been so many victims over the course of the day it was difficult to decipher which one had finally alerted the authorities. The bouncers came upon him and demanded he leave, but Gibby wasn't going anywhere until they got paid for the gig. Things started getting tense, and Gibby was in no state to deal with it. Somehow, before serious bodily harm could be inflicted, he escaped into the crowd, out the gate and back to the hotel to meet with the rest of the band, minus Paul.

Paul had remained behind, slightly less threatening than the others with his button-down shirt and short cropped hair. He hadn't seen his pals for some time though and was pushing his luck by standing by the cases of equipment donning the stenciled 'BUTTHOLE SURFERS' all over them. He drank an ale, every so often popping up on his tippy-toes to peer over the throngs of people milling about, praying he did not get recognized by security.

Realizing he alone, and that all the band's equipment was left behind in their mad dash to escape, Paul devised a strategy how to make his way back to the hotel without anyone noticing he was rolling cases of stenciled "Butthole Surfers"; the same band who had so flagrantly broken the law the whole day.

He took all the equipment he could, along with a trench coat he thought he had seen Gibby wearing earlier that day and dragged it as far as he could manage. He wound up stashing most of the equipment, along with the coat, in bushes in a park near the hotel after multiple trips back and forth and nearly collapsing from exhaustion.

The next morning, all the equipment was somehow still there. The coat was there as well, which, unbeknownst to him, had the money paid to them for the previous night's performance in its pocket. The same money Gibby had almost gotten the band killed for.

There was no way for Gibby to remember that payment had been given to him. He certainly could not be blamed. They all saw his state. If anything, it was the rest of the band's fault for entrusting him. But, alas, all was right with the world. With things in some semblance of order, they breathed a collective sigh of relief and continued to the next town.

It was a scene that would be played out nearly every night, Kramer recounts. Gibby would collect the bands payment and stuff it into his pocket, only to strip down to his underwear or some dime store dress he would tear off during the set. Loaded on whiskey and LSD, the clothes, and money would eventually be found stuffed under a drum bag or in a guitar case. In a moment of a blind, drug-fueled frenzy, Gibby would come inevitably come out screaming like a banshee.

Kramer recounts:
"'Who stole my fucking money???!!!! Some motherfucker stole our entire wad of cash, man!!!! 30 gigs of pay and it's fucking gone, man!!!! I've looked fuckin' everywhere and I just fucking know that some cocksucker stole it!!!! It was in my pants and now it's fucking gone, man!!!! I hate this fuckin' town!!!'"
[emails, Feb, 2012]

It often played out as Gibby stood there without any pants, sometimes out in the parking lot of the club in the dead of winter with police staring at the sight of a 6'5" hippie freak Texan tripping balls covered in beer and fake blood. The cops would get into their cars and drive away faster than Starsky and Hutch on a tip from Huggy Bear…best to give out beer tickets to the local high school kids than to write up a report from this madman.

The money was never lost or stolen, and it became just another aspect of being a Butthole Surfer for Kramer to cherish and laugh about. He was surely in heaven. The rest of the band, who were not as far removed from band business as Kramer, however, were not so sure where they were.

Europe was like another planet to these Texans. These people didn't eat barbeque, their TV was awful, and they only smoked Marlboro reds. From the second they stepped off the plane, they had an immediate impulse to turn around and fly home. They were fish out of water and had the look of fear in their eyes. Weird visions of German skinheads in bright green leisure suits singing 'Hare Krishna' left Paul a bit unhinged, but Kramer had seen this many times before and assured him that this tour would be the stuff of legends.

They would get often get bummed at the fact that many of the shows found them being billed as "The Butthole Surfers, featuring Kramer from Shockabilly," or "The Butthole Surfers from NYC," or even just flat out as "Shockabilly," but once the lights dimmed, and the set was in full swing, the kids seemed to really dig them. Money was tight, and many of the venues were left half empty, but Kramer did his best to ease their reservations.

Kramer:
"Trust me, Paul. No one has ever come out on stage with his right hand on fire and dove into the audience before. When these pussy Europeans see that right before their eyes, it will change their worlds. Trust me. You'll be back here in 6 months or a year, playing for ten times what you're being paid now..."
[email, Feb, 2012]

Kramer was right and by night's end, after the house lights came back on and blinded their bloodshot eyes, everyone, the fans, the press, and the promoters all knew exactly who they were and where from where they came. The Butthole Surfers from Texas!

Surely there were times when it was difficult to find a glimmer of hope and they might have questioned why they ever decided to ditch the accounting jobs they had forsaken so long ago. Perhaps Gibby could beg Peat Marwick for just one more chance…'I know I can be a good boy, now, sir…I strayed…I was wrong'. But, those thoughts only came up when times were at their worst. It was best to ignore the hunger pangs, language barriers, and strange customs and press on with the tour. And it seemed the more they pressed, the more the legend grew.

Kramer's faith in the band helped get them to Europe, but it sometimes seemed as if he was there more to get his own rocks off than to lend a hand on bass. While in Paris, he convinced the band to head down to a small town on the French Riviera for a week. Once there, he hopped on a train back to Paris to stay with a friend he knew.

Once, he decided to blow the last $10 the band had to their name to buy some chocolate for himself. Despite his help in booking this tour, and the profound friendship they felt, he and Gibby were often a mere glance away from strangling each other.

The rest of the Butthole Surfers whirlwind tour of Europe found them all narrowly escaping a savage beating in Stavanger, Norway, as well as playing successful shows in Oslo, Copenhagen, Berlin, and then back to the Netherlands, to play the Effenaar. After narrowly escaping a Dutch jail cell two weeks prior, they were invited back and now being hailed as the 'sensations of the Pandora festival' on promotional posters made for the gig.

It seemed that the more awful the experience, the more their reputation grew. The more horrible the nightmare was, the better the show was. It was a sign from above, and one which they would heed. Shows were meant to be circuses, hedonistic rituals, exorcisms, transcendental meditations. The band had always known how to stir up a crowd and create havoc stateside, and was gaining a cult of fans across the U.S. Now seeing how accepting the British and Dutch and Germans were toward them, their reason and purpose was becoming clearer. Perpetuate the horror.

The perseverance and drive to remain a band after the Mathews brothers had quit seemed completely insane. And it was completely insane, but it was no more insane than the Cold War that divided the European continent itself, or the CIA and KGB fueled guerilla wars which were sparking up throughout Central America. A world of insanity called for a band like the Butthole Surfers.

If the leaders of the Free World could act with such reckless abandon toward the end of assured mutual destruction of humanity, then an opposing force of insanity, equal in intensity, was needed to create a Tao-like equilibrium.

Paul and Gibby perhaps hadn't quite realized it in the beginning, at the time when they wrote songs for a goof and when every day meant another band name, before settling on the Butthole Surfers because it was the name they happened to be calling themselves when they earned their first paycheck. They were beginning to see a destination on the dark road on which they traveled.

They fell into being Butthole Surfers to eat, and to avoid having real jobs. They played shows for sustenance. They made music to entertain themselves and, slowly, gained their own following. Now, the formula was staying out of jail and then throwing out any and all formulas of what a band was supposed to be. Oddly, their single-minded vision seemed almost viable. Their oddball plan, which never really seemed to be a plan at all somehow seemed to be a winning one. And their shows, once merely chaotic, became completely hedonistic.

The crowds cried for blood, even if it came in the form of fake capsules stuffed into Gibby's boxer shorts. Like Romans at the Coliseum, they wanted to escape into the darkest recesses of their minds, and they needed a band like the Butthole Surfers to help take them there. Through the band's abandonment of laws, rules, and norms, they created a bible that fans could use as a roadmap by which to follow.

And the converted masses would themselves venture out and preach the twisted gospel of the Butthole Surfers. Soon, venues were filled with lost souls in need of saving. The band returned to the United States completely focused and energized to capitalize on their successes.

But the endless globetrotting was beginning to take its toll on these martyrs. Exhaustion and loneliness were starting to creep into their ranks, and with Teresa in particular. She was suffering, and her desire to return home, not just to their abandoned house in Winterville, but to Texas with her friends and family, was too deep to ignore.

As she longed for the stability and warm meals of home, she watched Kramer depart the group. Another casualty on their quest. Home tugged on the hem of her skirt, and as Gibby and Paul planned where they would go once they touched down in the states, Teresa planned her escape.

The Butthole Surfers were about to suffer their biggest blow since that scorching August night a few years back in Dallas, that early morning, when the Mathews brothers divided the band in half. Back then, the band's future was uncertain. Now, it would seem downright bleak.

Walk Away

When the band returned Stateside from the 1985 European tour, autumn was well underway. They immediately hit the ground running, hoping to capitalize on the startling success overseas. The tour of Europe, despite their initial reservations, had been a revelation, and as Kramer had predicted, promoters and fans were eager to see their return.

The shows in Europe didn't generate huge amounts of cash, but fans were fervent, the venues fair, and the food delicious, on the mainland at least. Prior to departing, plans were set in motion for their return the following spring, and it seemed nothing could stop the rock'n'roll train.

They headed to Detroit to boast to Corey of their exploits. They also played a two-night stand at Graystone Hall, a venue that Corey began booking as a promoter, further ingraining himself into the underground scene. From there, the band booked a two-night stand at Staches in Columbus, OH., followed by a stop in Chicago at the Metro. From Chicago, yet another two-night stint at the First Avenue in Minneapolis: a testament to their quickly growing fan base.

The two shows in Detroit were great coming home presents. The Graystone was packed and the Back Porch Video crew was there yet again to capture some more footage of the band. Plans were also ironed out for the domestic release of 'Cream Corn from the Socket of Davis'. Everything seemed to be falling into place before it all started falling apart. It was the calm before the house of cards was blown down. The beginning of the end, and the storm clouds were gathering on the horizon.

Just before the first night in Columbus, Kramer ate some rancid cod at the Blue Danube across the street from club. He recalls being hurled over with the pain of 100 daggers churning in his emaciated belly, and the show was canceled. Paul recalls how Kramer was almost immediately better after the show was called off. However, in an interview on VPRO Radio during their 1986 tour of Europe, Gibby does mention Kramer's 'attack in Columbus, Ohio.

As memories of these times are clouded and dreamlike, it's hard to tell where the truth lies. From accounts, one gets the impression that Kramer's dedication and commitment to remaining in the band was waning, be it for health reasons, personal ones, or both.

They were able to pull off the subsequent night's performance at Staches as well as the rest of the tour, but regardless the cod, Kramer was the feeling the intestinal strain of being a Butthole Surfer. The trip to Europe was a Ferris Wheel of dizzying highs and guttural lows, of brilliant performances, and blinding destitution. The days of adoration and quality hashish in Shockabilly were behind him, and the days of endless drives, and Mexican dirt weed were upon him. At first, it was a price he was willing to pay to be in his own favorite band, but the novelty was wearing off.

In the 4 months Kramer had been in the band, he hadn't been home to see his wife for longer than a couple of days, and he had not one penny in his pocket when he arrived. As he put it, he was 'a vegetarian, Jew from Long Island in a band full of Texans: who loved barbeque, drank warm domestic beer by the case, and ate LSD like Pez' [email, 2012]. It was a bleak existence.

Their itinerary, without the benefit of a booking agent, often meant they'd be driving hundreds of miles between gigs. Kramer would drive more often than not, he claims, having not done LSD since high school. It certainly seemed like the most logical plan to take. The rest of the time, he closed his eyes and held on white knuckled, fearing for dear life.

He had a studio in NY, and a wife, and the band didn't even have a home. There was absolutely no money for personal expenses, with every cent being invested back into the band fund to be doled out parsimoniously by Gibby from the pot set aside to subsist.

It's a gray November in Columbus, OH, and the bass player is puking his guts up in a public restroom. After sleeping 2-3 hours a night since summertime, his liver ceased cleansing his body of toxins.

He prayed: the last refuge of a man at the end of his rope…:

Kramer's prayer:
"'Please, dear God, if you really exist, make tomorrow a day that DOESN'T feel like some psychotic, living nightmare… Just one day during which we're not a cunt hair away from being arrested, shot dead, ripped off, mangled and bloodied by some schizophrenic bouncer, sickened by bad food, crippled for life in some gnarly highway altercation with a 16-wheeler, or beaten to death by some skinheads out to prove that the Dead Kennedy's are better than we are…please God….'" [email 2012]

Huddled in a quivering ball in the back of a van being driven a howling madman ripped to the tits on cheap acid, Kramer prayed. But there was no answer from the sky, just the persistent fever chills that left his muscles aching in pain. He needed some time to recover in his own bed next to his wife and not Mark Farner. Instead, he crammed himself back into the van for a 400-mile drive from the Windy City to Minneapolis: Land of 10,000 Lakes. His wife was angry at the lack of help with expenses back home, and the endless antics of Gibby and Paul along the way only made him wretch in pain. Their laughter butchered his guts like a thousand steak knives.

Finally, after driving from Minneapolis to New Orleans on a tour that hadn't stopped since he met up with them in Dallas, Kramer told the band the news that he was packing it in and going home. He had gotten word from his wife that the owners of Noise, NY were looking to sell the studio he had been renting, for cheap, and with the opportunity to fulfill his life-long dream to own, rather than rent, a studio, and to record and release material at his leisure, it gave him the final excuse he needed to walk away and bid the rest of the band a fond adieu.

Kramer, quoting Paul:
"Well that's just fuckin' fine, Kramer. If you just wanna be married and stay at home watchin' movies or sit on your ass in a recording studio and not be a musician anymore, that's just fuckin' fine, you go right ahead and do that. We'll just fucking go through all that fucking bullshit again and find a new bass player. What the fuck, we'll just do this every fucking month, I guess. Thanks a lot, Kramer." [email, 2012]

Paul says:
"Kramer was never really IN the band... I don't remember chewing him out for anything except the chocolate, and that was Gibby who chewed him out over it. We just went our separate ways." [email, January 2014]

King:
"...I don't think Kramer was ever in the band per se but helped us out for a couple of tours when we didn't have a bass player. He did the first European tour we did (where inevitably we were billed as ex-Shockabilly) and some shows on the east coast and mid-west. Basically, Kramer had a life to return to - a cool recording studio, a wife, a nice apartment - things that we didn't have and would in fact be an impediment towards.   He went back to his life after the shows were over and we went back to living in a van." [post 2006]

Despite the opposing perspectives on the end of Kramer's tenure with the band, one thing is clear, the band had seen the light in Europe. Their mission was given form and clarity. There were people in Holland and Denmark and Germany who got it. Kramer's prophecy was correct; Europe could be conquered. The rest of the band may have been hesitant at first but, by the time they were heading back to the States they would be revered by the few kids who saw them. And, six months from now, those kids would all be back with 10 of their friends. Much of the next European tour was already booked before they left the continent. The plan was in action. Kramer had been right, and now Kramer was bailing.

The band had been the center of Paul's universe for the past half-decade, and they were finally getting to a point where they could almost afford to buy their own groceries. It is easy to see how the frustration of another setback, just as things were finally beginning to gain some momentum, would have finally gotten the best of him.

It is also easy to see how Kramer's departure was little more than a bump in the road that the Buttholes seemed to forever be travelling. No matter whose account holds more truth, it seems the band was prepared for this day. And the fact remains that Kramer DID just want to be married and sit on his ass and run a studio. These were the thoughts of a rational human being.

His love for his friends and their music was strong, but he was not quite willing to martyr himself or his marriage for them. Any shard of guilt he might have been able to muster for leaving the band to fend for themselves was fleeting, overtaken by the pangs of being comfortable and warm at home with his wife and a brand-new recording studio in his name.

Kramer had a mission as well, and the studio would provide him the means to achieve it. He got the Butthole Surfers thinking globally. His job was done. But even the allure of being in the greatest band in the world couldn't change his mind. It had been a great run to look back upon, but these fond memories would be best viewed in retrospect, in a comfortable seat. Not hunched over some dirty throne in a rest area outside of Des Moines on a cold and cloudy morning. Not enmeshed in it every day. Then it was too real; too much for the sane man to give up his life for. Many tried, few succeeded.

Kramer would continue to make music on his own terms: as leader of Bongwater: with fellow Shockabilly alum David Licht and actress\artist\model, Ann Magnuson, as well as a solo performer and collaborator, but no longer as a Butthole Surfer.

Owning his own studio gave Kramer and a new crop of bands in the "Downtown Scene" a vehicle to produce and release their material. His Shimmy Disc Records gave rise to the next crop of underground bands. Bands like WeeN, Gwar, Boredoms, Ruins, Galaxie 500, King Missile, as well as the scores of others that called Shimmy Disc home for their earliest and most formative releases.

Shockabilly's notoriety was instrumental in helping the band attract the attention they so desperately needed. Though a short one even by Butthole Surfers standards, Kramer's tenure became legendary. His unmistakable method of playing his Hofner bass strapless, and previous experience covering the classics in Shockabilly seemed to give some folks that 'Ah Ha!' moment they needed to understand the Butthole Surfers in context.

The realization that punk rock was nothing but a state of being, and that the Beatles or Marty Robbins or Muddy Waters or Black Flag were all equal in their validity and inspiration, a thought that was almost as blasphemous within the strict, self-conscious world of punk rock. Now, punks could almost admit to liking Led Zeppelin in public.

Punk in its purest incarnation was just another way of breaking the rules. Gibby and Paul and King, and Teresa and Kramer had always felt as such, and now, with a connection established, there was a sort of a reference point to be drawn upon. They certainly won over the old Shockabilly fans in Europe, most of whom had no idea who the Butthole Surfers were before witnessing Kramer play bass for them. Those people were no doubt recruited. And, as for any of those few Dead Kennedys fans still confused as to whether the Butthole Surfers were just a novelty act, it was becoming more and more obvious that they were not.

It took a while to grasp, but once Paul and the rest of the band got over any hurt feelings, they realized Kramer was probably right. Maybe not the day Kramer stepped onto the plane and flew back into LaGuardia Airport, but eventually the sting gave way to a dull throb, and they understood that this mission was only for ones with the intestinal fortitude of a billy goat and that Kramer was not the John Rambo who could overcome the relentless onslaught. Paul and King both recall how they couldn't believe Kramer lasted as long as he had.

Before long, they would all forgive and forget, they for his departure, he for their sadistic lifestyle. Any hard feelings would blow over once everyone was showered and rested. They knew this day would come. Kramer would return to NY to be with his wife and that they would return to the roads of America on their endless tour. There seemed little illusion that Kramer would tolerate their lifestyle for more than a couple of months, and there was very little surprise, or anger, when he finally decided to leave.

The bass slot was, as the drum position had been when they were struggling in San Antonio, always fluid. This time, at least, the departure was not on the heels of a scheduled tour. This was a split that could be dealt with in a reasonable way. They had business to tend to, and the time was right to head back to Georgia. If it was to be without Kramer, then that was OK.

But, regardless of their feelings about Kramer's departure, the final outcome was still the same; the Butthole Surfers were once again left with a hole in their rhythm section. They were surely not going to allow their world to come crashing down merely because they lost another bass player, so they got right on the task of smoking the last of their weed and mulling over any old contacts and acquaintances they knew while driving the back to Georgia after the final show. Things would work out. It was not a big deal.

When they returned to Georgia just before Christmas, the house was dark and cold and looking stark and unkempt after months of being abandoned. The house objectified another cold, dark reality. The holidays were quickly approaching, and it would be yet another destitute and lonely one away from family and friends. This seemed far more depressing than the small joys any modicum of success could afford them.

Residuals were scarce and touring was the only way to make a living and the thought of the constant rehearsing they'd need to get a new bass player up to snuff was daunting, at best, and certainly didn't add to facilitate any festive mood. The reward of finding a new bass player would be the muscular atrophy, poor diet, and sleep deprivation of yet another tour. It was an unnerving thought, and it loomed over Teresa like a shadow. In the frigid house among the scattered beer cans and equipment cases, heavy with the stale smell of dirty ashtrays and the fog of a three-day old hangover, the approaching Yuletide seemed more like something out of William Burroughs than Charles Dickens.

And although Teresa wasn't really one for Dickens, she was beginning to feel the sentimental tug of the warm fires of home. It was after much deliberation that she decided that home, for her, was not in Winterville, but back in Austin. It was where she needed to be to regain her sanity, so she informed the rest of the band that she was leaving not just for the holidays, but to stay.

She had witnessed Kramer's transformation from lean and healthy to writhing in the throes of sickness. She had seen the toll it had taken on Terence, who had joined the group bright-eyed, clear-headed and focused, and who left emaciated and riddled with dysentery. She had not quite reached that state yet, but she reached the same conclusion. A serene realization that the time had come for her to walk away.

Teresa:
"...I called my parents and they wired me money to Atlanta, and I just fuckin' flew home. Then we got the stuff out of storage. My dad drove me all the way to Georgia and we got the stuff out of storage and I came home and got a job at a restaurant and my goal was to buy a video camera. We had a thing earlier in Georgia where I was asking Gibby if we could by a video camera, and he was like 'WE NEVER EVER BUY A VIDEO CAMERA'... So I went and got this job in Austin and saved up the money'... my whole trip was that I was gonna get a video camera and become a documentary filmmaker."
[phone interview; 7/26/2014]

Prior breakups had been based on altercations, hurt feelings, and lost arguments. Teresa's decision was made in the calm and cool manner of someone who actually pondered it, mulled it over, and had come to terms with the decision. It was clear-headed and defined, and though the same thoughts often entered each of their own minds just about every day, it was painfully and immediately clear that Teresa was actually going to do something about it.

When a girl makes up her mind and falls out of love it is usually well thought out and the decision final; based on hours of deliberating reactions and ramifications. They may walk away 100 times and come back, but when the decision is reached with a clear mind and placated heart, it is most certainly over for good. It soon became apparent to the boys in the band that she wasn't coming back. She wouldn't be turning around in a half hour and walking through the door after a time-out was taken. This was for real. Teresa was leaving.

Kramer's departure could be handled, but the loss of Teresa was devastating. The five-piece band was now whittled down to just a trio. Times were sad, and Christmas in their adopted hometown was just not the same without the girl they loved.

King:
"Teresa, on the other hand, did quit - she was in the band and it was a big deal.   Keep in mind that we all quit during that period, only to return hours or a day later...Living and working with four other people - day after day - for little money was pretty grueling.   Most sane people would have quit.   There were a lot of reasons why went through a lot of bass players.   It was tough and we weren't the easiest people to deal with, I reckon."
[post, 2006]

All of them felt the tug of home. They loved Georgia when their brief hiatuses afforded them the luxury of some time there. The Now! Explosion, WREK and the avant-garde 'Destroy All Music' happenings, the wild nights at the Celebrity club, the vibrant orange clay of their favorite swimming hole. Along with all the new friends they made in their new locale, King recalls them as some of the best memories of his life.

But the Butthole Surfers were forever Texans in their hearts, even if the scenesters in Austin had all but forsaken them as sellouts who bailed for Georgia. They only left Texas because they had outgrown the local dives they'd been playing as a fledgling punk outfit. Like the Dicks and MDC, Texas offered little else in terms of growth. Now, after branching out from the state, as well as from the strict confines of punk rock, they had the benefit of some money to call 'theirs', even if it all was in Gibby's pocket. They also had accumulated a small but fervent national following and the ability to turn a profit on the road, providing they all remained in a commune, but they were barely even a band now. Things looked bleak.

And though they were still not quite sure where they wanted to be, they were pretty sure they knew where they didn't want to be, and so they (apparently) notified their landlord in Winterville that they were breaking their lease.

Whether the lease was broken prior to the move to Europe, or after, is unclear even to the most lucid memories. But one fact was very clear; Teresa's departure left them reeling and they needed to shake themselves out of the funk that staying in Winterville was perpetuating. They moved back to Atlanta and began shacking up at the Mergentime loft near the Little Five Points section of the city. The loft doubled as both a practice pad for their pals the Easturn Stars, and home of that band's guitarist, Kytha Gernatt.

As in NYC, there were tons of artists and friends passing through the loft all the time, some staying the night, some leaving on extended vacations, some open-ended stays in the Big Apple to see what might be happening up there.

There were musicians and freethinkers abound, and it was not for lack of a pool of potential new recruits that the bass and drum positions went unfilled, but rather the difficulty finding someone who would be willing to give up their lives to dedicate to being a Butthole Surfer.

The band was on the longest hiatus since that fateful night in Dallas when fists flew and breakup seemed inevitable. Now the future of the Butthole Surfers seemed just as uncertain. They knew they needed to lick their wounds and move forward, but there was an empty space they couldn't quite fill. They awaited the news that 'Cream Corn' was ready for its domestic unveiling and then figured they'd try to grab anyone who'd sit in on bass just to get back on the road and away from Georgia and the malaise of a Christmas depression.

Things would get even worse when word got to them that their friend D. Boon had been killed in a van accident outside of Phoenix. It was a devastating blow during a time full of devastation. Sadness prevailed around the scene, and tears fell like rain in the Butthole Surfers camp.

It seemed the Butthole Surfers' reputation preceded them. It wouldn't be as easy to fool the next recruits into believing that they would have a life outside the band, or a home of which to boast, or hold a job for their own personal cash flow. Love interests were also out of the question. These luxuries would not be tolerated. Being a Butthole Surfer meant picking up on a moment's notice and going out on the road for tours that didn't end. It meant living together in the same house on the rare occasions you were not on tour. Splitting money, food and weed between everybody, giving up on school or much of anything that might take your focus off the band. Not surprisingly, there were no immediate takers for the job.

The first scheduled shows in Europe were mere weeks away, but the band was down to just three members, and prospects were running low. They asked their friend Steve Marsh, who was playing with the band Miracle Room at the time. When Steve asked if it was ok for him to bring his wife along for the trip, they crossed his name off the list

Jimbo Yongue was an obvious choice. As their first friend in Atlanta, they knew him well, and they all got along swimmingly. His prowess on a six-string and his uncanny ability to play Charlie Daniels' "The Devil Went Down to Georgia" on a tiny toy fiddle made him the perfect candidate for the position as well.

Gibby made the offer; $300 cash as well as food, lodging and all the drugs they could muster for his time in the band. It was probably a better offer than they were able to afford, and probably a better offer than any member in the band ever got, but time was short and they were desperate.

Jimbo was a guitar player, though, and his band at the time, Threshold of Pain, was doing pretty well locally: combining punk rock, metal, and country blues into a lightning fast, riff-fueled hoedown. They were opening for tons of bands at his home away from home, the Metroplex, as well as at other clubs around town. Gibby's offer was nice, but after some thoughtful deliberation, he politely declined. The band was bummed, but although he himself wasn't ready to be a Butthole Surfer, Jimbo mentioned a friend of his who he thought would be the perfect fit to take over the helm.

Jimbo recommended an old friend of his named Jeffrey Pinkus, who was a already a huge fan and who also, coincidentally, played bass guitar. He had a decent handle on most of the material too, so the time breaking him in wouldn't be such a tortuous slog.

Jimbo Yongue:
"I received a call from Gibby asking if I wanted to tour Europe for three months with them on bass. He offered me all necessary food, lodging, drugs and $300 when all was said and done. While this is a tempting offer, I was a guitar player with a burgeoning local band, Threshold for Pain, and wasn't sure about being a bass player.
I thought of Pinkus, who was a huge Butts fan and already knew all the material.
I put the word out I was looking for him, and when I finally called him and said hello, he said 'YES! YES! I'll DO IT!'" [email 9/19/12]

At the tender age of 17, Jeff was considerably younger than the rest of the band, but his age was actually a benefit, as it left him with few ties to tether him to Atlanta. Word that the band was gearing up to tour Europe again in the spring left Jeff with but one course of action. He gathered his few meager possessions and started playing and practicing for his new role as a Butthole Surfer.

Teresa with King 1985,
courtesy of Ralph Pepper

hair. A flannel shirt and knee-high leather moccasin boots made him look like an outsider even among these outsiders. With Kramer, the band had become a well-seasoned workhorse. With Jeff, they had a player destined to become yet another footnote to the laundry list of bassists since Scott Stevens had abandoned the post just a few months into their existence. Based on their prior history, it was nearly impossible to have high hopes for anyone taking on the role of bassist.

But Jeff was young and eager…or desperate and high. Either way, after the first practice, with him jamming on some Black Sabbath and Blue Cheer covers, they told him the job was his if he wanted it. The only requirement was that he would have to stick around long enough to complete the European tour and not leave them in the lurch, lest he take on the new role as 'Most Hated Man in America'. After the tour, the choice was his as to whatever he wanted to do. With nothing left to lose, and the tour only a handful of weeks away, he agreed.

Jeff:
"Jimbo and Gibby actually sat down and Gibby called me up from a pay phone, and [Jimbo] assured me it was him… So two of my ex-girlfriends, brought me down to the warehouse that those guys were at…we just jammed on some Black Sabbath and Blue Cheer shit, played a couple of real easy ones of theirs…and I remember them saying, "Do you want to be in the band on this European tour thing', and I was like, "Well, sure,"…and (later) Paul goes, "Well you can be in the band for as long as you want, and I said, 'alright"…and that was it…that was our big talk…" [phone interview, 6/20/14]

In Jeff, they had a nubile young buck ready to join them on their quest. The band was still interested in being a quintet, though. Teresa would not be easy to replace, but they continued to probe everyone who passed in and out of the loft with an inquisitive eye. The Eastern Stars had in its ranks a group of friends and artists that were more like a performance troupe than a conventional band, and touring was not anything that was even bantered about. Among their ranks was a girl named Kathleen Lynch, who had been bouncing back and forth between her native Atlanta and NYC, where she first met the band after introducing herself after a show at the Tin Pan Alley.

Kathleen had become somewhat of a local phenomenon for her visceral and earthy performances at places like 10th and Juniper and Weekends. Her outlandish antics and eccentric humor blended well with the Butthole Surfers ethos and they had really hit it off during the band's tenure in Atlanta.

Through the haze of smoke someone brought up the notion that the Buttholes should hire a dancer to share the stage. The subject also broached of replacing Teresa. Some say the band was ready to ask Kathleen to fill Teresa's vacancy, but Jeff mentions another girl (name?) whom they had intentions to ask. Whatever the case may be, and whomever the target was of the band's interest is unclear, but what is clear is that when all was said and done, Kytha agreed to join the band as their second drummer.

Kytha:
"My heart band, Easturn Stars, which included Rozzy Moray, Laurie Nevada, Opal Foxx, myself and Kathleen, was officially breaking up, after Kathleen had moved to NY,. Playing as a 4-some was just sad. I was performing as Karsyn O'Genic in that band, but I changed my name with every new project I did. So, I changed my name to Kabbage Galore (all my names had/have K and G in them, was KMG-259 for a while etc.). My girlfriend was having an affair with my roommate. I was ready to rock and roll, and move on, obviously. So, when the offer came to join them, I did not hesitate." [post: 2020]

After some awkward laughter, the band figured they'd run with it. The lease was up on the Winterville house, and the loft was all they had left in Georgia during these waning days of December, 1985. They could practice there, and although she might not have seemed lthe perfect person to take Teresa's place, Kytha, or Kabbage she began calling herself, was passionate enough about her new career choice to hopefully make up for her lack of proper skills behind a drum kit.

Paul states:
"I remember there being some confusion at the time. I think we all thought we were getting someone who could somewhat play the drums, which Kabbage couldn't. But Kabbage was willing and she had a place to crash and practice in a warehouse in Atlanta."

Paul's memory is rock solid on this one:
"There was a time at that warehouse where we were all sitting around, and

someone had left a crusty macaroni-and-cheese pan sitting in the middle of the room with a spoon in it. Kathleen demonstrated for us her ability to pee a full teaspoon of urine without spilling a drop, then put the spoon back in the dirty pan. A few minutes later, Felicia the drag queen came in and picked up the pan and took the spoon and started eating the old macaroni-and-cheese. We all shrieked at him to stop, because Kathleen had peed in it, and he looked back us scowling and said, 'But I'm eating from the sides.'" [email: 6/27/14]

And so, with that, there was obvious work to be done if they were going to get the band back to the well-oiled machine they had become in the months leading up to the surprising and devastating departure of Teresa. A bass player still hungover from his 18th birthday and who had never been in a touring band before, and a drummer who had never really played drums before would be challenging, but with 'Cream Corn's release date just days away, the band jumped back into the fray; working on songs and immediately booking a trip back to the west coast. Moving forward as they always had, by the seat of their collective, soiled trousers.

Kytha says:
"The truth is I had never even heard of the Butthole Surfers before I met them, and I was the guitarist in the band they found me in so, we kind of a had a rocky road between us. I loved performing and I guess they saw that in me - that I would do just about anything for entertainment. Add booze and dope to that and it really was anything goes. I appreciate the experience, as it was my first real adventure outside of Marietta Georgia. A butch-dyke traveling in a cargo van full of equipment, props, 4 straight boys and dog was not the most comfortable way to see America, but once on stage, it was a lot of fun."
[email, July 18, 2014]

Joining the band along with Jeff and Kabbage was a little crippled midget lesbian boy named "Johnny Smoke". The newest addition to a set already laden with unreleased material, "Johnny Smoke" showcased Gibby's story-telling skills and the band's penchant for southern fried psychedelia. Stealing its concept from an old anti-smoking PSA, the song was a galloping, bastardized "Ghost Riders in the Sky"-style romp that dissolved into a stream of consciousness story about the little person who stood 10-foot tall with a knife.

Johnny's legend would grow to epic proportions as his exploits were ad-libbed each night. The Butthole Surfers were not as lucky, still floundering to rekindle the flame of yesteryear. Their first show together was more like a house party than a concert. Like they did in Texas to earn money for their trip to CA, they opened for themselves to collect more money from the door. This time instead of Brown Circus they used the moniker JackOfficers. It was a performance art assemblage of sights and sounds as they stuffed trigger mics down their pants which cued samples of old 'Davy and Goliath' episodes when they tapped on their crotches. Jeff hadn't played a show as a Butthole Surfer yet, but he was already a JackOfficer. He would stuff mics down his pants and tap his crotch for money. *"They were business majors, I was more of an acid major."* [phone]

It had been a long dry spell with no means of support and the band had Europe in their crosshairs, as spring was quickly approaching. With Jeff and Kabbage, they could finally start earning some cash again. The well had been running dry since playing their last shows in early December with Kramer and Teresa, barely surviving off residuals from records that were selling modestly at best.

It was now January in the year of our lord 1986, and they were unveiling the new Atlanta contingent of the band to their hometown crowd at the 40 Watt Club in Athens, most of whom were friends from around the scene. While not quite the mighty force they had become before the split, the band was at least grinding back into some sort of motion after weeks of doing little besides milling around the loft. They had high hopes that, with some time together, they could work out any kinks in the set and again become a cohesive unit.

Along with the domestic release of 'Cream Corn from the Socket of Davis' now in stores, Terry Tolkin had been spending the last few months commissioning songs from some of his favorite bands around the scene for inclusion on a compilation he was putting together for a release he dubbed 'God's Favorite Dog'. The record would soon become the calling card for Corey's fledgling label.

The release of 'God's Favorite Dog' was like a rebirth for Touch & Go, and for the punk rock scene as an entity. Featuring an entirely new stable of bands rather than just Corey's old hardcore buddies, the compilation featured some of the Buttholes' old friends from Texas, Scratch Acid, as well as Chicago's own Big Black, Hose from NYC (featuring a young Rick Rubin, who was already promoting records on his new Def Jam Records endeavor, and who would shortly after produce one of the biggest records of the 1980's, the Beasties Boys' 'Licensed to Ill'). Rounding out the line-up were the Happy Flowers from Richmond, VA, and Madison, WI's own KILLDOZER.

The compilation was a decidedly different direction for Touch & Go and was a brand-new foundation for the label that built its reputation releasing far more straight-forward hardcore records by Corey and Tesco Vee's pals in the Midwest hardcore scene.

The music on 'God's Favorite Dog' was violent, atonal, and industrial strength. The songs were filled with odd time signatures and dirges about serial killers, pusticles, and car accidents. With many of the old U.S. punk bands breaking up or crossing over to capitalize on the more lucrative genre of heavy metal, this new wave of "punk" bands used noise instead of speed as their weapon of choice.

And it was the Butthole Surfers who were at the forefront of this new musical movement. Corey's plan to make the band the cornerstone of his label was finally coming to fruition. With Touch & Go's new stable of bands worshipping at the same alter as the Buttholes were, Corey was given the validation of what he had known upon hearing them years prior; that the Butthole Surfers could be a mainstay for Touch & Go label to build its reputation upon, and the foundation to help afford the him the freedom, and finances, to sign just about any band that he wanted.

Still, as 'Moving to Florida' started getting adds at college radio stations across the country, and 'Cream Corn' started to shift units, even Corey must have been a bit taken aback. The Butthole Surfers name was now being spoken over the airwaves at some brave underground radio stations, though many station's Program Directors opted to use "BH Surfers" or "The Surfers" rather than risk the heavy fines being doled out for violating the recently enacted FCC decency standards by stating their full moniker. And though not quite affording them the sums they needed to hire Sammy Davis Jr to dance for them, the EP did afford them the purchase of a TRUE touring RV, some better equipment, and the guarantee to get out on the road and sell out most every venue that they played.

Like 'Cream Corn', 'God's Favorite Dog' featured an older, and more seasoned incarnation of the band: this one with Trevor and Teresa. Jeff was the new bassist, but the band still had a closet full of old recordings that stretched back nearly two full years and several different line-ups from which to cull. Rather than jump into the studio to record new versions of the songs with Jeff, they instead released and toured behind the material that had been recorded months, and even years prior. Who could really be sure, after all, just how long this line-up was going to last. Why spend the money on the studio time when you could be earning money on the road? Use the money they saved for weed and a new effects box, replace a bullhorn, or put some gas in the vehicle.

The band never stopped to release a record and then formulate a tour behind it. The records got released while they were out on the road. They often played songs that wouldn't be released until years later. Records came out when cash permitted, sometimes released mere weeks apart; often from tapes comprising several different line-ups, featuring bassists who had long since run away, screaming in horror at the very mention of the name the Butthole Surfers.

One song on *God's Favorite Dog* entitled "Eindhoven Chicken Masque", was an outtake from the Detroit sessions that Corey had arranged when Trevor had joined. It was a spaghetti western style romp, replete with a mariachi-style horn accoutrement. A "Ring of Fire" Southern revival held in the same town just north of the Rio Grande from where Johnny Smoke lived. It was so far removed from anything they had released to date, it was easy to fool the public into the belief the song was a recent addition to their repertoire and not a song they played a few times in the studio and then shelved for almost a year prior to its release on the compilation.

The other piece, "The Legless Eye" was an even earlier recording, a sound experiment that Gibby and Alan Tubbs recorded of Alan's coffee percolator at his apartment in Brooklyn, when the band had first departed Texas, that life-time ago. Fed through a forest of effects, and closing the record on an endless loop, the noise was foreboding and hypnotic and was yet another example that the band had no rules or limits, and that Corey had absolutely no tether to prevent them from creating whatever whimsy popped into their heads. It was a symbiotic relationship, theirs, and eventually, it led to the Butthole Surfers choice to remain Touch & Go artists into the foreseeable future.

Within days of their first show with the new Atlanta contingent, the band was in the RV and heading west for some gigs at Mabuhay Gardens in San Francisco, Club Lingerie in Hollywood, and Fender's in Long Beach. The hiatus was officially over, and the Butthole Surfers had once again beaten the odds. It was after this handful of gigs on the Pacific Coast when they got word from Terry about doing a two-night stand at Danceteria in New York City. Terry was interested in a sort of *God's Favorite Dog* record release party and the club was ready to offer the band an unheard of sum of $6000* for the two night event. Floored by that amount of cash, they immediately ditched any idea of booking their way across the U.S. and decided instead to drive the nearly 3000 miles straight to NYC to make it in time for the early February booking. The band was no stranger to the road, after all, and the handsome purse was certainly enough of an incentive for them to change any plans they may have had and make a B-line back East.

The shows would mark a turning point in the band's career. No band coming from the school of punk rock was garnering that kind of money. With most surveyors of the scene screaming that punk rock was dead, the Butthole Surfers were demonstrating that it was merely evolving, moving from the back alleys and onto Main Street, USA.

This had been what punks had wanted, and feared, since the first strains of the Damned's "New Rose" blasted from a pair of stereo speakers in 1976: a forum. A venue in which to show straight society that their world of bloated patriotism, bloody guerilla wars in third world countries, and nuclear stockpiles were not accepted blindly by the masses.

There were outsiders who believed in Sanity, even if what constituted sanity seemed most insane through the eyes of the ordinary, Reagan-loving American. To most punks, it was America's finger-on-the-trigger foreign policy, and Meese

Commission \ family values-driven domestic policies that seemed more insane than any bevy of blue mohawks.

Those concerns were best left to others. The Butthole Surfers were just a band scraping by on a few dollars a day. Politics and politicking were the luxuries of those who knew where their next meal was coming. For the elite who knew where they'd be sleeping that night. $6000 might not solve America's woes, but it would certainly go a long way in solving the woes of the Butthole Surfers.

The air was bitterly cold when they piled out of the RV and into the Big Apple. They arched their backs and stretched their legs after driving for days with hardly a rest stop. Once they arrived, they got in touch with Kathleen, who had been in NY a few weeks now, and who was still searching for some gainful employment. Her latest failed endeavor had been a brief stint at a peep show in Times Square which ended when, in her Grand Finale, she blew out a blast of diarrhea onto the floor, held up her hands and exclaimed, 'Ta-Da!"

Jeff the black-haired guy, Gibby & Kabbage, 1/25/86 Fender's, Long Beach, CA
© Kirk Dominguez

Clearly, in that blast, Kathleen knew she was destined for better things than a Times Square peep show: She was an artist, a genius, and a compatriot, and she now would be commissioned to become the Butthole Surfers interpreter for the world. When they asked her to come and dance for the two gigs at Danceteria, Kathleen emphatically agreed, and the scene was set for something truly magical.

Long-Haired, Drug-Crazed Hippies

A small crowd was beginning to mill around in front of Danceteria on this frigid, February afternoon in hopes that tickets were still available for the evening's performance. Tonight's bill featured the Happy Flowers as openers and both bands were ready to bring the house down on top of the seething masses.

A few hits of acid and a clean batch of MDMA had been procured, and the scene was sure to be an extravaganza. MDMA was a drug that was known as "Adam" when it sprung up in the nightclubs of Dallas a few years prior but was now going as 'Ecstasy' on the streets of NYC after the drug's popularity sprung up overseas and boomeranged back to US shores. Terry Tolkin was the ringmaster and oversaw the celebration of Butthole Surfers' triumphant return to New York after the months of trials and tribulations. They had weathered yet another storm and they remained, different, but intact. Kramer was on hand as a spectator now, as was Michael Macioce. Alan, Mary and Cheryl Dyer as well. Friends from far and wide. The band in high spirits and ready to conquer the Big Apple again.

Ticket sales were brisk, but, without prior notice and for reasons still unclear to this day, Danceteria canceled the second night. The band, who had driven for days straight from the west coast due to the promise of a handsome purse, was now being told that they would only be paid the half the amount they were originally offered. Sorry.

Gibby headed straight for the bar and commandeered a bottle of Johnny Walker Red for himself. Not even the MDMA, long administered to treat victims of PTSD, could alleviate this trauma. No, this night was not a celebration. This night was a ritual. Dark clouds conspired. Evil thoughts stirred behind the eyes of the beast. The prophecy had been foretold. The deal had been broken and the die was cast. There would be blood by the light of the new day.

As the moon took control of the sky, a murder of punks, geeks, art-snobs, long-hairs, and general riff raff began loitering the corner of 7th Avenue and 21st Street. The Buttholes hadn't played NYC since the previous August, nearly 6 months prior; a God's age in Butthole time. The cauldron was beginning to boil in anticipation. The energy bubbled like a stew.

In the street, a bottle breaks, and profanity echoes within the sunless valley of brownstone apartments. A beat up 1979 Volare farts a plume of foul smoke, 'Frankenchrist' blasting from within to drown out the wheeze of its rusted exhaust pipe. Closer to the club, ticketholders huddle in circles on either side of the street, smoking stuffs, their lighters flickering like fireflies. Inside the hall, the band makes preparations for the Black Mass they are to hold; a eulogy for the $3000.00 they had stolen from them in the blink of an eye.

'I've always got a knife in my back...no matter where, no matter when...'

Drink up. Gibby & Kathleen 2/7/86
© Chris Schneider

According to legend, Kabbage and Kathleen take turns peeing into the little holes on the bottoms of a couple of plastic, Fred Flintstone Wiffleball bats they bought that day. Gibby is stomping around the club, smashing the walls and swigging from his bottle like a pirate on shore leave, clothespins adorning his nappy hair. Several dresses are draped over his immense, lanky frame, one on top of the other, each drenched in the whiskey that he has drooled down his chin from his monstrous swigs.

Off in the distance, a small steam ship comes loose from the moorings of his mind. The journey begins to the mouth of a river, then steadily upstream into the dark, foreboding jungle. Happy Flowers take the stage and the sound stirs those standing outside into the bacchanalia. Plumes of cigarette smoke rise up from the crowd, drift into the stage lights; white to blue to orange. A roar of feedback squeals and the laboring motor of the hulking steamer riles the savages, who batter themselves in ritualistic frenzy.

The Happy Flowers draw to a violent end. The natives' yelping bleats beyond the lip of the stage. A plush, red curtain drops between performers and spectators and traffic criss-crosses the stage preparing the grounds for the main event. Night has fallen. The moon peeks out behind a veil of pendulous clouds, black as ink.

Dressed to Kill 2/7/86
© Chris Schneider

As the tiny craft ventures deeper into the dense brush, some chirps begin to emanate from the guitar, like bats stirred from their cave. The natives begin to cavort again around the altar.

Is everybody in?…is everybody in?…The ceremony is about to begin.

WAKE UP!!

The curtain moves violently as a pair of hands blindly hatchets in search of the opening. Once found, Gibby's hands, and then his head, peak from behind. With a vacant and violent scowl, he surveys the landscape and eyes the followers with contempt. He unscrews the cap of his bottle and draws in a deep gulp. It is dangerously empty by this point and he disappears back behind the lush, blood-red veil, lumbering and off kilter.

The chirps grow manic to a squeal. The curtain divides like, thick jungle undergrowth, to reveal our lost demigods. They foretell of doom through a soupy haze of smoke and tumultuous rumble of tribal drums.

Darkness
© Chris Schneider

Jeff, Kathleen & Paul 2/7/86
© Chris Schneider

You will lie in the graveyard… you are rotting away…

Gibby spits out the words so vehemently that he struggles to gain his breath before the next line of the song. Kathleen twirls around the Wiffle Ball bat piss wands, spraying the crowd with urine like a wild beast marking her territory. She wears a sack on her head, and her body marred in green war paint. A long black wig drapes around her naked, heaving breasts. King's wiry frame appears caked in mud, whirling and disheveled:

Well I talk to you daily….you've got nothing to….

A group of onlookers further back from the proceedings flog themselves in time with the music. Gibby tears off his dresses down to his boxers by the time Jeff rides the opening notes of the next song, the *Children of the Grave*-esque, "Dum Dum". Gibby clutches at the waistband of his briefs as the speed he's been devouring like cocktail weenies for the last few hours leaves his hands involuntarily in need to fritter and toil and clench at everything within reach. The dresses he wore are in tatters from his talons and by the time their third song "Suicide" smashes to a close, he stands before the crowd completely liberated of all his earthly vestiges.

High on a horse
© *Chris Schneider*

The light pours out of me...
© Chris Schneider

He grabs a plastic hobby horse they bought earlier with the Wiffle Ball bats and shoves it between his legs to conceal himself, but it's no use. All sense of sanity has been terminated with extreme prejudice. The bourbon and hallucinogens begin to soak deeply into the spongy recesses of his mind. The crowd itself, like the crew of that fateful steamboat *Nellie* is brought along for the ride, deeper and deeper into the heart of darkness.

And there stood Gibby, like a model of Kurtz himself. Once a star student, Accountant of the Year, and captain of his college basketball team, now a rogue element in this foreign place. He has been reborn as the New Messiah and his mind degenerates into dark, inhuman thoughts, consumed by power, and deep feeling of betrayal. He is lost.

The crowd wallows in a dense fog of sweat, staring like zombies at the strange medicine men brewing their potions. A strobe light pulsates toward the inevitable bloody conclusion.

Well I see you, in my concubine...

Here, where sex and death have no boundaries, Kathleen and Gibby begin to play and wrestle about on the ground. Demonstrating a power far beyond her tiny frame, she picks up his 6'5" hulking mass and spins him like David conquering a Goliath. Instruments melt and vomit in the background. Gibby playfully rolls around with Kathleen as they tussle in complete liberation. A tangle of naked limbs rise from the floor.

U.S.S.A…U.S.SR…U.S.S.A…U.S.R…

Small fires burn about the stage as Gibby cries and moans out an elegy to his lost sanity. He comes stumbling out of the wreckage. He has a weird look on his face, and he trips, and as he trips, he holds out his hand, taking out a section of King's drum kit, spewing drums everywhere. Recoiling backstage in horror to the small room relegated to the band, King resigns himself from the carnal rituals taking place onstage.

The show dissolves further into the abyss, with the crowd being dragged along into the depths. According to Paul's account, he grabs a screwdriver and begins to puncture holes in the monitor speakers. Kabbage and Kathleen embrace and frolic on the floor and Gibby and Paul get behind the drum set. The guitar loops a heinous discord and sirens wail endlessly as, finally, the band, exorcized, stumbles off stage.

Completely lost, the soundman kills the stage monitors. "The Crusher" begins to pump out of the house speakers, which signifies to the stupefied crowd that they need to attempt to collect themselves and leave the proceedings. They need to try to gather the pieces of their useless existence and return to what they had been prior to this experience: denizens of a civilized society. They need to go back to their average homes and go back to their ordinary lives. They need to try to sleep, to shower and to try to wash themselves clean of all they had witnessed.

Shortly after the 'set' was over, the backdoor of the club flies opens and then slams closed. A blathering Gibby is ejected out onto the cold NYC streets, naked and violently incoherent. The door reopens from the inside and he leaps back inside the club, hurling obscenities at everyone within earshot. He rips up the check he is handed as payment. Screaming and banging his frame against the walls of the club.

Security grabs him, and he once again is tossed out into the cold. This scene plays itself out several more times before Gibby eventually accepts the check for this complete blur of an evening. Perhaps, if he can muster up a memory, he may recall the damage the band has caused to the club. Perhaps it makes up for any of the remaining, unpaid fees they are owed. Perhaps there is some small, and expensive, victory for the band.

Falling for you
© Chris Schneider

Pretty in and out of Pink
© *Chris Schneider*

Kabbage & Cockroaches
© *Chris Schneider*

John Beers aka Mr. Horribly Charred Infant (Happy Flowers):
"...as for the payment issues...Gibby kept tearing up the check when he was asked to sign it. He'd sign it, then rip the pen through the check. I remember he did it at least twice. If I recall correctly, the check was for $3K." (email, 2009)

At some point, Gibby throws on some stray rags which he had discarded earlier and the band collects their gear and they slip back into the night, their heads echoing with the voice of the club owners screams: '***YOU WILL NEVER PLAY THIS TOWN AGAIN!***'

The horror....the horror....

Like a Boiling Dove

A mere five days later the Butthole Surfers are waiting to take the stage at CBGB's across the street from their home base at Terry's loft. They were not only playing NYC again, but for more money than they were guaranteed for the canceled second night at Danceteria. Their skin was still stained with green food coloring from the antics of that night at Danceteria, and despite being near exhaustion from stuffing their heads with large doses of leftover acid and MDMA all week, they managed to pull off a short but, spirited set in front of a full house at the tiny club.

It was sweet revenge for the hellacious cross-country journey they had endured only to be denied their due pay. No one could have looked upon the Danceteria debacle as a success at the time, but reviews of the show spread like wildfire. Not just in New York City, but across the country. Before long, the naked tussling between Gibby and Kathleen became an 'on-stage sex show'. The underground publications ran with it. The band could barely remember the performance, but the patrons in attendance would never forget it, even those in the back of the club who couldn't see a thing.

Danceteria became Madison Square Garden, and each one of the 30,000 people who claim to have been in attendance each spin their account of the mayhem. The story got more mileage than the RV on their drive from the west coast, and the show is still the stuff of legends. Looking back in time, the show cemented their reputation as the most dangerous touring band in existence. By abandoning all rules and laws at the door of the club, and then out on the roads of America, they created a new society, one which they didn't necessarily rule, but curated.

At the time, however, the band was just trying to make enough money to get to Europe, and the nearly non-stop drive from Los Angeles to NYC for half the money they expected to be paid left them pissed and reeling. Danceteria reviews were still being written as they drove out of town to their next shows, trying desperately to recover.

After NYC, they headed up to Boston, for a Valentine's Day gig, enduring a harrowing stop on the way up that had cops emptying their RV out in a Holiday Inn parking lot in the middle of a blinding snowstorm. The cops claimed the van didn't have a proper registration, obviously ignoring the papers Paul had presented to them upon their request. The officers informed them that they would not be allowed to proceed further into the state. A tow truck was called to haul them and the vehicle across the state line back into NY. 90 mins later, with the snowstorm still raging, they crossed back into MA, hoping they wouldn't be spotted by the same Highway Patrol officers who had stopped them earlier that evening.

Thankfully, the rest of the band - and the drugs - were in Terry's car ahead of them on I-95. When Gibby and Paul finally did arrive at the club, they found most of the crowd wildly stumbling around with psychedelicized eyes, none of them minding that the band was scheduled to begin an hour or so earlier. It turns out that Terry had been handing out the rest of their doses to keep the crowd at bay. They managed a 40 min set before the club's curfew chased them off the stage, and they fled back into the cold, windswept night and onto the icy New England highways for another harrowing drive back to New York.

Terry Tolkin:
"...as we approached Hartford, CT. all hell broke loose in a snowstorm. I mean blinding! We lost sight of each other. King and Chris (Gordon) and I got there with just a few minutes to spare. Despite the weather, there was a line around the block. Gibby and the rest of them had been pulled over by MA Highway Patrol just over the border into the state. They had been playing shows all week and Gibby's skin was still stained with the cheap food coloring that he used on stage. The cops made them unpack the entire van in a Holiday Inn parking lot in the middle of the worst part of the snowstorm. Well, the pigs didn't find the drugs (which I had) and they got there late, but no one seemed to mind. I had been dosing the audience with liquid MDMA and we all had a lot too.
At the end of the show, I went up to the owner, who spoke through one of those voice box amplifiers, and he tried to short me $500.00 with some kind of excuse. I simply went and told Gibby. As I stood off to the side, I watched in glee as this idiot tried to pull one over on Gibby. Suddenly, Gibby reached up and in one motion smashed the voice box into the brick wall, shattering it. The guy then went behind the bar and got them the rest of their money."
[email 2010]

The exhaustion of the previous week finally caught up with them the next night at a small show at Vassar College in Poughkeepsie. After a 45 min set, they gave up on playing; opting to tell jokes and tour stories for the rest of their time onstage.

Gibby: *Let's have a talk show?...*"Did anyone see us on the Scott & Gary Show?...no no no really...what was it like??...I never have seen the video...and my mom did...it freaked her out...I swear to fucking God.*

As soon as he realized that the music portion of the show was over, King braved the freezing cold to get out to the RV. There, the 3000 miles drive from sunny California to the frozen Hudson Valley, coupled with the insanity of a 'sex show', copious amounts of acid, and violent snowstorms finally wreaked havoc on his immune system. He passed out shaking and heaving with fever chills.

The place was packed despite the foot of snow which blanketed the Hudson Valley, but the band's schedule over the last two weeks leading up to the event barely afforded them the opportunity of a single night's sleep. The sound system was miserable and they were exhausted. The show dissolved as they took a brief respite to sleep, per chance, to dream, only to get right back out on the road.

This time, instead of working their way from west to east as planned before the Danceteria debacle, they booked the reverse course and headed down the east coast, through Jeff and Kabbage's hometown of Atlanta, through Austin and Dallas, then back to the west coast for some unfinished business there. Winter was giving way to spring and the nice weather was also helping the band mend back to health after the nasty flu season.

Teresa had stopped by the show in Austin, to say hi to her former bandmates and see how they were fairing since deciding to hang up her drumsticks. She had taken a job at an upscale restaurant, Chez Fred, and though not quite the whirlwind of excitement of touring the world's highways and byways, it paid well and afforded her the chance to buy the video equipment she wanted but which Gibby wouldn't budge upon. The dry Texas heat did wonders for her and she was in much better spirits than she had been the last time they saw her in Winterville. It was with a tad of relief, and a tinge of jealousy, that she said goodbye to her old friends, and new ones, and bid them well wishes on their journey westward.

To Dallas, then to the Golden State for a huge show in Sacramento with the Circle Jerks, then an even bigger one with the Jesus & Mary Chain, down the street from their old apartment on Pico Blvd, at the Santa Monica Civic Center. Finally, a more intimate show at the I-Beam and they were done. After nearly three straight months of non-stop touring, they finally had a break: their first since acquiring their new rhythm section.

The European tour was set to start at the end of April, and they needed to be back on the east coast again for the flight overseas. This time, though, with *Cream Corn from the Socket of Davis* in stores and selling at a decent clip, they had some rare money in their pockets. It was decided that they should take a little reprieve from the madness of touring their way back to the East Coast and make the journey east on their own schedule. Instead of booking their way back across the continent, playing two sets a night under different monikers to horde cash, they took a much-needed vacation, and stopped for a few days rest at Bryce Canyon National Park in southern Utah.

The pit stop was a chance to let the breeze blow through their hair and to survey, not only the stony outcroppings before them, but also where Butthole Surfers were as a band. It was the first time since leaving Texas, nearly two years gone, that they had stopped long enough to enjoy nature, and not watch it speed past them through the dirty windows of their RV.

Rembrandt Pussyhorse,, the record that "was never going to be released," according to Alternative Tentacles, was in Corey's hands, and due to come out in a couple weeks' time, and "Moving to Florida" was still lighting up college radio phone lines across the country. Their shows were selling out in nearly every town they played, as well. And yet here now, on the edge of this vast precipice, there was silence.

A bird singing a gentle tune. The lingering scent of a desert rose. An endless, blue sky filled with cotton ball clouds. No crowds, no promoters, no people begging for interviews: nothing. The spur of the moment stop in the country's Badlands reinvigorated their souls. For the last two years they had been mindlessly bounding from coast to coast on a tour that never ended, leaving the strewn bodies of bass players in their wake. They had almost forgotten about being human, that there was a place of solace and beauty which existed outside of their vehicle and outside of the smoke-filled clubs.

Teresa:
"Sometimes we would treat ourselves to little vacations so that it wouldn't be so horrible. We'd spend money and try to have a good time, but I think because of some of our issues, and alcohol and drugs, we'd end up in the middle of something that we meant to do, but one of us would have some kind of breakdown. And then it would be like, 'oh no we spent all this money…"
[phone 7/26/14]

Time drew nearer to their scheduled departure back onto foreign soils, and the few days of peace and tranquility did them well. It was time to get back into their RV and continue on the quest eastward, head to NYC and to John F. Kennedy airport and get on the seven-hour flight to oblivion. As they pulled out onto the road, though, they began to realize how badly it was all beginning to stink. Not just the endless stretches of boredom and open road, but, the actual ply-board interior of their battered vehicle.

Kabbage's unspoken vow to avoid laundry detergent had not waivered, even though her skin was getting red and shiny and raw. Now, what began as a musky, earthy aroma was turning into a nauseating stench and was beginning to penetrate every fiber of fabric within the confines of the van, and permeate through the smell of beer farts, cigarettes and stale weed which had masked the malodorous fumes in the past.

Kabbage had also found a stray cat while on the road and had brought him into the RV, where he proceeded to mark his territory by spraying the entire interior in cat piss. It only added to the stench and to their queasiness, and to the feelings of resentment.

Live, the band had taken to giving her only one drum to play. And when that didn't seem to help, they tried not even bothering to mic it. But, now as they lay immersed in the stench of months of gigs and cat piss, they began to not only lose all faith in the hope that Kabbage would eventually learn how to play, but not care if she did.

Their eyes watered and the hours passed like the road underneath them. As the band hit the border of Tennessee, they finally decided that enough was enough. As Kabbage slept, the rest of the band conspired. They gathered up her stuff, woke her up, and bought her a bus ticket from Knoxville to Atlanta. Not even King, who was now left to pull the duties of two drummers by himself, was in dissent of the decision. They opened the windows and sped away as the groggy, ex-drummer stood alone at the bus station trying to conjure up what just happened and gain some semblance of where she was.

Kabbage:
"They dropped me at some bus station, I don't remember which. When not on stage or in the hotel rooms, I spent the entire tour in the way back of the van with King; both of us laying on our backs on a platform set on top of all the equipment. We never saw much of the actual 'road.'
Yep, a bus ride home was the sum total of my severance package (or any payment for that matter other than meals and hotel rooms). This was soon after Gibby had a rage fit on me on our way to get dinner and literally threw me out of the van on the side of the road. Somehow, I found my way back to where we were staying and luckily they let me back in. So in that light, looking back, I guess a bus ticket was a genuine kindness from them." [message, Sept, 2014]

With Kabbage gone, the remaining Butthole Surfers were revitalized. By paring down to their minimalistic core they gained a renewed sense of self-confidence and vigor. The boys crossed the bridge back into Manhattan with a new outlook and, also, some new material that they had written while rolling on the long slog cross country.

One song in particular, a reworking of Black Sabbath's "Sweet Leaf", featured Gibby once again leaning heavily on the effects box he had used on "100 Million" and "Comb." Now, however, he not only used heavy delay and loops, but also changed the pitch of his voice, and overlaid multiple tracks of vocalizations, one on top of another.

184

The result is a trance inducing flight of fancy threading the audience into a cocoon of subliminal screeds and meanderings. The rape of desire. Brian Wilson's "Smile" echoing through the chasms of hell.

Their lone show as a quartet stateside was at Irving Plaza, and it showcased a Butthole Surfers that was a completely different entity than the one that played NYC only two months prior. Whittled down to just four men for the first time since Teresa had joined the group, this new line-up was a stripped-down machine. An industrial strength psychedelic, punk freak out. There were no "sex shows," no green food coloring, no MDMA or piss-filled waffle ball bats, none of the gimmickry or distractions of their last stop in the Big Apple.

What the crowd got was a glimpse of the new band beginning to gel into a cohesive unit. Ditching Kabbage had helped Jeff immeasurably. Since he joined the band, he was forced to stand in front of her bombasts. Now with her gone, he was able focus solely on King's steady command behind the kit. The legendary rhythm section they had become known for was beginning to return to form. King had to step up to play the parts of two drummers, but it was a challenge he accepted and conquered.

And it was King who was running the show. He opted to remain standing, playing without the aid of a kick drum, as he had since his days with the Hugh Beaumont Experience. But now, for the first time since his very first couple of shows before acquiring Teresa's help, he stood alone, like Patton before Old Glory.

His arms flailed and spun like a tumbleweed in a dust storm. Acrobatic agility like Ray Bolger dancing on the hood of a car in a traffic jam. When mic'd through Gibby's FX box, his drums swirled and swept in a sound that abounded, and resounded, and rebounded off the ceiling. It took 5 seconds to realize that this Butthole Surfer band had a new sense of purpose here on the planet. It was all space music. No dresses or clothespins or bags full of paper cockroaches, just four men and their music, which was growing ever stranger and more beautiful.

Rembrandt Pussyhorse had finally been unveiled on Touch & Go the day before the Irving Plaza show, and it too revealed an altogether different Butthole Surfers. Despite being recorded more than a year prior to its ultimate release, the record was a complete change of direction from its predecessors: equally as deranged, yet more subtle, perhaps even melancholic.

Upon finally hearing from Alternative Tentacles that there was not now, nor would there ever be, a Butthole Surfers record named "Rembrandt Pussyhorse," any thoughts of continuing to fantasize of a full-length record on the label were finally put to rest. The Butthole Surfers would now be full time Touch & Go recording artists. The band agreed, in turn, to keep 50% of all money earned for any records sold, and Corey and Touch & Go would get the other 50%.

It seemed like a fair split, and since the band was seeing basically nothing in the form of residuals from the sale of the two EP's they released on Alternative Tentacles., it at least ensured that money would keep coming in from their record sales and that they would be able to eat. Corey had kept his promise to focus all his energy on the Butthole Surfers, and they had kept theirs by promoting themselves on the road until members dropped like flies. Corey's belief in the band paid off, and now, with the band fully committed to being on Touch & Go, they would work hand-in-hand to conquer the universe, or at least their small corner of it, and *Rembrandt Pussyhorse* was the next projectile fired in their quest for world domination.

The record threw everyone who thought they knew the band, and underground music for that matter, for a complete loop. It featured disquieting organ pieces, manic backward-looped fiddle excursions (which they found already on the tape at the BOSS before recording), a bastardized cover of the 'Perry Mason' theme song, and even an acid house rendition of the Guess Who classic "American Woman". The album was in stark contrast to the sloppy, southern fried punk found on *Another Man's Sac*, even though a vast majority of it was recorded right around the same time.

Rembrandt Pussyhorse was more polished, refined, and almost commercially viable. It showed a slightly more high-brow side of the band, one toward which their previous efforts had only alluded. Most people would assume the band was heading toward a new direction in an attempt to capitalize on the modest success of "Moving to Florida, but they would be proven wrong, yet again.

For the extended EP that was meant to be their first full length on Alternative Tentacles was a journal entry of where they had been, not a roadmap to where they were heading. Any cries that the band might be 'selling out' were certainly, at the very least, premature. But, again, with no indication as to where or when the songs were recorded in any liner notes on the record jacket, nor anywhere else, nobody knew what to believe. Some might have feared the worst: the Butthole Surfers had been tamed. They only needed to witness the band live to know that the Butthole Surfers were not toning down but were venturing deeper into the depraved depths than ever before.

In fact, much of the material on *Rembrandt Pussyhorse* remained unplayed even after its release or had been ditched from their sets years before. Like the Jimi Hendrix Experience's *Axis: Bold as Love*, the record was released with little acknowledgement from the artists themselves, despite the strength of the material, nor the fact that the record contained another quasi-hit that alternative college radio latched onto in "American Woman".

"Perry" hadn't been played since the Mathews brothers days and instead of promoting *Rembrandt Pussyhorse*, live sets consisted mostly of tracks that had still yet to see a proper release. The Butthole Surfers always seemed light years ahead of their recorded output, and they often were. The tracks on *Rembrandt Pussyhorse* were recorded with Teresa, and with Paul and Trevor on bass. They were now a four-piece without Teresa, and with Jeff, and they were about to head off to the UK again to embark on their second tour of Europe.

Europe '86'd

The boys were a bit out of their element and on their own in the UK, but the love that had been shown to them on the previous tour had given them the moral support they needed and made them into true warriors ready to stampede across the continent. They had a bit to learn about touring logistics though, and how to prepare for their working vacation abroad. After just one of the two scheduled gigs in the UK, they were kicked out of the country for failing to obtain the proper work permits.

For some odd reason, Paul recalls, English officials at the airport insisted that the plane pull away from the gate without the band. They were then personally escorted onto the tarmac and onto the plane for departure. The flights attendants assumed they were men of privilege, and they crossed the channel as kings with a complimentary bottle of champagne given to them in their honor. Finally, they were being treated as they deserved to be treated, and once on the mainland, things only got better.

They stopped in the studio of Holland's VPRO radio, for an in-studio interview and performance on the weekly "Backline" program. The show was broadcast across the entire country and showcased the band to a much wider audience than any stop on the previous fall tour. The last time they were in Holland, Gibby had nearly been arrested, and rightfully so. He had every right to be locked up and left to rot for his art like the Marquis de Sade. But the legendary stories that had swirled around about that day, and subsequent shows in Nijmegen and Eindhoven, only added to the legend that preceded their return to the land of Danes. Towering at nearly 10 foot tall, standing on a chair; with clothespins pinned to his matted hair, and wearing a grandmother's dress stained with blood. Gibby was exalted as some sort of an acid-drenched Demigod.

Now, Gibby had returned like the ghost of Hamlet's father, armed with a new voice box that echoed wild tales and fearful warnings. While they were still working out some jet lag issues, the 'Backline' performance showcased a band that was nearly unrecognizable from the one which had been in the Netherlands just 6 months before, both in membership of the band and in the material that they played. They had slowly transformed themselves into a behemoth, growling like a bear awakened from a winter's slumber.

The punk band that visited the continent the last time had undergone a metamorphosis into a lumbering prehistoric mammoth. Guttural moans growl like a mammoth beast haunch-deep in quicksand. The high-pitched chirps of the scavengers conspire an around to pick at the fresh flesh as the sweet smell of death permeates the air.

Another live VPRO broadcast from the Paradiso two weeks later revealed even more new material and found the band in much better form. It was clear that they were no longer the Butthole Surfers of Scott Stevens, or Andrew Mullins, nor of Quinn or even of Bill Jolly, not of Terence or Trevor or Kramer or Juan. This was the Butthole Surfers of Jeffrey Pinkus.

Both broadcasts featured many of the tracks that had comprised their sets each night, but which were nowhere to be found on wax. It gave the European freaks not only the opportunity to hear the Butthole Surfers forging their new sound long before their American counterparts, but also gave bootleggers the chance to steal the food right out of their mouths. The broadcasts began popping up on 7"s and full length LPs, pressed up in a jiffy to capitalize on the small but rabid fan base who needed to hear every fart note the band blasted out.

Yet even as the band was getting incredible press, drawing crowds, and selling product, money from the tour seemed non-existent. With each show, the band and the promoter were finding themselves deeper in the hole. Their first return since the previous autumn with Kramer was anticipated by freaks far and wide, but no one could explain why, with every gig, the debts kept mounting higher and higher.

As the tour was to continue from the Netherlands to Norway, the tour manager asked for her payment for the tour to date. She had run up some serious debt using the proceeds to book three separate hotel rooms each night: one for herself, one for the soundman, and one for the band: all 4 stuffed in a room together. As bad blood began to boil in both camps, the band figured it was in everyone's best interest to terminate the relationship. They told the tour manager about some friends they had in Brussels and asked that she take them there and be rid of them for the good of all involved.

The band gathered up their belongings and got in the van. The plans were set. But, as the band slept in back, the van made a detour. They weren't going to their friends' house after all. Instead, the van was heading to Brussel National Airport.

Paul states:
"Our tour manager had the sound man drive us to the airport in Belgium after we told her we wouldn't play any more shows for her. Every night she'd use our show proceeds to get three hotel rooms - one for her, one for the sound man, and one for us. We had no money for food. We were about to leave Belgium for Norway when she told us how much money we owed her, and it just got to be too much. We told her to take us to Brussels and that we had friends there, she could drop us off and be done with us. Instead, she took us to the airport and told the police we'd tried to rape her at gunpoint. They came out and nudged us out of the van with machine guns. We were asleep in the van at the time. I'll never forget the look on Jeff's face when a cop woke him up nudging him with a machine gun...I guess they didn't take the story seriously enough to have us arrested. They just told us to get out of the country immediately." [email. 12/12/12]

The van drove off out of sight and there they stood: a motley assortment of scrubs left on the curb, penniless, groggy, no doubt high, and now being accused of aggravated sexual assault.

It's hard to tell what she was thinking or trying to convey to the cops, other than that she believed she was raped financially. Perhaps she was just hanging the band out to dry after her plans to make a windfall of cash off the band's anticipated return had failed to yield her the dividends she had anticipated. Whatever the case may be, the band was now being encircled by several large customs officials, with M-16s drawn, and in some serious need of an interpreter.

Not that the cops or customs agents necessarily believed the promoter's story, per se, but, there was one thing they could tell just by looking, and smelling, this unsavory ilk: these Americans with their greasy hair and bulging red eyes had little to contribute to Belgian culture. Pigs from any good standing country would have wanted these dregs gone, and the blight they created in their wake wiped clean from the streets of their fair city.

These brave men in blue were no different. They were more than happy to make sure the Butthole Surfers would be leaving on the soonest flight out of their proud country and that they would remain securely detained at the airport until such time as they could.

A call was made to Gibby's dad back in Dallas, waking him up from a peaceful slumber to explain their precarious predicament. The dreaded '*a funny thing happened...*' phone call from a child is always much funnier to the child than it is to the parents, but Mr. Peppermint jumped out of bed and into action and wired the money for the boys to purchase their 4 plane tickets back to friendlier shores.

It was the first and only time the boys ever called for a financial bailout in their long and storied meager years. Starvation and broken-down vehicles, Homelessness and destitution, all were dealt with, and the challenges overcome, but a foreign prison on a trumped-up rape charge called for an intervention, and a call for mercy was necessary. Jerry Haynes was always there for Gibby, showing his support by coming to all the Butthole Surfers shows in Dallas, and letting him off the hook from his change in career when the world seemed like Gibson's oyster.

Many parents would not have been so understanding, but Gibby's dad put his full and eternal faith in his son. This incident might have put that faith to the ultimate test, but Gibby and his friends were in some serious trouble. So, Jerry wired the money to them as fast as he could and before long, the boys were in the air on their way back home.

Once back in New York, they decided to hang low, bouncing between Cheryl's, Chuck's, Terry's and Alan and Mary's place in Brooklyn. While in the Big Apple, they tried to discern how much money they had, and how much was lost and then to make plans to get to Detroit and check in with Corey.

It didn't seem long after returning stateside that the whispers and the rumors began to swirl around the laundry room of punk gossip circles of the how and why the

European tour was cut short, and of how the Butthole Surfers must be comprised of a group of drug-addled sexual deviants of the worst sort. Combined with the fact that the ink from the Danceteria reviews were still wet on the page, the dye was cast. The band began being painted as a clan comprised of the most surly and unsavory characters imaginable.

With no girl in the band to help quell the myth, and with the band's focus on entertaining themselves rather than the ridiculous and unfounded rape allegations, they became misogynists; criminals; miscreants of the worst sort. No one could explain how a band of rapists was still allowed to roam freely among civilized society, but fanzines and scenesters from around the globe continued to spin tales of sexual debauchery and dungeons filled with innocent maidens that the band used towards their own sadistic ends, including, but not limited to, ritualistic Satanic blood orgies.

Still, even most fans were in the dark about what had actually happened, and they could do little to defend the band against the throngs of riot grrls, gossip mongers, or human rights activists who seemed to be just looking for a reason to hate them. An interview with Forced Exposure magazine finally revealed, off-handedly, the band's account of the story, but, nearly a year after the actual debacle took place, it was ignored by those who already had their opinions etched deeply in their belief systems.

Paul :
"Funny thing about that story is that we brought it back and told it to everyone. It wasn't a story that followed us, it was a story we laughingly shared."
[email, March 2014]

If their experience across the pond had been bad, then the political climate at home was downright deplorable. Musicians from across the spectrum, from John Denver to Twisted Sister to Frank Zappa, were being hauled before a congressional committee to determine whether their music and lyrics were driving kids to behave as the mythical Butthole Surfers did.

Jello Biafra was now fighting to keep his label afloat and his band intact after a mother notified the Los Angeles County prosecutor and CA State Attorney General on behalf of her 13-year-old daughter, whom Santa Claus had gifted with a copy of the DK's 'Frankenchrist' LP. Upon seeing the poster by famed 'Alien' artist HR Giger included as an insert in the album on that fine morning, the mother's eyes bulged three feet out of her skull. Shortly thereafter, cops burst into Jello's home and offices in the middle of the night, dragging him off to jail, confiscating records, and charging him and the label with 'unlawful distribution of harmful material to minors': an offense that, if convicted, carried up to a year in federal prison.

The Reagan Administration openly backed the efforts made by such groups as the Moral Majority, the American Family Association, and Focus on the Family to uphold decency, and dismantle artistic expression, for all Americans. Along with North Carolina Senator Jesse Helms, the Reverend Jerry Falwell, and Reagan's own Attorney General, Edwin Meese, a war was waged against anything deemed to be "anti-family", "anti-Christian", or "anti-American", and they now had rock music targeted in their crosshairs.

Forced school prayer, outlawing all abortions, even in cases of rape, incest or saving the life of the mother, and opposition to ratification of the Equal Rights Amendment were not only being spoken about, but were gaining traction with, not only the conservative powers-that were in charge, but with everyday Americans as well.

In showing its allegiance to the Moral Majority, Reagan's new FCC deregulations gave the agency unbridled ability to fine media companies for anything that might be found to be indecent, while also giving conservative stations the right to push their agenda without worrying about supplying the Equal Time statute that was contained in the recently overturned Fairness Doctrine.

Now, another group in line with Reagan's own Gestapo of the Decent, the Parental Music Resource Center, or PMRC, was targeting artists and musicians based on their own, often faulty, interpretation of lyrics, and imposing the view that music should be suited for 9-year-olds or else be censored or banned.

The PMRC was comprised of several senators' wives from both political parties, obviously taking advantage of the conservative climate and its trade winds blowing across the continent. Now, alongside the National Endowment for the Arts funding being gutted due to 'objectionable art', rock music was again targeted as the culprit of America's decay, just as when Elvis started gyrating his hips around like 'the negro'.

The PMRC saw its opportunity and struck while the iron was hot as they released a list of the "Filthy 15" songs to call attention to the 'problem' pop music presented. Among these violent and pornographic songs, the horrific and obscene "She Bop" by Cyndi Lauper, which led children down the path of the unrighteous by promoting masturbation. The Mary Jane Girls "In My House" was also targeted for apparently inviting a partner into the debauchery.

Though the PMRC only specifically targeted 15 specific songs, the backlash was felt throughout the music industry and the RIAA (Recording Industry Association of America) was on high alert and re-examining any artist who might comprise the next 'filthy' list the organization generated.

Jello Biafra and the Dead Kennedys were an example of what could happen to more mainstream artists like Prince, Metallica, Madonna and the Beastie Boys should their material be deemed too offensive. Chain stores were clearing their shelves of records and record companies were running for the hills as their artists were dragged before congress in this new version of McCarthy era paranoia.

And as Reagan's popularity soared, the conservative policies that would normally be laughed off the floor of congress were now being passed into law. It was a scary time for those Americans who believed in freedom of expression. There was an honest fear that, without vigilance, any view outside of the mainstream love of 'God and Guns' could lead to arrest and imprisonment.

Be that as it may, living free on American shores still beat the shit out of being held at gunpoint by the federales in Belgium, by a long shot, and the band knelt and kissed the ground like the pope himself upon their touchdown home. They were still homeless, with their last known residence being the floor of Kabbage's loft in Atlanta some 6 months ago. They needed a place to settle and take a break from the madness of their nomadic lifestyle, to regain some semblance of sanity. So, they crashed for a couple of days in NYC to muster up enough cash and motivation to head back on the road again.

Georgia had been nice for the little time they actually spent there, but it wasn't really home. With a rare spell of no shows booked, they decided the time had come to retreat to a place where they had friends and family and the feeling of comfort and belonging. After a brief stop in Detroit celebrate a gig with their pals in KILLDOZER, Scratch Acid, and Laughing Hyenas, they headed back to Georgia, packed up their stuff, and drove off, once and for all, to roll like daddy's meat under those glorious singing stars of Texas.

Juan Molina:
"Athens was way too 'pop' for the Butthole Surfers. Even the grungier bands from there were just pop with a little distortion thrown in. They definitely didn't 'get' the Butthole Surfers, and maybe that translated into hate. Gibby was pretty outspoken about Stipe too, which probably didn't earn any brownie points. REM pretty much put Athens on the map, and that's the way they liked their music there – melodic, mainstream –definitely not experimental. To put it into perspective, Athens didn't exactly embrace the B-52's until after they were famous. They didn't 'get' them either." [email, Feb 6, 2007]

Once back in the Lone Star State they found a small dump located right off Interstate 183 in Austin that they dubbed 'The Compound', and they immediately began building lofts and setting up their rooms. Paul ran miles of wire through the walls and converted the kitchen into a studio just like he had back in Winterville. Still not most ideal digs, but they finally had some space and a place of their own after so many years of outlasting their welcome on the floors of every friend they ever made between the two coasts.

So long deprived of even so much as a decent mattress, they might now catch a few nights' sleep in a row, or maybe gather their stuff from storage, family, and friends' garages and put it in their very own closets. The house was a dump, but it didn't have 4 wheels on it and that seemed like a good place to start.

One of the first friends who came to visit was Teresa. She welcomed the boys back to town and then, shortly thereafter, began practicing with them again. She had the previous 6 months to detox from her life as a gypsy and it was nice to be able to step back from the insanity for a little while. Now, though, with the rest of her mates settling down in the Lone Star State again, she had stabilized enough to ease back behind her drum kit and see what might come of it. Before long, she was spending nearly all her time at the house with Gibby and the rest of the guys, jamming and recording tracks in their home studio, which was becoming pretty state-of-the art from all the money they had invested into it.

A mixing desk and a multi-track recorder. Effects boxes and monitors, guitars, amps, microphones and miles of cords cluttered the tiny kitchen where they all lived. They'd wake up in the morning, pull some bong hits, and immediately start laying down new ideas or tinkering with old tapes they had laying around. They would contact Corey for an advance to record some new material, then buy more weed and record at home for free. Hundreds of hours of tapes were strewn about the tiny shack. It is hard to know if the band themselves even knew how much material they had buried beneath the ashtrays, bongs, and empty beer bottles, so vast was the cache.

They had already released 'Cream Corn' and 'Rembrandt Pussyhorse', as well as contributing tracks to the God's Favorite Dog compilation within the first 1/3 of the year since Jeff had joined, and now, with the year half over, the 'Blind Eye Sees All' video filmed by the Back Porch kids in Detroit got its proper release as well. They were taking full advantage of having a label that was excited to put out their material, blowing the dust off of old recordings and getting them out to fans.

Still, though, nothing they had released in the first 6 months of 1986 showcased the Butthole Surfers that had recently reunited and was annoying neighbors around 1401 Anderson LN. As a five piece again, the band began to soar to new heights only hinted at when listening to their most recent releases. Songs began stretching out to 5 and 6 minutes or more. Goofiness turned to Godliness as compositions became heavier and denser, filled with looping guitar solos, vocals slowed to s guttural groan, and now, for the first time in what seemed eons, the dual drum dynamics of our space-aged womblings.

Jeff had matured incredibly quickly since his first practices in Atlanta and was now settling comfortably into his role as bass player in the Butthole Surfers. He had seen more of the world in the previous 6 months than he had in his entire life and his

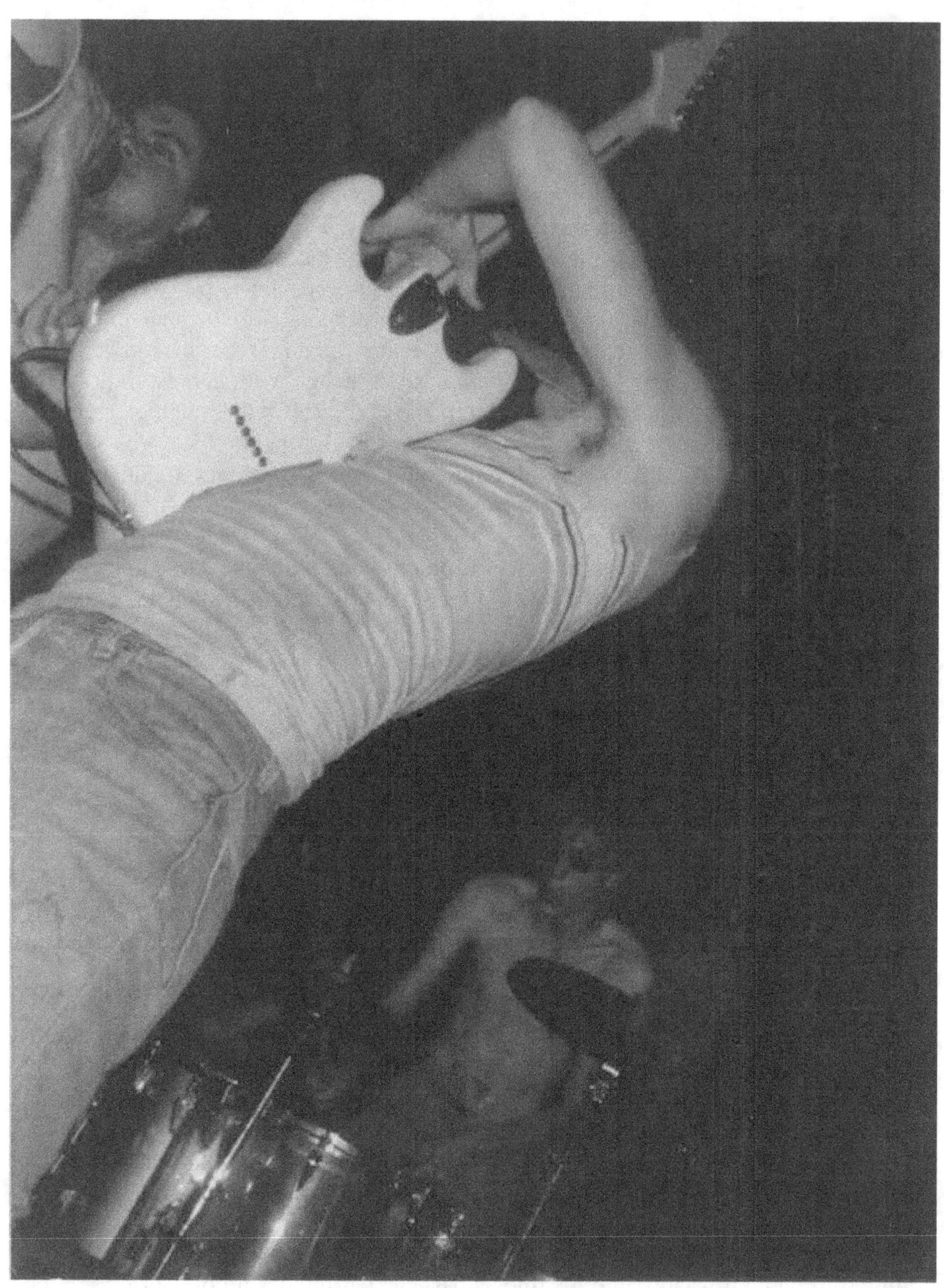

Back in Texas 7/26/86 Woodshock
© Jessica Goldfinch

a worldliness far beyond his 18 years. Where the other bass players before him had left the Buttholes to move on to adulthood, Jeff was growing up as a member of the band, like little Webster in a family of white folk.

Although he had still not been featured on any of recorded output to date, Jeff's influence on their developing sound was becoming blatantly obvious. He shared the band's love of 60's & 70's power rock: Blue Cheer, Grand Funk Railroad, ZZ Top: grabbing Jefferson Airplane by the throat and shaking violently, and he was able to exorcise these spirits during performances, allowing Paul and Gibby to work their magic creating their wigged out sonic emissions. Like The Fall or Wire before them, the Butthole Surfers began deconstructing the concept of rock'n'roll. Unlike the British post-punk bands who stripped rock music down to its most primal core and exposed its bare bones, the Butthole Surfers reconstructed it into a new monster with their own set rock rituals. They began showing films behind themselves as they played, in a sort of Joshua Light Show revisited. Smoke machines bellowed a dense and foreboding fog, creating shadows and hallucinations within a haze of blinding strobes and heavenly halogen lamps. They upped the ante of the 70's style rock stage shows from over the top, to out of the stratosphere, in both a loving tribute and a satirical jab at rock'n'roll excesses.

They conjured up demons from acid rock to punk rock with little concern that punks weren't supposed to admit to liking Led Zeppelin or Black Sabbath. Before grunge bands started recycling 70's cock rock riffs without even the slightest hint of irony, the Butthole Surfers were irreverently paying homage to the token rock Gods and forging mammoth blues riffs with a mighty hammer that destroyed any clichés by repeatedly bludgeoning them over the head until they were completely disfigured.

Aside from a small contingent, the amalgam of punk and acid rock had barely even been alluded to since the days the MC5 had pummeled the stage at the Grande Ballroom in the late 1960's. But, unlike the MC5, who were destroyed as much by politics as drugs, the Butthole Surfers dealt only with the idea of the ID: the Here and Now. You could decide what it all meant if you made it back home from their show with your mind still intact.

There was no John Sinclair to rabble rouse the audience. Instead of 'taking 5 seconds to realize your purpose here on this planet', the Butthole Surfers invited you to planet far removed from this one, where freedom was truly yours for the taking. The only constraints were those the listener chose to put on him or herself, not set by some false figurehead with an agenda hoping to start a new religion, revolution, or social movement. Theirs was a true freedom away from the dogma and corruption that inevitably springs up around any new movement that claims to espouse individual freedom.

Jeff and Teresa, August 1986
© *William McConnell*

And as the oppressive summer heat bore down on Texas, the time had come to spread this new gospel of liberation across the country. Not a new home, nor the PMRC, nor Edwin Meese, nor the climate outside of the borders of TX could stop the Buttholes from doing what they knew best: touring. It seemed like the only time they were comfortable was when they were in motion, and enduring the most horrid of living conditions. There was a certain comfort, and some much-needed money to be made there on that road, and they were going out to claim it as their own.

They proclaimed their return in a blistering performance at their old haunt the Ritz on Independence Day, 1986 and within a few weeks were back on the road as a 5-piece band: up to the west coast, then down through Texas, then up the east coast, then back down the east coast, through Texas, and back up the west coast again: like skaters on a half-pipe, up and down and back again.

Though their new home in Austin didn't hold them too firmly in place, it did keep tours a bit more structured and the schedules a bit more sane. A home in Texas allowed them the ability to stop between coasts for a couple of days to recoup before heading out and doing it again in reverse.

There was still work to do at their new home. Although they already had released a wealth of material during the first half of 1986, they were working on a project that was far more ambitious than anything they had recorded to date. A project that would keep them rooted in Texas for the next several months as they gathered the material, ironed it out, and committed it to tape.

Of course they still continued to play one-off shows, sometimes flying, instead of driving, to major markets to try out their new material live, and earn extra cash, but most of the fall of 1986 was spent in the kitchen, recording and mixing, splicing and experimenting with tracks from the stacks of old tapes they recorded while back in GA, just after Trevor had become the 'Most Hated Man in America'.

The recordings were made on the same crude Ampex 8-track machine they used for 'Cream Corn', only now with Paul's ever-increasing expertise in mixing, editing, and multi-track bouncing, they had room for dozens of tracks and overdubs, and they used all of them.

Their original intent to release a 7" of a new song entitled "Human Cannonball" was quickly nixed as old recordings began to manifest into actual songs, and new inspirations began to take shape. They soon had a wealth of new material from which to draw. And while the songs recorded years past were merely tinkered with, these new songs were slaved over, fucked with, and skewed. Timing, pitch, and tempos were changed, sometimes mid-song. One of the new studio creations overlaid 64 simultaneous kick drum tracks and 17 different guitar solos into an maniacal, cacophonous racket.

Over a Christmas respite, when all the rest of the band had split the house to be with friends and family for a few days, Paul stayed behind: gouging into the band's stash and turning knobs and levels like a stoned Dr. Frankenstein. Carolers may have been outside, but Paul was inside huddled in the dark kitchen and laughing to himself, checking his dials and mixing his potions.

Guitar tracks were reversed and sped up to 78rpm. Vocals growled and spoke backwards in incoherent, ancient languages. No turn was left unstoned. The band came back to the house from Christmas break and were given the most unholy of belated gifts: "the O-men", owing its name to a local metal band, the Omen, and their song "Termination" which inspired the lyrics about "cyborg lust".

August 25, 1986 Cat Club
© Robert Carillo-Cohen

A collection of call-in radio show clips that emanated out of Paul's amp one practice (remember kids, there's Butthole truth and then reality) was taped and sculpted into a harrowing glimpse of domestic abuse. The façade of the Midwestern housewife is exposed to reveal the hideous truth underneath. Life on the farm is not what it appears. '*They seemed like such a happy couple at the penny social*', until an anonymous late night phone call to a therapist's radio program reveals the demoralization behind the smiles they wear to Sunday church service. The cattle moo outside in their stalls, while the farmer's wife weeps in hers.

By running the same tape backwards at high speed, "22 Going On 23" becomes 'Hay', a flurry of Chinese stars zipping perilously passed to our heads. Nothing was sacred or off-limits. One early mix of "Graveyard", a track they had been playing religiously for the previous year-and-a-half, was slowed into a lumbering ox, belly-deep in mud. Another live mix was also put into the "Keep" pile. Left to their own devices, there were no limits, no rules, and no boundaries.

And as Ronald Reagan oversaw the speech restrictions at home, and the Soviets began their own political awakening dubbed *Perestroika,* the boundaries of freedom and oppression became blurred. The U.S.A was looking more and more like the U.S.S.R. The song "U.S.S.A." was a frenzy of paranoia amidst the book burnings and abortion center bombings that was as immediate and poignant as any political manifesto Biafra could conjure up in his 3-page lyrical screeds.

So, the two song 7" grew like fungus in a Petri dish into a full-length LP. As packaging and art began to fall into place for its scheduled release early in Anno Domini 1987, it quickly became clear that this was no ordinary record. It embraced the radical ideals of the 60's and then dragged the listener through the drug and sexual revolutions of the 70's, before burning them on the pyre of the punk movement of the 80's. It left a skid mark across the underwear of rock music and cultural history. To the throngs of people who were becoming believers that the Butthole Surfers were the most important band in existence, this new release would be their generation's 'Trout Mask Replica'. There would be but two eras in the history of underground music: life before its release, and life after its release.

Locust Abortion Technician was not a mere genre defining work, it was a genre creating work: perhaps creating several musical genres without a thought in the world about it. At a time when punk rock was dying, and long before anyone knew anything about 'Alternative', the Butthole Surfers bridged the precipice between; or rather cleaved a path and drove a semi-truck right through the fukker.

Soon after the release of *Locust Abortion Technician*, bands began to spring up from coast to coast whose music was rooted in punk rock but who incorporated classic rock and psychedelic overtones. From Jane's Addiction out west, to Dinosaur Jr. in the east, and everywhere in between. It seemed a new psychedelic renaissance was taking hold. These bands may have been around before *Locust Abortion Technician*, but now, they would be recognized and celebrated and, soon, form a scene all their own, free from the chains of what had been called punk rock. From the ashes, rose the phoenix of a new brand of underground music, and the Butthole Surfers were not as much fanning the flames, as igniting them.

The bands who would later cite *Locust Abortion Technician* as an inspiration would go on to sell millions of records, garner huge major label record deals, become darlings of MTV and commercial radio and become the faces of the emerging alternative rock scene. What those bands took away from *Locust Abortion Technician* was the spirit of freedom and experimentation, for surely any band that was planning any semblance of fiduciary rewards for their art would certainly not be emulating what they heard within the record's grooves, but rather the single-minded vision of the work, along with complete lack of restraint from label or critic or even fan concerns. This made the record an inspiration to anyone who believed in their own work as art.

Locust Abortion Technician is one of the most commercially alienating records of all time. The comparison here to Beefheart's Trout Mask Replica stems from nearly the same set of circumstances as how they both came to be. Both Don Van Vliet (the Captain) and the Butthole Surfers were producing the record solely for themselves, not for a label, or a manager, or a record company PR man. Beefheart was finally finished appeasing company brass, as well as band's squeamishness over the material, and untethered his genius to make the record he dreamed of making. He assembled a new band and brought his ideas to his pal Frank Zappa, who had formed his own Straight Records. Zappa agreed to let Don Van Vliet do whatever it was Don Van Vliet wanted to do, no matter how insane the idea. All Zappa was responsible for was to help commit all Beefheart's insane ideas to tape.

The Butthole Surfers had Corey, who after finally convincing the band to commit to Touch & Go (and reaping more financial success from them than he and his fledgling record company could ever have imagined) was ready to turn them loose to do whatever it was they wanted to do, without constraint.

Even Zappa must have tossed an eye roll on occasion from inside the control booth. Corey was 1400 miles away in Detroit. The Buttholes did this entire project without any filter or edit to their creation, and they compiled a monster out of the decaying corpse of rock music.

Locust Abortion Technician would become the new archetype for anyone trying to make a record on their own terms, without the burden of commercial appeal and without concern about alienating old fans or attracting new ones. The Butthole Surfers made their money on the road and it was this freedom that allowed them to put to wax almost any fleeting fancy they could conjure. Strung together, their thoughts became almost a stream of consciousness concept album.

> *"Locust Abortion Technician is a concept album where every song is a concept unto itself"*
> - Gibby Haynes, MTV, 1987

With the last few remaining punk bands on life support by 1987, the Buttholes released a record that was a big fat 'FUCK YOU' in the face of mainstream rock and the entities that pushed it on the masses. Without a thought or care that the PMRC would censor them, whether stores would stock it, or people would buy it, *Locust Abortion Technician* was easily as 'punk rock' as anything released in the 1980s. In fact, it almost harkened back to 1970's, when bands as diverse as Throbbing Gristle, Devo, The Residents, and Pere Ubu were cranking out obscure and challenging records that were called punk simply because there was no other pigeonhole in which to drop them.

The record was a revival back to a time in music when anything was possible, where independent labels and publishers sprung up in small towns and released art, poetry and music to their friends without fear of censorship or marketability. Surely, if organizations like the PMRC were going to be defeated, it would be by artists using

Cat Club, NYC
© Robert Carillo-Cohen

their First Amendment rights without fear of reprisals, and the Butthole Surfers did just that.

At a time when America's youths needed to be called into action, the Butthole Surfers were unwitting and unlikely generals. They had no desire to be the next Dead Kennedys. They were not trying to change the world, and yet, by ignoring the politics of the day they became a symbol of what a band could do when they were not shackled by their record company, nor by the fear of arrest from the right-wing conservative sect. By simply ignoring all the codes of the day, they became crusaders.

It wasn't as if Tipper Gore was going to try to challenge the Butthole Surfers to explain themselves in front of a Congressional Committee assembled to review the adverse effects of rock music upon America's teenagers. She had a much easier target in Jello Biafra and the Dead Kennedys, whom she could parade in front of the country as treasonous letches. She could point to the blasphemous lyrics and politically charged propaganda of the posters and lyrics to submit as evidence. "I Kill Children", "Too Drunk to Fuck", "Let's Lynch the Landlord". There was enough fodder in the Dead Kennedys for any sexually repressed Stepford wife to play out her dominatrix fantasies without having the word "Butthole" echo through the hallowed halls of the Capitol building.

The Buttholes remained free. Free to be the Satan worshipping, drug fueled rapists who roamed the countryside like lawless rogue warriors drinking blood and eating the brains of children on a never-ending coast to coast death race.

Shhhhh...Peaceful

It was a bucolic plot of land about five acres in size and about an hour's drive outside of Austin, in a speck on a map called Driftwood: far removed from the traffic and noise of I-183. Huge moss laden trees shaded the front lawn and swayed in the gentle breeze. A large meadow filled with deer grazing lazily was just across a narrow access road. It was a ranch style home built into the side of a hill, with some small storage sheds peppering the landscape. The nearest neighbors couldn't even be seen from the main house.

Flynn Mauthe, like so many of their old pals, had given up playing punk rock in the Marching Plague and grew up and get a real job. He was their real estate agent, now, and he brought them to this gorgeous slice of paradise in the country. Once they saw it, they knew they had to buy it. The band had been cooped up at the 1401 House in Austin for the better part of a year. It was cramped and dark and right near a highway. They were in constant danger of being evicted and the house being condemned by the city.

With this new property, they'd have meadows to walk through, space for Mark Farner to roam, and a place to play without fear of disturbing the peace. An idyllic setting far from the cities where they spent their nights when on the job. King didn't drive, and opted to stay in Austin for convenience's sake, but the rest of the band all living together on a ranch conjured visions of chainsaw massacres and rooms containing exquisite statues fashioned from human skeletons. A commune of freaks not unlike The Family or the Branch Davidians or The Weavers: in self-imposed exile to escape the prying eyes of the authorities.

But the stockpile kept at this compound was not guns or bibles, but guitars and drums: a new multi-track recorder with PC editing software, delay pedals and microphones, smoke machines and strobe lights, and miles and miles of tape and cables. So, when the UK division of Caroline Records approached the band with an offer to release a compilation of artists handpicked by the Butthole Surfers themselves, it was a great opportunity to try out their new home studio.

They coaxed long-time pals Stick Men with Ray Guns over to record some tracks, and finally got some of their product released to an audience outside of Texas. They also recorded some tracks by prolific avant-garde musician \ filmmaker \ artist and agent provocateur, Steve Fitch, whose mom and dad were both morticians. The Buttholes themselves contributed two tracks to the compilation, as well as featuring a musical savant who had drifted into Austin the previous summer named Daniel Johnston.

With two of his own songs, as well as his collaboration on the Butthole Surfers tracks, Daniel Johnston was truly the featured artist. It would be several years before the rest of the world would take notice of Daniel's talents, largely due to Kurt Cobain donning a t-shirt of Johnston's 1988 debut LP release, *'Hi How Are You'*. (released several years earlier as a homemade cassette). The songs that Johnston contributed to this compilation were some of the first professional studio recordings he ever recorded, and certainly the first with any sort of real distribution.

Johnston's story reads like a modern day Roky Erickson. His history of mental illness and trouble with the law has become almost as notable as his prolific recorded output, most of which he recorded himself onto cassettes at home directly into a boombox. The low budget quality and starkly honest lyrics about love, ghosts, and comic book heroes were like a scented, cool breeze blowing on a cavity. His songs are beautiful and sad, triumphant and defeatist, and so heartfelt it feels as if you are intruding on his personal breakdown.

If not for Kurt Cobain bringing him to fame, few might have ever heard of Daniel Johnston. If not for the Butthole Surfers giving him first real break, he may have gone completely unknown other than to those who actually played the tapes he gave them as they walked down the street, his main way of distributing his work before earning a record deal.

At the suggestion of Caroline, the compilation was named 'A Texas Trip', and shortly after its release, Daniel Johnston would visit NYC to record his debut professional recording, '1990', with none other than Mark Kramer at his Noise, NY. Daniel's 1994 LP 'Fun' would be produced by Paul. His songs have since been covered by such luminaries as Tom Waits, Beck and Mike Watt, but it was the Butthole Surfers who offered him his first recorded output that had any kind of real distribution outside of Texas.

The Butthole Surfers songs that were contributed continued in the vein of Locust Abortion Technician: overlaying dozens of tracks, each so drenched in effects that one's skull was endangered of being crushed and added to one of the statues at the band's own horror ranch. Their new studio passed the test and gave the band the chance to keep the advance money paid by Caroline to fund other endeavors…like putting their weed dealer's kids through college.

With the release of *Locust Abortion Technician* and 'A Texas Trip', as well as their recent contribution to the 'Smack My Crack' compilation (put out by NYC poet\performance artist and ex-Andy Warhol confidant, John Giorno), the band took a deep breath for a couple of weeks before hitting the road. It was the final chance to get out and see the dappled sunlight play off the tall grass in their meadow before piling back into the RV.

Venue sizes had been increasing, and theatre-sized shows in major markets were now almost guaranteed sellouts. This time out they would leave no market unscarred, shocking audiences not just in the big cities, but across the four corners of the US with a brand new aural \ visual assault.

Teresa & King, Liberty Lunch, 12/13/86
© Pat Blashill

Shortly after they had settled into their new digs in the country, mail began arriving addressed to Dr. Gibson Haynes. Films he had requested from medical schools, acquired for "educational use" after searching the ALA archives for the treasure trove held within. Officer Gibson Haynes also got packages to the house. Libraries and film archives, the prestigious Mr Haynes contacted them all in hopes of adding new films to his growing archive of cinematic oddities.

Soon, stacks upon stacks of 16mm projection reels were amassed of everything from old 'Charlie's Angels' episodes to penis reconstruction surgeries, Bridge collapses to car accidents, Electroshock treatments, Coral Reefs, and Desert Oases. When put to music the films became a journey into the very soul of Man: a voyage into the subconscious mind filled with horrid nightmares, rapturous beauty, esoteric allusions, and mundane trivialities.

The last national tour was done by a band in transition, still experimenting with new songs and new gadgets like a smoke machine and a strobe light. This time, they would storm the country as a 6-piece ensemble, replete with an interpretive dancer who made Stacy from Hawkwind look like Peter Pan.

Kathleen Lynch had been bouncing between in NYC and Atlanta since first abandoning the 'Now Explosion' scene in Atlanta for the seedy core of the Big Apple. The love she had uprooted her comfortable existence for had not panned out, but she did find a different kind of love the in the vibrant streets of the Lower East Side, frequenting haunts around Alphabet City like the Pyramid and A7, where all the fun was happening long before Mayor Giuliani had the cops 'clean out' the squatters, queens, and junkies in and around Tompkins Square Park.

She had friends and compatriots in some Atlanta transplants like Lady Bunny, who would go on to create the iconic annual 'Wigstock' drag festival, DJ\ Club Promoter and former owner of the Celebrity Club, Larry Tee, and even RuPaul, who got her start at the Celebrity Club and frequenting many of the same clubs the Easturn Stars used to play back in Georgia.

Downtown was where the queens hung out and it was ground zero for all the good parties. Kathleen had continued to craft and hone her own art and music and even danced a couple of times for the Buttholes when they rolled through New York City, well after the dust had cleared from the Danceteria show, but she never had the motivation or desire to market herself like the other freaks had. Her art, like that of the Butthole Surfers, was created in a vacuum.

She had many close friends who were the flamboyant characters running the shows, but she was rather shy and private about her personal life, in stark contrast to the personas she created through her own music and onstage in her performance art. Kathleen's raw sense of humor and highly eccentric personality, both on and off stage, left her a complete enigma to all but her closest confidants. The vow of silence she took shortly after joining the Butthole Surfers left only her alter ego, Ta-Da The Shitlady, to speak for the girl formerly known as Kathleen Lynch, channeled through her interpretive dance.

Teresa:
"When Kathleen first joined us, she was reading the 'Book of Urantia'... And she would be like studying it and like underlining and highlighting passages. And then she went through that no talking thing. I was like 'Kathleen you can talk!' I was like, 'Some people in the world can't talk, but you can fuckin' talk!'... She would just write down in her little pad what she wanted to say..."
[phone interview, 7/26/14]

Kathleen, Spring 1987
© William McConnell

For all her talent, it was onstage with the Butthole Surfers where her true muse took flight. Her playful antics at the Danceteria show only alluded to the horror and beauty she could conjure and manifest when lost in her oracles. She would now be the band's full-time dancer. And as a member of the band, she guaranteed every night would be a carnival freak show that was sure to amaze and mystify.

A seaweed boa wrapped around her neck, her face painted kabuki white with a mock Fu Manchu beard dangling from her chin, her teeth covered in tinfoil, dressed in a loose-fitting diaper, when dressed in anything at all, TA-DA was truly a sight to behold. She was the complete embodiment of the band itself: Impish, childlike, grossly horrific yet tantalizingly beautiful. She was like a pixie writhing and luring you ever closer into her world, and into the world of the Butthole Surfers, where Man feasts on the souls of children.

As absurdist and humorous as TA-DA was to the Buttholes new stage show, she seemed completely uncontrived. It was as if she sprouted out of the stage or wandered in from the cold, summoned and conjured up by the shrieks and growls of the rituals performed both onstage. Band and audience were now one, and since the band never knew what tricks she would pull out of her hat either, both band and audience were often equally enthralled and aghast at each new ceremony.

There was little doubt after she started performing every night, that Kathleen was a member of the band, and not just a performance artist or go-go dancer who pranced naked around the stage. She was a living, breathing embodiment of the world they created each night, and each night became something magical.

Teresa:
"Sometimes people refer to [Kathleen] as "the stripper". And I try to be really clear to people that I was never in a band with a stripper...She would glue that green beard onto her chin.. Some shows she stood on her head the whole show and shit like that. So we called her the naked dancer. But I never liked it when people would say "ya'll had that stripper". I wasn't in a band with a stripper..." [phone, 7/26/14]

It was these six members, as well as jack of all trades, Danny Flaim, projectionist Bill Daniel, and soundman Ric Wallace that comprised the small army they needed to put on the Greatest Show on Earth. Being able to bankroll even this small staff was light years away from picking through garbage dumpsters for meals like they had in NYC. They now could support themselves and finance the stage show they always dreamed of presenting; filled with thrills, chills and excrement.

Paul:
"I went to sleep one night with the TV turned on and I woke up at two in the morning and the TV was flashing this white light; and I opened my eyes to this flashing light and I realized I was looking at a rock concert on the TV and it was just blinding, flashing lights and billowing, plumes of smoke, and belching flames, and explosions and I was like, ' YEAH!, That's a fucking rock show!', then I was like, wait, that's US!" [Matador Revisionist History Podcast, Episode 13, March 2024]

In spring of 1987 they finally unleashed this unholy beast on the road: from Texas to Albuquerque to LA, from Oxnard to Berkeley, across the Bay Bridge into San Francisco and then north up the coast into Canada. Off to Denver, Minneapolis, Chicago and then to Detroit to see Corey and their pals at Touch & Go. Up to the Northeast quadrant and down the coast down to Florida. A juggernaut tour that left no market spared. The addition of Kathleen left fans in awe, and club owners reeling. All age punk shows replete with pyrotechnics, films, and Kathleen naked as a jaybird in spring.

It was a bit more than most club owners and promoters could handle. The dangers of the club burning to the ground as Gibby played with rubbing alcohol and a lighter were bad enough, but some 12-year-old telling his parents he just saw a sex show at the local punk matinee was a whole different can of worms.

Teresa:
"Teenage boys. That was the first live naked woman they ever saw. And so their jaws would be dropped, but then at the same time they'd be repulsed."
[phone, 7/26/14]

When they got a booking in early May at City Gardens in Trenton, promoter Randy Now was waiting, well aware of their stage show and their new interpretive dancer, Kathleen. They had played NYC a couple of nights earlier and smashed 4 guitars during their opening song. General insanity was to be expected at a Butthole Surfers performance. One learned quickly to expect the unexpected, but with the City Gardens show an afternoon all-ages affair, Randy requested they forego the use of Kathleen's services in hopes of keeping the proceedings PG-rated for the kids in attendance.

Jeff's new haircut, and Ta-Da in LA, 4/3/87
© Krk Dominguez

"Gibby said' 'OK', which really meant 'fuck you'. – Randy Now
[No Slam Dancing, No Stage Diving, No Spikes: *How City Gardens Defined an Era."*, Amy Yates Wuelfling]

Kathleen danced the first song, "Graveyard", in a t-shirt and large adult diaper, but as the music grabbed hold of her during the next song, "U.S.S.A", she dropped all vestiges confining her to this world and revealed herself to anyone who could see passed the smoke, snuff films, and steady heartbeat of blinding strobe lights.

With a blood-thirsty, sold-out crowd enveloped in the ritual, Randy had little choice but to grin and squirm as Kathleen writhed and channeled her other-worldly hallucinations bare breasted at his all-ages show. Parents who had brought their kids screamed at him in the back of the club, but all he could do was shrug. He told the owner of the club, Tut, to go into the back room to count liquor bottles to distract him from the proceedings unfolding onstage. The plan almost worked, but when Tut emerged from the back room and found Gibby performing his latest trick: lighting a drum cymbal on fire and smashing it with a drumstick, exploding a huge mushroom cloud of flames that blossomed into the air, he became unglued. The jig was up.

Safe in the arms of security, City Gardens, 5/3/87
© Ken Salerno

He screamed at Randy to yank the huge lever which controlled the main power to the stage. The lights on Paul and Jeff's amps immediately went black, and with no power to the stage, Gibby shouted into his bullhorn to command the attention of the crowd.

Teresa and King walked off-stage, but Jeff, with a joint dangling between his lips, jumped behind King's kit and began bashing away. Kathleen threw a t-shirt on her back, knowing she may need to vacate the premises in a hurry, and she jumped behind Teresa's drum set. Power or no power, this show was not over until the band decided it was over.

Security rushed the stage with a fire extinguisher spraying a thick plume of smoke covering the stage in toxic foam, as the crowd starts chanting: "BOUNCERS SUCK, BOUNCERS SUCK!…". Small fights begin breaking out in the crowd, first in one section, then another. One bouncer grabs a beer and throws it on the cymbal to prevent any more fires, but Gibby, instead, drenches him with his rubbing alcohol accelerant. He flicks his Bic several times, threatening to ignite the burly hulk. As the guard readies to knock Gibby unconscious, an equally large bouncer, realizing that the place could really ignite into a real tinderbox if Gibby gets punched, grabs his pal and drags him off-stage by his t-shirt.

210

Riot on the dance floor - City Gardens, 5/3/87
© Ken Salerno

Paul instigates by mockingly screaming like a frightened schoolgirl at the madness around him and jumps into the arms of a bouncer to protect himself, '*save me!*'.... The side doors into the parking lot fly open, as fights spill out from inside the club into the outside parking lot, and into the blinding light of the evening sun. Beer bottles are hurled at cars and shatter against the walls of the club. As Rome burned around them, the band hung around inside, waiting to get paid. Once they collected the other half of their guarantee, they bolted out and off to the next show.

This scenario played out in even scarier fashion in Tampa, FL, where Kathleen was dragged off the stage and into the crowd. That night Paul swung his guitar around to get a group of skinheads off her and her backstage to safety. As he did, more kids stormed the stage and smashed another of Paul's guitars to splinters, ending the show after just 15 mins.

Despite any myths to the contrary, the band was never more violent than the crowds they attracted, but they seemed to enjoy stirring crowds to a breaking point. It was as if the projections behind the band were of Emmanuel Goldstein, and the crowd the citizens of Oceania during the Two Minute Hate ceremony. Reactions were sometimes violent and extreme. No one could be sure if this was all for the greater good of humanity or some twisted plot by the Ministry of Truth to manipulate to masses. 1984 was over, and though many in the United States of Unconsciousness believed we had survived the fate of Orwell's dystopia just because 3 years had passed since the book's setting, the few who knew better were growing in numbers, and were growing more frightened.

For those few who understood, the Butthole Surfers were the saviors who had come to liberate us from Big Brother. Those who understood were left shuttering in fear and awe, but also with hope: a hope springing from the realization that, though the numbers were few, they were not entirely alone. And though their antics might demonstrate otherwise, they were not the ones who were crazy after all. They were the byproducts of that which was fed to them. There were other denizens of this Military Industrial Complex who saw it too, and they believed as you did. To those few but fervent fans, the Butthole Surfers were the world's last\best chance at survival.

As club owners screamed and begrudgingly wrote checks despite all the damage to their halls, and as crowds bubbled and bordered on rioting, the band would simply hop back in their RV and move on to the next town, like serial killers wrecking innocent lives and then hitchhiking down the road to their next unsuspecting victims.

The sensory overload of the live experience was too much for some. Even the strongest among us wilt as the bandages surrounding a 10-foot-tall, bloody stump on screen behind the band are unsheathed; the mangled remains of a penis of some unfortunate farmer who strayed too close to a combine. Strobe lights pulsating, dry ice smoke creating shadows and monsters as maniacal voices loop and feedback screeches from somewhere behind the veil of sweet-scented fog. We are jostled back to a spot we can discern some silhouettes moving through the haze. Naked bodies. Flailing Limbs. This was violence itself, and it would sometimes manifest itself in confrontations among the patrons. It was just one more reason for detractors of the band to cite as a reason to hate them. They were the senseless chaos without merit who fought against everything the best of punk rock was supposed to be.

But, when one holds a mirror up to an ape he can get confused and lash out at his own reflection. And that is exactly the response of the self-righteous punk when asked to confront his or her innermost and darkest thoughts. When shown true freedom, some will think and breathe and blossom, and some will destroy and submit to the basest impulses of the ID, threatening the very freedom for which they so yearned. For them, the chaos of a Butthole Surfers concert was too much. It merely became the excuse to lash out in blind, anarchistic rage.

It was a problem that had plagued punk rock since its infancy, but the Buttholes often took the rap harder than many other bands of the day, either because many of the older punk bands were breaking up or changing styles by 1987, or because the band themselves never had much to say at all regarding the shows or their meaning. The band had insisted, when prodded, their stage shows meant nothing. They were mere theatrics: complete existentialism meant only to entertain and amuse. And while, for the band members at least, there was more than a grain of truth in that fact: the shows they staged, and which so terrorized their audiences, were merely flights of fancy, what the audience glommed from the experience was something altogether different and, often, more holy than that.

For the band, the films were interesting and the nickel-and-dime Joshua Light Show in which they immersed themselves simply accentuated their own buzz. Bashing away on a 10-minute jam without a melody while prancing half-dressed and cross-eyed was just a way to get a laugh. The audience, however, were like rats in a lab. For some, this blitzkrieg of lights, images, and sounds became an excuse for a violent release of their own. To others, the frenzy of subliminal images and media propaganda set against the screaming sirens and wailing guitars was a call to arms: a cry for help in a world gone mad.

Some vomited and passed out, some fought, some danced, some held their ears in apparent disgruntle and dismay. No one left without being affected in some way, which seemed to be the rallying cry of the early punk pioneers when they first started banging on their instruments. Make the listener *feel* something; love or hate…ANYTHING but indifference. Inject feeling into an unfeeling world.

Teresa:
"There's this unspoken code, and this is sort of what happens in a dysfunctional family, but we had a code among us that nobody told what the deal was…. If we knew how Gibby got an inspiration for a lyric, and then later someone said, 'hey what's that song about?' We'd be like 'shhhh…'. That was how that song "Perry" came about. Because everybody kept asking Gibby what his songs were about, and he was like, 'it's about this it's about that…'
'It's about lovin' yourself, it's about lovin' your mum' that was all because people kept asking us what the songs were about. And we just had an inter-thing where we didn't talk about the way that we came about inspiration…that was a secret. And I can see that Gibby's still… he's an artist, he's a very talented artist. And I think he has trouble letting people inside of that world." [phone interview, 7/26/14]

The opening band that day at City Gardens was obviously moved by the 'riot on the dance floor.' It was their first real show in front of a crowd and as huge fans of the Butthole Surfers, the boys of Ween got a lesson from their idols on how to emulsify a crowd into a froth, which they used to gain their own legion of loyal followers.

For those who had seen the Butthole Surfers prior to the metamorphosis that was spring 1987 tour, there was something entirely different about the band now. The fetus that had been incubating inside of body of Kane had reached maturity, and the Alien now tore out of his stomach in a bloody expulsion of guts and gore: a true Mechanized Death of the old Butthole Surfers had taken place, and its rebirth spawned a 10ft tall beast with teeth like razors and blood like acid. The band had been simmering like a gumbo in the Texas heat since Teresa had rejoined the group, playing some dates around the state, and some quick one offs in major markets to keep the mortgage paid, food on the table, and the bong tightly packed. Now that the lid was off the pressure cooker, they hissed out violently onto the roadways of America again.

Few who witnessed the new stage show and its visceral intensity were left with any doubt which independent band had the greatest live show on earth. When the tour reached its conclusion at the end of May, and they arrived back in Texas for their typical brief respite, awaiting them was another new stack of film canisters, and their 3rd tour of Europe just beyond the horizon.

It would be their most ambitious endeavor yet, hauling their full stage show across the Atlantic and storming the continent like the Allies on D-Day. Their two previous tours of Europe eluded all but the most diehard contingent of fans: Dead Kennedys fans who had read Jello's meanderings about the band in some magazine, Shockabilly fans checking out Kramer's new project, Subterranean interns who heard the first record by chance.

Most punks had read the glowing reviews the band received in Sounds or Melody Maker long after the band had left town. That last tour of Europe was over a year prior as a struggling quartet. This tour was a high tech, psychedelic freakout that was miles beyond what had been presented to the fans overseas previously, and the Buttholes were realizing their full potency.

Kathleen hadn't even bothered to pack a suitcase before the plane took off from NYC, and she crossed the pond with only the pair of shorts and t-shirt she had on upon departure. All that she needed she was wearing, and with the absence of any spoken words, all that she expressed, she expressed through her art. At the first show in London, an uptight councilwoman screamed at Blast First president Paul Smith to get her to put some clothes on, he snapped back…'

"You want her to do that, then you tell her! she's right there in front of you!"

The back and forth yelling obviously distracted Kathleen, who wasn't going to stop dancing to engage. Instead, she had honed the art of peeing to that of a master, and without breaking stride, peed the most elegant ark ever seen across the councilwoman's shoes from a good 5 feet away…

Paul Smith (Blast First Records)
"I swear Kathleen never splashed a drop on me, but women's shoes were soaked. The women went very pale, and promptly left, never to be seen again. Kathleen never even broke her dance step rhythm.'"   [email Sept 2013]

When she got chilly that night at the room provided for them at the Columbia Hotel in Lancaster Gate, she cut herself some leggings from the queen-size comforter. The blanket was left on the bed with two perfectly cut leg sized holes in it. It was often difficult to tell when a Butthole Surfers show ended and when it began. Kathleen would often walk into hotels ahead of the band, according to Jeff…:

Jeff:
"We'd get bummed out because she'd always be the first one in…with a shaved head and hairy legs, all covered in dye…then we'd come in and try to get a room…"
[Chris Smart interview, 2001)

But, when the lights dimmed, the smoke billowed out, the projectors spun to life and the music belched forth its hideous racket, it was hard to be bummed. Jeff knew it as well as anyone. Kathleen standing on her head for a full 15 mins while being battered by a barrage of lights and sounds was truly a wonder to behold, and every night was another spectacle of the beautiful and the grotesque. They floored the unsuspecting crowds with the mayhem that ensued. Those in the know had braced themselves for the usual anarchy of a Butthole Surfers show, but few were prepared for the full-frontal assault that greeted them on this trip. Films, lights, pyrotechnics, Ta-Da the Shit Lady; it was this barrage that they brought to the UK in August 1987, and the one which John Peel witnessed for the first time.

Peel noted that the band "force you to re-evaluate everything in your life, really…". This from the man who had witnessed nearly every pop artist since the late sixties as DJ on his own Radio One Programme. He was left nearly speechless. It was an amazing compliment of the highest order.   John Peel had given Jimi Hendrix some of his first studio time as a solo musician, after Jimi fled from the United States to the UK in frustration. Unlike the USA, British kids soaked up the influences of black blues artists of America like sponges and repackaged their riffs as their own. The Brits understood the context of Hendrix's material long before the youth of America did. It was only in the context of America's escalating involvement in French-Indo China that kids in the US began to feel the real blues and welcomed Jimi back with open arms. Peel, however, got it first.

Peel had also afforded a rock band like Pink Floyd the opportunity to play their brand new "Atom Heart Mother Suite" with members of the London Symphony Orchestra, something which had never been tried previously. Through the ages and stages of rock'n'roll, Peel touted the genius of artists like Captain Beefheart and Gang of Four and the Jam and the Fall when they were all still unknowns to the rest of the world. He had lived through the Love Generation and the Punk Explosion and the New Wave of rock. He had not only seen it all, but he helped expose it and promote it on one of the few truly independent radio shows in the world. Now, upon seeing the Butthole Surfers, he was re-evaluating everything in his life.

Peel invited bands into the Maida Vale studios in London to record with a producer for free, and the bands often used the opportunity to record new material. Everyone from David (Bowie) Jones to Led Zeppelin, to Joy Division to The Who had used the time to try out brand new songs, showcase new directions, revamp old staples, and play covers of their favorite artists. Peel oversaw it all and now was touting the Butthole Surfers in the same pantheon as the legends of rock'n'roll he helped bring to super stardom.

Upon his transformation at the Clarendon Ballroom (ironically dubbed by Paul Leary as one of the worst shows he's ever played), Peel dug through the vaults of the BBC and found some songs which the BBC had recorded live on the band's first tour of the UK, with Kramer. He aired them on his very next program, spreading the Word of his new gospel to the uninitiated masses.

Peel, as many others, realized that the Butthole Surfers in concert transcended mere music. Shows were religious meditations. Fans rocked back and forth and mumbled in tongues like monks in a trance. Most of them flippantly boasted about the amount of drugs they were scrambled on, but the obvious sex, drugs, and rock'n'roll clichés couldn't come close to describing the power of the live experience. Anyone who had a heart could see, not just those with spiked mohawks too fucked up to pee straight, but also those who donned their wire-framed glasses and clutched their Nietzsche books close to their chests.

It was all the hippies had dreamed about in their acid test visions. The endless possibilities of freedom once you discovered your Self, and the part one plays in the world. Live concerts became a warning cry: a call for insanity in the sane world. The sane world, you see, was teetering on the brink of a nuclear holocaust. Sanity conducted covert CIA operations in Central America, funded by US money funneled through Iran. Sanity built a wall that divided a city in half to appease two spiteful

Playing with fire, 12/12/87 at the Ritz, NYC
© Ken Salerno

Making love under the strobe light
© William McConnell

Superpowers. It was obvious that the only way to fight Sanity would be to battle it with Insanity, and our small army of traveling minstrels were the foot soldiers in this war.

Like Hagbard Celine in the 'Illuminatus Trilogy', the Butthole Surfers were the captains of the Golden Submarine headed for Atlantis and away from the evil Illuminati who control the universe. It was not just a mere concert, it was a catharsis: a metamorphosis, a rebirth of Self: an emergence from chrysalis into butterfly, where you could flutter and break away from the cocoon of the self-absorbed Me Generation and into the flower of the enlightenment to see the potential of life as it could be.

1987 was the true rebirth of the band, as well. From their compound out in the country, they orchestrated a violent overthrow of commercial music and the corporations behind it. They were finally making enough money to not have to tour constantly to support themselves, and yet, they were still out on tour more than they were at home. When they were at home, they jammed for hours at a clip: writing, playing, recording, and editing their own material.

What the Butthole Surfers shared with punk culture was the do-it-yourself ethos; the mentality that it could be done cheaper, and without compromise if it was done by yourself and for yourself. And while punk irritated the powers-that-be like a

218

diaper rash, it was a small sect that could be contained and dealt with. There was something more dangerous with a band who raged apart from the machine instead of against it.

Teresa:
"That trip to Europe was a huge awakening because we had been on the road non-stop for three years. And we were treated like shit everywhere we went. And it was just one disaster after another. And people trying not to pay us and just bullshit... People trying to shut us down and all this. And we got to Europe and they were like, 'here's all your separate hotel room keys and this nice ass hotel', and they were like, 'we'll do press and you'll be meeting with New Music Express, and at 2 you'll be meeting with this magazine, and different clubs and.' all of a sudden we were like 'whoa this is like being a rock star.'" [phone, 7/26/14]

The European tour was highly successful, especially by Butthole Surfers standards, and they received amazing support throughout the continent. Press was glowing and they became the 'must see' band. Somehow a band that mainstream press all but ignored, labels wouldn't touch, and commercial radio completely shunned was gaining, not only notoriety, but accolades. They returned to Texas at the height of their powers and immediately got back to work on new material.

And in their latest batch of new songs, they pushed the boundaries of 'punk rock' music even further out into the stratosphere. Songs like "Backass" and "Jimi" stretched out to over 6 and 7 mins a piece in a live setting, and the aptly titled "Psychedelic Jam" pushed passed the 10-minute mark on a good night.

Barely home from Europe for two months, the band hit the road again, debuting the new material they had been road-testing over the previous month across the European continent, along with yet another cache of new songs. King took a seat this tour, and added a kick drum to his drum set for the first time since the earliest days with the Hugh Beaumont Experience. This new element now allowed sets to blossom into marathons. Teresa, in a true test of endurance, still stood, bashing away with her long, auburn locks violently whipping into the air for the full two-hour tour into the outer most regions of the stratosphere.

The fall 1987 tour of the US was a true Ludovico style sensory overload. They had tested and honed their treatment and were now conducting a total reconditioning of the subjects in attendance. The crowd strapped down and defenseless, their eyes transfixed as if a speculum held them open, forced to endure the ultra-violence as it played out. Many could not do it. The penis reconstruction surgery was often the final straw in the virtual baleful of manure shoveled onto their psyches. The band's motto seemed to be, 'let's spread the shit and see what grows from it.'

By the time the last of the leaves of autumn had fallen, they had accosted most of the land with their traveling freak show. They had taken to playing covers of Grand Funk Railroad's "Paranoid", REM's "The One I Love", as well as most every song that would comprise their next release, and now as a winter snow blanketed the northern reaches of the US, they decided to book studio time at January Sound in Dallas, the same studio where Christopher Cross mastered his hit song "Sailing" nearly a decade prior, according to Paul.

The band hadn't recorded with an engineer or producer since they had gotten their own multi-track recorder back in Athens, and even before that, Paul had handled all but an occasional stray session himself. But, they decided that with all the material for the new LP in the can already, they could make haste of the process and get the record they knew they could make if not so preoccupied with recording, mixing and engineering the entire project at home themselves.

They had been playing most of the songs that would comprise "Hairway to Steven" for more than a year, and "Johnny Smoke" had been a staple of their live set for two years by the time they entered the studio during the first weeks of 1988. They took a day to record the 9 songs, with their live soundman, Ric Wallace, manning the board. They returned shortly thereafter for overdubs and within a week of starting they had gotten most of the record finished.

The collection of recordings that would come to be "Hairway to Steven" was just as much of a skullfuck as those that made up *Locust Abortion Technician*, but for many, vastly different reasons. Filled with acoustic guitars, and songs you could actually hum along with, it was the work of a band at peace. A band that had seen days of sunshine which were not filled with hours of excruciating driving.

It was a record that invited you in and left you ever wanting to venture further in to see what new and fascinating things you would find. The truckloads of effects which molded the sonic landscapes of *Locust Abortion Technician* were left at home in Driftwood. Instead, "Hairway to Steven" was almost pastoral. Almost…

Paul's pants, 11/7/87
© Krk Dominguez

Loafing in NYC, 12/12/87
© Ken Salerno

I'm Soiled, Soil me...

The opening track of *Hairway to Steven* was the Butthole Surfers magnum opus. It picked right up from where *Locust Abortion Technician* had left off. "Jimi" was a track that had been beaten out over the course of the previous year or so: released in one of its infant stages as "Flame Grape" on 'A Texas Trip', it was now a fully realized piece, and the one that most fully encapsulated the live experience on record.

Live, the song culminated in a bombast of feedback and mayhem, but in the studio, they tacked on their "Grantchester Meadows"-esque ballad "Cartoon Song" to the frenzy of feedback, stretching it to over 12 minutes in length.

Like 22 Going on 23, "Jimi" told the tale of domestic abuse, but this time instead of being voyeurs, we are thrust inside to live the nightmare ourselves. A father's satanic growl:

What do you know about reality?...I am reality...

Fingers scrape down the fretboards as time and space slow to a crawl, like the endless span of a final breath. Fear renders our tongues speechless as the demon rephrases the question:

What do you know about death?...I am death...

"Jimi" ends like a violent struggle between good and evil, cloven hoofs clutch one stony cliff, the feet of the Savior stand on an opposite peak, like the vision of Father Merrin and Pazazu in the Exorcist. We watch from the precipice below, as thunder bolts roar and lightning cracks the desert sky.

A child cries:
Crazy, crazy fucking world...crazy goddamn world we're living in...

The demon taunts:
Have a baby, slap its face...

The ocean floor cracks open as the maelstrom subsides and our descent into the Malebolges of Hell is followed by an ascent into Paradise and to the Gates of St. Peter...

You Rang...

In death there is rebirth. A rising up through the clouds on shaft of light, which gently places us into a plush green garden; where a waterfall gently pools, and a stream meanders passed. Floating upon it are all the things we held as precious before our souls were shed of their earthly vessels: a competitive match of bowling; a rooster welcoming a dew filled morning, the gentle cry of a newborn babe. To Hell and back all within the first song.

As a wrought iron gate creaks open at the beginning of track 2, we are warmly welcomed into another strange and beautiful world. An immense, rolling grassland, where herds of raptors scamper and pterodactyls pepper the deep, azure skies.

Brother and sister imps smile and dance playfully around the spaceship parked nearby. They giggle and dance to a tribal rhythm as our cordial mad scientist host enquires…

Oh, won't you tell me, what's your name…?

"Ricky", an homage to their soundman Ric Wallace, is a warming fire on a cold winter's day. The drum sound is rich and harmonious. The bass tone is thick and milky. Gibby's use of his voice modulator, or Gibbytronix as it has come to be known, is subtle and subdued, weaving a web of sound around a prog-rock riff that dips and swirls like a Pteranodon in a phugoid.

"X-Ray" spins a tale of child-like wonderment at the beauty of the seemingly 10-foot tall dental assistant, whose needle we willingly accept into our flesh just to have the glory of her standing over us. We catch a quick glimpse of her perfect breasts down her shirt as she injects the serum, and we drool from our numbed lower lip onto our plastic apron.

'My God, it seems like just the other day, but it might have been one hundred years before…'

"X-Ray" ends in a guitar solo that hovers like a cloud of nitrous oxide radiating the crepuscular rays of the sun.

The ad-libbed sermon of John W. Smoke Jr gives way to a song that was written with the hopes of getting Roky Erikson to sing it. Although "Roky" retained its name despite the disinterest of the legendary singer of the 13th Floor Elevators. Roky, the man, had his bouts with mental instability in the past, and the day the Butthole Surfers invited him over to the ranch for some BBQ, he spent much of the time locked in the bathroom spacing out on the psychedelic wallpaper that adorned the walls.

Jeff:
"I remember he'd been in trouble for stealing neighbors mail and maybe a little fire at his mamma's…I wrote the melody for the song on bass for him to

play to. [It] never happened 'cause he stayed in our arty bathroom the whole time. I think he realized I ripped off an Iron Butterfly song. (jokes)"
[Jeff: forum post, 2007]

Though the demo the band played for Roky Erikson didn't move him into the recording studio to lay down a vocal track, they did get to spend a pretty surreal day with one of their musical heroes, walking the grounds of the ranch, smoking grass and gaining a newfound perspective from a legend who, much like themselves, eluded real success while imitators lived in mansions in the Hollywood hills. Left with little else than an enigma upon Roky's departure, Gibby laid down the vocals himself.

Oddly, though, the walk through the haze of scattered memories was just as fitting for Gibby to profess as it would have been for Roky himself. The previous eight years were like the blur of a lifetime, from his detour from star accountant to his destiny as a Butthole Surfer. Few bands that had been around twice as long could boast such exploits, from near starvation and homelessness to a palatial ranch in the country, and still be able to cite a body of work that was so unabashedly uncompromising.

It appeared that Corey Rusk had delivered on his promise to promote the band while still letting them do whatever it was that popped into their heads on any given day. And the band had delivered on their promise to Corey as well: that if left alone to create their art with no tethered restrictions, they would reap financial and reputational rewards for his label. They did, and the success of Touch & Go Records could be directly linked to the success of the Butthole Surfers. A new Butthole Surfers release was like an event.

In a time before the Jesus Lizard had formed and after Big Black had broken up, the Butthole Surfers were able to keep T&G afloat despite the fact that no other band on the label came even close to moving as much product or generating as much revenue. Their acquisition in 1984, along with Terry Tolkin's business savvy, salvaged the label from certain financial ruin. Now, their success afforded Corey the ability to shape Touch & Go into the label he had could only have dreamt about when deciding to go into the business of selling music.

Hairway to Steven had been one of the most anticipated releases of 1988, and upon hitting the streets that April, the Butthole Surfers became the little band that could do no wrong. The album wove a tapestry of preternatural beauty hiding behind a veil of grotesque faces and crude, representational drawings that stood in the place of proper song titles.

The artwork on *Hairway to Steven* left Ric Wallace as baffled as it did the fans. For as the fans were left scrambling to decipher song titles and lyrics, Ric was left wondering why all the work he had done recording and co-producing the record wasn't credited anywhere on the sleeve. Paul brought the proofs to his house to check out, giggling, and Ric sat there stunned.

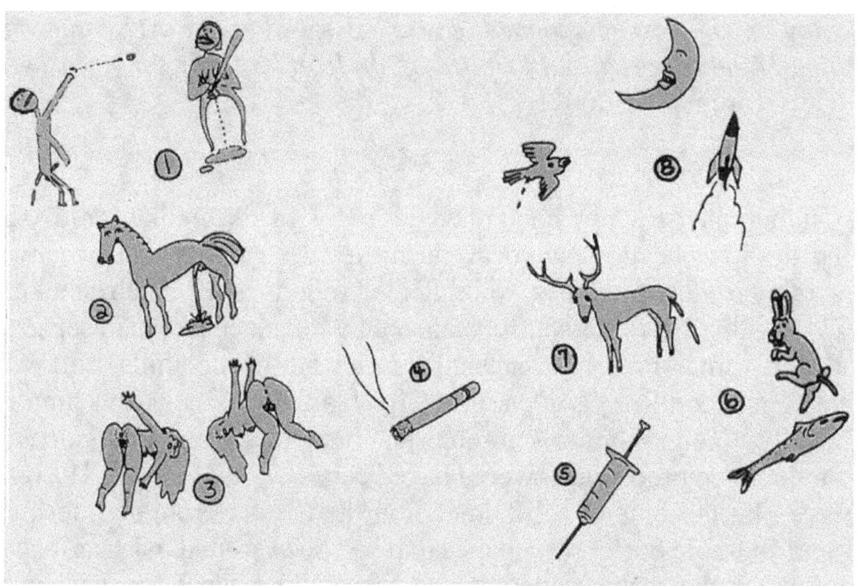

Hairway to Steven *track list (all rights reserved)*

❧

Ric Wallace:
"Whoa...where are the credits and song titles, Paul?....Oh, there is no writing or printing or anything except a bunch of fucking nonsense little pictures?... Paul, what the fuck?? And of course [Paul] thought it was just the coolest thing in the world: an album without any titles or credits." Of course, they never compensated me for all that work either. But I loved the band and took serious pride in what I was doing so I stuck around anyway. Sheesh, I never really forgave them though." [email, 2010]

❧

Ric had been recruited onto the Buttholes' own Mothership and felt the same calling and sense of purpose as Paul and Gibby. What the Buttholes were doing was something extraordinary, and something that had hardly been attempted before: a punk rock acid test.

Gibby
© *William McConnell*

Some could argue that bands like Chrome, Swans, Throbbing Gristle, or Sonic Youth were first to incorporate the aesthetics of the counter-culture revolution and excesses of the 60's and 70's into punk rock, but few could deny that many of these artists were, themselves, anxiously awaiting a new Butthole Surfers record, if only to see what they were going to do next.

What the Butthole Surfers did on *Hairway to Steven* was bridge the vast expanse once thought to exist between classic rock's hedonism and punk rock's visceral immediacy. It was an album that hippies could "get", and punks still respect. It was psychedelic, but not pretentious. It was welcoming yet imposing, crude, yet sublime. The nasty brown stain they left on the carpet of rock music had been steam-cleaned into a gleaming, sweet-smelling shag, rife for rolling around upon in an uncontrollable bliss.

While keeping their convictions intact, *Hairway to Steven* showed that the Butthole Surfers were not just a bunch of stoned guys with lots of effects but were a bunch of *talented* stoned guys {and a gal} with lots of effects. They happened to be strong players, and solid song writers, and even, by golly, commercially viable. It wasn't long after its release that major labels started taking serious notice of the band.

What major labels were beginning to see was that underground music could be modestly lucrative. A few scant months after *Hairway to Steven* was released, Warner Brothers would unleash Jane's Addiction's *Nothing's Shocking* upon the world. *Nothing's Shocking* was a Bauhaus-meets-Led Zeppelin styled platter that garnered rave reviews from critics everywhere, and even produced a quasi-hit single in "Jane Says", something that would have seemed impossible just a few scant years prior.

Back when record companies were making HUGE profits from manufactured pop artists, there was very little incentive to risk the almighty bottom line for artistic integrity. Prince, Michael Jackson, and Madonna, and producer assembled boy bands like New Kids on the Block were not only selling records like wildfire but were merchandizing machines.

Everything from t-shirts to toy dolls with their likenesses flew off the shelves of toy stores everywhere. There seemed to be little reason for labels to nurture new bands, and even fewer reasons for impatient labels to sign a band without the safety net of knowing there was going to be a hit song. In this time before internet downloads record sales were brisk and the bread winners were rock stars, not punk rockers.

But underground bands like Husker Du, the Replacements, and REM were prolific tour de forces. They booked their own tours and produced their own LPs, from songs to cover artwork. They designed and manufactured their own t-shirts and handled all aspects of merchandizing. They were self-sufficient micromanaged machines by necessity, and they had been doing it steadily for years. They were seasoned veterans of all aspects of the business of music and their ardent fans were like a graveyard full of loyal zombies, constantly craving more: more shows, more records, more brains. Fanatics of the Butthole Surfers spread the almighty 'word on the street' that they were the greatest thing since the Beatles, and when even mildly chided, were inclined expound with the exacerbation and vehemence of a bug-eyed Al Pacino in *...And Justice for All.*

Fans of the Butthole Surfers had appeared as guests on the David Letterman Show, touting their name as the show's producer scrambled for the edit button. They starred in major motion pictures and wore their t-shirts while walking down Hollywood Blvd. They themselves were in bands that were selling millions of records, as well as roaming major labels record company halls as interns.

Soon it was difficult for labels to ignore these bands and their DIY ethics. And with underground bands looking for little else other than some tour support and some

228

small pittance of advance money to record, the label would need to do little else than to front some studio time and distribute the resulting product. And so, little by little, some staunchly independent bands began to make the jump to the majors.

But the Buttholes were not that all that anxious to have a major label record executive watching over them, just yet. Labels, in this time before Nirvana's breakthrough, were notorious for snatching up small bands, choking the life out of them, then dropping them, leaving them to wallow in bargain bin obscurity. For many bands, even in this age when punk rock was little more than a fleeting memory, signing to a major label was still considered the kiss of death.

For unless a band was willing to sell out its values, there seemed little way that a major label was going to support their drug habits and artistic vision for the drop in the bucket they garnered. Jane's Addiction's modicum of success was a fluke, and even with the seemingly new precedent set of being able to market a band with some substance, most of the majors weren't quite sure they could sell a band named the Butthole Surfers.

The Butthole Surfers were living comfortably doing everything they wanted the way they wanted. They were in no rush to be major label artists. And, while some tour support would be nice, and a signing bonus would be even nicer, they were content with being the highest grossing independent band in the world.

Fine Whiskey and Women

After recording and mixing wrapped on what would become *Hairway to Steven*, the band took a short excursion back to London to do a couple of shows and some advance press promotion. The mayhem which ensued was a testament to just how lofty their reputation had grown over just the last 6 months since their previous visit. Disappointed fans resorted to rioting in the streets when the first of the two shows they booked sold out, practically before tickets were made available to the general public.

The British press ate it up, and the riots harkened back to the earliest days of punk rock itself when worker's unions took to the streets and tensions between blacks and whites seethed to a boiling point. The chaos in front of the club, where scores of hoodlums were attacking ticketholders as they walked up to the door, only added to the frenzied atmosphere inside the club: the Chicago National Convention relocated across the pond.

The Mean Fiddler was oversold and the walls were wet like a cold beer can in the hot summer sun. The band arrived at the club after they ate some dinner and the restlessness outside was already well underway. With the array of cops and riot police lining the streets, they figured that there was no way the show was going to happen. But as the situation was brought under some semblance of control outside, the lights inside the club dimmed and they strapped on their instruments, inviting chaos in.

In the blind revelries of those few lucky enough to have gotten hold of a ticket, Gibby gets hit by an errant bottle thrown out of the darkness. He sneers into to the crowd, ensconced in echo and a slight flange: "Die…blow your head off…" Blood mats his hair, already drenched in sweat and beer, and forms a trickle down his cheek, as Jeff's bass swirls into "Backass".

There were no films behind them this night, no lights, and no *Ta-Da the Shit Lady*. None of the theatrics of their previous trip. Just the music, and that would suffice.

It was a violent and a mesmerizing culmination of nearly a full year of non-stop touring. Another show two weeks later at the University of London was forced to sell advance tickets only and forego any ticket sales the day of the show at all in hopes to thwart the angry hoodlums from showing up. The show was sold out a week in advance anyway and went off without a hitch, though many were still left outside in the cold. After the ULU show they took off from Heathrow as heroes. Critics and fans alike were left in amazement at the potential of this band to change the world.

Most critics in Europe were suspect of hype. Bands from America were ogled with an especially leery eye. An American band as outrageous as the Butthole Surfers would have a lot to prove. A multi-media light show and a film barrage on a shoestring budget would draw yawns if not backed by something of substance to sink their notoriously bad teeth into.

But even amongst the critics who found the band crass and cacophonous, there seemed also to be a respectful recognition of their potential. The power they exhibited on stage transcended mere music and art but forayed into politics and psychology as well. Even the most jaded among them couldn't help but to find the Buttholes intriguing, if not necessarily enthralling.

They may have been base and juvenile, but there was a certain childlike playfulness in their music and presentation. An innate and primal fascination with torturing the audience which evoked Pavlov's reflex and response studies: the Sudden Conversion methods which stretched the Trans-Marginal Inhibition rate to its breaking point.

The bizarre mixture of violence and sex is something which Freud might have attributed to some trauma during the Infantile Sexuality period of their lives. They abide by an Altered- Reality Principal; where the ID rules all, with no rationality of the ego, and no guilt of the super-ego. They were anarchic and apolitical, with a tongue-in-cheek humor not unlike an HL Mencken. Their espousal to a rule of law in which there is no rule of law creates a platform that becomes a political movement itself, as the community of freaks who follow them create a scene all their own, outside of the clubs and long after the band has left the stage.

Often, the criticism hurled at the band was that they didn't seem to have any agenda behind it all, other than to simply fuck with people's heads. These critics were looking for the Butthole Surfers to create a Bill of Rights for their constituents to adhere to. If there was none, they would contend, then it was the Butthole Surfers who were held responsible for those led astray in the battle against the bug-eyed, boll-legged normal man. If only the freaks would rise up, we could win. The Butthole Surfers seemed to be our last, best hope, and if only they realized this fact themselves, perhaps the world could be saved.

And what if the Butthole Surfers did win? What if everyone decided that they weren't going to work and that they were going to paint and write and make music and do drugs and roam the country like 'Easy Rider'. The rabid fans who travelled the countryside to witness the band brought with them inevitable visions of the Butthole Surfers as the next Grateful Dead. The fire on the mountain sparks a movement and the movement makes a community.

There was a belief for a fleeting moment that it could happen. The riots, the madness, the music all proved that there were other people who believed it too. Despite the detractors, there were also the believers, and a certain idealism that the band created and fostered among them. They led by example and showed that the dream was possible. That true freedom could be attained if you just ignored the oppressors and did whatever you wanted any old time.

By offering a code of ethics, the Butthole Surfers would be repudiating freedom. By carefully explaining an agenda, they themselves would become usurpers, idols, messiahs.

They were just a band. They weren't Jello Biafra or Bono or Billy Bragg. They had no desire to become preachers or politicians. The job of interpreting and analyzing was left up to the fans and critics. So little did the band care to become the voice for a lost and disenfranchised generation that they didn't even bother to title their songs or print their own names on their record sleeves.

The unveiling of *Hairway to Steven* to the public in April of 1988 brought with it an eerie quiet. With most of the record having been unleashed over the previous summer and fall, the band saw little reason to kill themselves with yet another grueling tour back and forth across the United States once the record hit the streets. The true *Hairway to Steven* tour took place seven months before the album came out. They kept themselves relatively grounded, playing some local gigs, while also hitting some major market venues in California and the Northeast, but avoided another tour in favor of letting their fans steep for a while. Commanding as much as $15,000 per gig meant the band could drop into a city and hang out and party for a few days before returning to Texas to play some basketball, visit a local swimming hole, or work out some new material in their elaborate home studio.

Touring was certainly not what it had been in the old days. Hauling trailer loads of equipment and films, merchandise and staff. It was no longer a matter of hopping in the gutted "Lady Killer" and booking shows in transit as they drove from shithole to shithole. Tours needed to be charted, guarantees needed to be made, and assurances given to ensure losses were kept to a bare minimum. A punk ethos was fine and dandy, but if an independent band was going to stay alive, itineraries and business matters needed to be closely monitored. And under Gibby's watchful eye, the business of the band was thriving. The Buttholes realized long ago that nothing kills a band faster than meal shortages and destitution, and they were not ready to die just yet.

But with the summer of 1988 beginning to wane, they were finally coaxed off their asses with an invite they simply couldn't refuse: an offer to record some proper tracks at Maida Vale studios in London for broadcast on the John Peel radio show. Coupled with an invite to co-headline a slot at the Futurama Festival in Belgium, it gave the band just the fire they needed to get out of Texas and make another trip overseas.

Both shows gave the band an opportunity to unveil upon the European freaks, yet again, the newest batch of songs they had written during their short respite from traveling. A trip over the pond was also a good way to get some relief from the searing Texas heat. Without the burden of a grinding tour upon them, they had spent most of that summer forging even more new material, much of which soared into the heavens like thundering, sonic landscapes.

John Anson Ford Theatre, 6/10/88
© Krk Dominguez

The new tracks brought the focus further away from lyrical content and further into a kaleidoscopic prism of sounds and colors. They ensconced the listener into an "Altered States"- like hyperbaric chamber. The sarcophagus which holds our vessels cannot contain the spirit, which journeys upward and outward like Helios riding his chariot across the dappled sky. There was a cosmic life-force, and on a particularly good night, the band held our hands into the mysterious abyss.

The frustration of music, Jimi Hendrix once lamented, is that you can drink it in but never feel quenched; can feel it but never touch it; love it, but never hold it in your arms. But if we believed in the message and held it in our hearts, then music can transcend mere auditory stimulation. It could infect and enrapture into enlightenment.

It was everything Charles Manson and David Koresh used to recruit their followers, minus the messianic rock star worship and megalomania. The spirit of Art born from the belief of love and beauty, is an energy that creates the epiphany.

> ***'In order to find the truth, we must look to the poets, not the politicians'***
> ***- Plato***

The Butthole Surfers never felt they needed to say much of anything at all on the subject. One didn't have to ask what songs were about or for a reason behind what they said or did. Many interviewers tried and failed, so it was of little use to even pose the question. By merely inviting the listener in to their strange and magical world you became a denizen of it. A place where you are free to dance and sing and love without fear or inhibition. It was the embodiment of the spirit of punk without having to stand on a soapbox or stab a safety pin through your eye.

But as the Butthole Surfers gained a fan base outside of the stodgy old punk rockers that made up the crowds of yore, and ticket prices crept up to $10 or $15, the mumbles and grumbles became audible from the streets that the band was selling out their ethics and abandoning their original fans for new ones.

It was a no-win situation for the few bands that had escaped the deathtrap of a career in punk rock alive. Newer bands could get away with higher ticket prices because the precedent of a $3 show with the likes of the Big Boys, the Dicks, Butthole Surfers, and the Offenders had been set. Selfish punks would seemingly rather have their favorite bands starve or break up rather than to be forced to pay the few extra dollars to support the bands and the scene.

But the Butthole Surfers were committed to staying together and making music for as long as possible, not starving. Indeed, though, nothing lasts forever, and though the band didn't know it at the time, this trip abroad would be their last together. The Peel Session they recorded in September of 1988 would be their last formal studio session of the year, and their last ever as a 5-piece unit.

Time marches forward, and it leads to an inevitable end. And when times at their most pristine and sublime, as they were for the Butthole Surfers in the fall of 1988, it's hard to imagine anything else other than the wonder, amazement, and infinity of the present moment. The never-ending possibility of the Now. It was how the band seemed to live, and how they challenged their listeners to live as well. Time, however, was drawing ever nearer toward the end.

The band flew to London in the waning days of summer and settled into Maida Vale studios to produce a session of unparalleled brilliance. The three unreleased songs they recorded, "Nee Nee", "Edgar", and "Blindman", were a bacchanalian trinity of raucous hedonism. Their debut here on Peel was like a door being thrown open at the Roman coliseum. Growling Tigers, and doomed contestants and the roar blood-thirsty spectators, swirled together into a blur of silken tapestries and disemboweled gladiators.

Manic guitar solos layered over our twin drummers scrambling about their kits behind a dizzying wall of vocal effects. These were just the sort of ingredients fans had come to expect, and this new crop of sticky buds was inhaled as some of the best material in the band's already rich catalogue of primo shit.

The session put an exclamation point at the end of the long, beautiful story that had begun in the infancy of the Reagan White House. Now, in a cloud of conspiracy and controversy, his tenure was also drawing to a sunset.

Paul 10/24/88 I-Beam
© Greg Hubbard

The Iran-Contra hearings had played out in front of congress involving the sale of U.S. arms to Iran in exchange for hostages they held. Money from the sale of these arms was funneled, against the Boland Amendment, to fund US-backed Contra rebels involved in a bloody guerilla war in Nicaragua. Reagan's vice-president, George HW Bush. was a former CIA director and his claims of ignorance seemed dubious at best. But, instead of securing a lengthy prison sentence, he secured the GOP presidential nomination. Perhaps it was our own president and senior staff members who were the ones living outside of the rule of law, not the Butthole Surfers.

The Butthole Surfers stood as the polar opposite to Ronald Reagan and the "Me Generation" he fostered in during his time in office. The Butthole Surfers and The Reagan administration spent the entire decade proving the Law of Polarity. They were the Yang to Reagan's Yin, and it appeared to the naïve that, since the Butthole Surfers had somehow outlasted Ronald Reagan, that the Just and the Good might be able to prevail against the greed, hypocrisy and warmongering which had run rampant during his administration. The Butthole Surfers were on top of the world as Reagan, the Moral Majority, and PMRC were exiting the scene. The war was over! We won! MISSION ACCOMPLISHED!

Not many opposing forces survived conflict with Ronald Wilson Reagan. His will was carried out by the Moral Majority at home, the Military Industrial Complex stretching across the European continent, and the CIA's tentacles dipping into the banana republics of Central America. His goal of bankrupting the Soviet Union by engaging in a costly and dangerous nuclear arms race was nearly coming to fruition, and his legacy as a hawk stretched back to his governorship of the state of California, where State Troopers beat and opened fire upon student protestors at People's Park in Berkeley, killing student James Rector, and injuring hundreds more.

"If it takes a bloodbath, let's get it over with", he was quoted as saying around the time of the People's Park protests. His methods were so successful in his home state they were soon adopted at the federal level by the Nixon Administration, who less than a year after People's Park, sent National Guard units to open fire on protestors at Kent State, killing four students, and wounding nine others. There is no substitute for effectiveness.

And now here were the Butthole Surfers, just weeks away from outlasting 'Old Cancer Butt', as Gibby referred to him. When the band struggled to find drummers and bass player, it seemed impossible they would make it to see the end of Reagan's first term, but now they were watching the Gipper ride into the sunset back to his Rancho del Cielo just outside of Santa Barbara, CA: ex-President of the United States.

Winter was coming, however, and darkness was looming on the horizon. Playtime was drawing to an end. As Reagan passed the torch to a new commander-in-chief, so too would the Butthole Surfers come to pass. There was still life to be lived for this Butthole Surfers line-up, however, and it was to be cherished as a newborn babe in spring.

No Man is an Island...

By the time autumn's wind blew chilly and cold in that year of 1988, the band was in the middle of their longest U.S. tour in over a year. They were finally hitting markets neglected since the release of *Hairway to Steven* six months prior. Kathleen, who had been dancing with the band steadily since early 1987 decided to head back to NYC, making a mere handful of appearances on the tour. She would go on to shed the shackles of Ta-Da the Shit Lady and focus on her own, true persona. She released several harrowing 7"s with her friend Jason Young under another of her alter egos, LIVIIING, then got a band together she called the Beme Seed.

It was the sad end of an era, but the Butthole Surfers were no longer the band whose shows might dissolve into an onstage "sex show", or find Gibby stumbling dumb-founded about the stage wearing nothing but his birthday suit. They had matured into a more high-brow art. Shows were more religious exercises than free for all Roman orgies, and the band were the high priests of the festivities. Their live shows became like rituals performed by shaman who were moved and possessed with a light from above. They channeled their energy from far beyond the earthly realm and became the experienced captains on their voyage into the cosmos.

The band that had dissected rock'n'roll to its most primal core was now putting the flesh back onto the bones and unveiling an entirely new monster underneath. Beautiful and grotesque, it stood to be gawked at like Joseph Merrick on a pedestal at a London Hospital.

As the lights dim, we prepare ourselves for the specimen that is about to be revealed. A menacing hum drones on from the depths of our souls. It changes pitch, as if we are surfing on a sine wave; up and down and up again our stomachs grow queasy with dread and anticipation…the steady drone punctuated every so often with a rapid-fire pop of gunshots,until finally the hum fades off to oblivion. Birds chirp and dogs begin to bark a frenzied warning, as a disjointed curator welcomes us all to the proceedings.

Brothers and sisters in the front row….

The air implodes as if a vacuum sealed bag is being popped around our head. White light fills two movie screens and forms a star of glare on the steel rim of one of the two drum sets at the back of the stage, like a vast array of cold steel Victorian medical devices shining under a surgery lamp. Another rapid fire pop startles us out of our transfixion.

Brothers and sisters…brothers and sisters…brothers and sisters…

Sirens wail in the distance. A steady burst of a single strobe light reveals the horror before us. The words echo that of a diatribe by Mark Farner on Grand Funk Railroad's '*LIVE ALBUM*'. Here, however, they become like the paranoid ramblings of an inmate in 'Titticut Follies'.

There is a person out there who may call himself your brother, but he's not…So when he tries to hand you something…don't take it…don't take it…

Through the darkness a shadow play of figures, each casting a silhouetted likeness against the screened backdrop, which has changed from stark white to the contorted visage of an electroshock therapy treatment: much like the one we suspect is in store for us should we venture deeper down this jungle trail down which we've embarked.

Brothers and sisters….brothers and sisters…brothers and sisters…

The voice repeats as our beloved brother and sister twins begin to conjure the rumble of an impending thunderstorm. An uneasy fear settles over the spectators. Anxiety, combined with the disconcerting dichotomy of light and darkness. The danger signs which our brains would normally innately heed plead for us to run away and save ourselves, instead we stand doomed like lab rats injected with disease under a mass of infected bodies, each clawing on top for escape. Alive with Pleasure.

As the scene plays out, all our senses are attacked in a blitzkrieg of lights and sounds: the flash of bombs raining down onto the streets, and the rapid return of anti-aircraft shrapnel screeching toward the heavens. The participants stand, shell-shocked by song after unreleased song, trying to decipher the melodies through the suffocating billows of smoke wafting in their faces and the intertwining vines of limbs riding the crowd and flailing spastically through the clouds like incapacitated birds being sucked into a jet engine.

Slowly, a rumble of a bass guitar emerges from the soup, sounding as if it is being played in reverse, the chaos slowly subsides into a steady, churning stew. A disembodied voice rises from the broth, unseen, the orator hiding off in the shadows to the side of the stage, twisting knobs like a maniacal puppeteer dangling his marionette…

I don't recall you, so I won't involve you, the window's quite small so I might need a symbol to fly…

A cathedral sized riff plays as 17 voices speaking simultaneously in wild tongues cavort, growl chortle, and endlessly weave a tale, like the bride of Odysseus endlessly weaves her husband's funeral shroud.

Shadowy men on a shadowy planet, 12/12/87
© Ken Salerno

It's pretty simple, your body's a temple, it looks good on paper, but paper's not here….

The bass is as thick as soup, and the guitar squeaks and squeals like a freight train's wheels: cold steel upon steel:

I've never seen you, your flesh and your body yields only a symbol so that we can fly….

Those who have chosen to participate in the proceedings are confronted with visions of their own mortality. The legacy of senseless suffering that came before our birth. The passage of time leading to our inevitable end: the end of our existence, but not the eternity of senseless suffering.

Teresa:
"We salvaged beauty from an immersion into the depraved."

And as the last rambling screed from Gibby's fades into the darkness, and the house lights cause our eyes to ache and squint, we are not the same person that entered the hall some 90 mins earlier. Like church or the grainy films of a Nazi concentration camp, we've come face to face with our own mortality and our darkest curiosities. The part we play within Nature, and the part we play in perpetuating the cycle of horrors.

This relentless maelstrom played out night after night, town after town. The crowds stood frozen and stunned, exhausted, and disoriented. But, after the show was over, those masses went home, sobered up, and went to bed. The band didn't have that luxury, and the stress and strain of this constant bombardment of the senses began to exhaust its toll on the band, both mentally and physically.

Teresa, 10/24/88
© Greg Hubbard

Teresa began suffering from extreme vertigo and on several occasions dropped limp behind her kit, vomiting and convulsing, forcing King to finish some shows alone behind his drum kit. It was a heavy price to pay to entertain, especially when most people in attendance seemed content to just get high and slam dance into a stranger or two or loiter near the bar.

Although the tour schedules had certainly become more rational than in the early years, the unrelenting attack on the senses their shows had become was like a Navy Seal stress test. Where the audience had some time to heal it was the band that was at it again the next night, and the night after that. It was like treading water with 50lb weights attached to their waists.

The brutal three-month long jaunt finally culminated with a New Year's Eve performance alongside the Cramps and the Dead Milkmen at the Warner Theatre in Washington DC. It's one of only a few times that King recalls feeling star struck. Sharing the stage with Lux Interior; clad in leather and wearing size 13 stiletto pumps. His darling wife Ivy Rorschach beside him chewing gum with ennui as he rolled and writhed around the stage. It was true success to be coupled with these icons of rock'roll.

King had grown up listening to the Cramps, and although they had been creeping out audiences since before the time of the Sex Pistols, the Cramps were one of the few bands who could rival the Buttholes on stage. After nearly 15 years they were still holding strong with their own psychotic hillbilly beach parties that some people called concerts. Along with the Buttholes full blown freakout in effect, it was sure to provide all the insanity necessary to put the icing on an insane year.

The year of 1988 was going out like the blast of a champagne cork. The Buttholes were at the height of their prowess, and the height of their popularity and the theatre was tightly packed long before the Cramps took the stage to see the Butthole Surfers opening set that night.

It seemed like they could not be stopped. 1988 was being bid a fond farewell, and the hope and anticipation of a new year was on the horizon. But with all the hope and celebrations, came some soul searching that often left more questions than answers. Amidst all the success, where was the money? Why was it that Jane's Addiction and the Pixies and the Red Hot Chili Peppers were signed to big label deals and the members of the Butthole Surfers were still living together in a single house?

Teresa:
"We ran into the Chili Peppers after they had their first round of success... and Flea told us they all went out and bought a car... like a retro kind of car. We were like 'Nooo... Really?!?!'... The only way we were able to keep recording was to not take money personally... We would have fallen apart."
[phone 7/26/14]

The Butthole Surfers could definitely draw a crowd and had an avid following both in the States and around the world. They had been headliners on bills that were filled with major label acts who were getting paid twice as much money per gig, plus some actual tour support from their record companies. And while concerts and t-shirts provided a healthy cash flow, it didn't translate into brisk record sales. The road was where the Butthole Surfers made their money, and it seemed like the only choice was between staying off the road and not eating or touring and not sleeping.

What could be the reason they couldn't translate the concert windfalls into record sales or a major label contract? Could it really be the word "Butthole" in their moniker? The PMRC had all but been vanquished in the previous year, appeased by record labels slapping warning notices on all records containing profanity and questionable content.

With these warnings secured, the flood gates had been broken open. Major labels like EMI and Columbia began releasing records by rap artists like NWA and Ice-T, who pushed the boundaries that had been avoided since the PMRC had begun its Witch Trials.

It didn't take long before labels saw the chance to use the warning stickers to their advantage, and make huge profits based on controversy. By slapping a label on a record, all bets were off. Now kids everywhere were pumping their fists and singing along to songs like "Fuck Da Police" and "Girls: LGBNAF" (that's "Let's Get Buck Naked and Fuck").

Political rabble rousing by bands like Public Enemy brought the revolution off the television screens and into the bedrooms of mainstream America. The housewives had gotten their WARNING labels and now that they had been warned; there was no limit to what record companies would release. Soon the labels and novelty acts they signed were releasing anything guaranteed to shock and offend to generate quick sales.

Conservatives whined and burned CDs in piles outside their churches. The Moral Majority changed its moniker to the Christian Coalition and as rap music came out of the ghetto and into the houses of middle-class white people, cultural and racial lines were blurred. White kids soon were buying rap records and embracing what came to be known as hip hop culture. It was called much worse by the fear-mongers who believed tribes of black headhunters were snatching white children from their clean, vanilla suburbs.

But this trend showed that white kids were just as pissed off about the bigotry and class warfare of their parent's generation. They had grown tired of the economic inequality and of being disenfranchised by The Man, and white kids became the meal ticket for artists who once could only be heard in small clubs in the Bronx. The turkey of nearly a decade of conservative leadership was now coming home to roost.

And yet still, after 8 years of Ronald Reagan reigning with an iron fist, his former partner in crime, George H.W. Bush, was readying himself for Inauguration Day. If it wasn't clear enough already, it was becoming clearer by the day that Washington was not the place to look for solutions to the stagnant economy, divisive class warfare, and worsening unemployment levels. The rich got richer, and the poor got ignored. There had always been an element who protested the injustice of inequality, but with the widening chasm between the haves and the have-nots, the mistrust of politicians that had prevailed since Watergate festered into rage.

Many of the new rap artists, like the punks and hippies before them, were kids who saw the politicians, as well as cops, teachers, and even their own oblivious parents, as part of the problem, not as the solution. In 1983 the Big Boys sang:

We are all white niggers \ We are all white niggers \ We won't be white niggers no more...

In 1988, NWA sang:

Fuck the Police coming straight from the underground \ a young nigga's got it bad 'cause I'm brown \ and not the other color the police think \ they have the authority to kill a minority.

Both NWA and the Big Boys could point to James Brown as a major influence. Both band bucked the establishment and each could relate to being enemies of the mainstream 'normies'. By putting themselves on the frontlines of a war against stupidity, punks had gotten a glimpse at what many black youths had seen in ghettos in everyday in every city in Amerikkka and could feel a kinship.

Though the racism sung about in songs like Public Enemy's "Fight the Power" was far beyond the scope of what most suburban white kids could truly understand, the punks had been hassled by cops for years. They were beaten up for the color of their hair, not for the color of their skin. Punks could respect bands like Public Enemy and were on a similar wavelength, if not necessarily on the same page.

Often, though, as rap artists flooded the market, hip hop became a trend and a farce: the next generation of plastic, talentless acts that A&R reps fed like Pabulum to America's youth. Rap, and hip hop culture became another fashion statement. Another compartmentalized genre that turned kids into robots, much the way heavy metal become, or punk rock for that matter.

With warning labels on records, anything could go, and record companies seemed to look for any artist who could conjure up sales through some First Amendment battle on a TV talk show. It seemed that nothing, indeed, was shocking, as rap and rock bands alike jockeyed to make records more violent, profane and sexually explicit than the last; replete with TV audiences rioting and breaking Geraldo Rivera's nose or bloodying up Morton Downey, Jr on air. It was a multi-media blitz of the ridiculous and the sublime.

Yet, as shock began to sell, it was the Butthole Surfers, who could certainly shock and offend, who were in danger of becoming a footnote amongst myriad of artists who stole their histrionics, but who far too often missed the point completely.

Straight from the Underground...

The Butthole Surfers are from Texas and Texas is a world all its own. The hype and the nonsense that was going on outside the boundaries of their insular little prairie land mattered little to these citizens of the Lone Star State. Texas had seen trends come and go and they continued to thrive by ignoring them all. Any new fad was greeted with little more than an eye roll and the Butthole Surfers, as consummate Texans, continued to create their own art in a vacuum.

Paul was becoming an expert in production and soon Gibby and Jeff began getting proficient with all the new electronics scattered about their house in the country. As their answer to the recent techno dance craze, they started recording under the moniker of the JackOfficers. Although it sounded little like the Butthole Surfers, the JackOfficers celebrated the free spirit and experimentation of the band. After spending a few weeks at home recording, they now had some songs on a cassette to play before gigs.

The Butthole Surfers carried the JackOfficers tape with them to LA and Phoenix, before playing a show in Austin on February 10. Much the early months of 1989 were spent in their home studio combing through hundreds of hours of DAT tapes they had recorded on their last trek across the USA, in hopes of finally releasing a live record. It was a long time past, and many bass players ago, since they had given fans a live document. It was about time to showcase the band they had become since Jeff had joined.

Certainly, without the benefit of visual aids, a live record could do little to capture the sheer spectacle of the band, but the eventual release of 'Double Live' on LP cassette and on the emerging media of CD could allow the listener to focus on the songs without any of the distractions, something that would be impossible for the actual concert attendee. Stripped of the lights and the films and the theatrics, one could focus on the rich and varied material spanning the band's entire career.

Though the release of 'Double Live' in May of 1989 did little to quell the tide of illegal bootlegs, and the limited pressing of about 20,000 LPs, cassettes and CDs meant that only among the most ardent fans would own one, its release on their own 'Latino Bugger Veil Records' gave the band a chance to sell the album without the shackles of splitting the proceeds 50\50 with Touch & Go, nor worrying much about promotion at all.

The recent advent and huge popularity of the CD format meant fans were replacing entire discographies of LPs, and money began to flow in again from formerly stagnant sales of older material. This infusion of cash was graciously welcome and prevented the need for a huge tour, something that was becoming increasingly difficult, demanding, and dreadful.

The excitement on the streets of a live document showcasing the band they loved left fans in a frenzy of excitement, but it did little to change the increasing unrest within the band's ranks. Slowly but steadily, over the past months, they had been drifting apart. A commune for so long, they could barely remember what it was like to lead a normal life, nor what a normal life even was.

For years, 'normal' meant grueling drives and endless tours, followed by everyone piling out of the RV and into the house they all shared, or onto the floors of some understanding friend's apartment. Recording in their kitchen and pooling their money to buy equipment, food, and beer. Any productive period spent laying down tracks at their makeshift home du jour would be followed by everyone climbing back into the RV and starting the process over again.

It was the only thing they knew and this ethos had given them the modest success they enjoyed, but after nearly a decade together, it was becoming increasingly obvious to everyone, especially the band members themselves, that this was not how normal people lived.

Drifting apart didn't have to mean breaking up. It just meant going home to a life that wasn't focused solely on being a Butthole Surfer 24 hours a day, 7 days a week. Paul was falling in love and was spending less and less time in Driftwood and the sense that someone was missing other than King, the lone Renaissance Man who attempted a life apart from the band, might have been the slap in the face that awoke them from their slumber.

But when Teresa finally decided to pack up and leave, it was a not-so-subtle sign that she was distancing herself from the band for real. She was not taking another brief hiatus or some respite to re-gather herself. Not this time. This time, Teresa's departure was a sign that she was not only leaving the house, she was leaving the band for good.

Teresa:
"I was in the midst of a full-blown nervous breakdown. I was doing drugs, mostly speed at that time. And going away from the band in Austin and doing speed on the side. I'd come back and be all frazzled. It was like I'd skip town and show back up and they'd be like 'what have you been doing?' And I'm like nothing...' I started having horrible fear of plane crashes. And not only was I gonna crash on the plane, but I was out at my parent's house.. my parent's had gone outta town for like three months, and I was housekeeping out there and I kept like taking cover under tables and stuff because I thought a plane was gonna hit the house... So I wasn't doing well. I ended up clearing up later when I decided to stop drinking and got on medication." [phone: 7/26/14]

Teresa's last show with the band was a poorly planned rally put on by the National Organization for the Reformation of Marijuana Laws on the National Mall in Washington DC on the 4th of July. Perhaps befitting, it was a debacle that saw rioting between cops on horses and fans and open weed smoking on the steps of the Lincoln Memorial, while just across the mall Henry Mancini was entertaining the members of congress and high-powered elite: brilliant in concept, but an outright disaster in practice.

NORML's complete lack of preparation for the event left fans, bands, and crews in danger. Fans were beaten and arrested en masse, payments were scarce to non-existent, and the cause bruised due to the cliché stoner ineptitude. It was not quite the fitting farewell to the girl who help advance the Butthole Surfers into the stratosphere, and who became their anchor during the times they were being accused of being women hating sexual predators. But the setting on Washington's National Mall was perhaps an ironic testament to the political force they had become despite their lack of political agenda: the mirror image of the power-mongers swaying to "Moon River" just across the Mall.

The air was rife for riots this particular 4th of July, as the White House had been making a strong push to criminalize flag-burnings and the Supreme Court, in a ruling handed down just a day previous, Missouri v. Reproductive Health Services, ruled in favor of a states right to severely limit funding and counseling a woman's right to choose.

The music became the soundtrack for the crowd lighting their joints from the blazing threads of Old Glory. It was the background music as cop cars were overturned on the streets of the Capital. All this as the day's protests turned into the evening's rock concert. China's Tiananmen Square was packed with students demanding freedom from their government, and it was difficult to see the difference between what was happening there and what was happening on the National Mall here in the Land of the Free. The plug was finally pulled on the concert after about a half-hour and the band retreated to the make-shift backstage area to wait for the tear-gas smoke to clear.

As Teresa pondered her time in the band, she confided in King that she believed what he had done in separating himself from the everyday grind was probably the smartest thing for the sake of sanity. King only declined to leave Austin because he didn't have a license or a way to get into town when he needed, but the point she made was indeed a valid one.

The band had taken its toll on her health and on her personal life, and it was time for her to get it back to some semblance of reality. There would be no hiatus nor hope she would return. Teresa was leaving for good and the Butthole Surfers were again reduced a quartet.

Teresa:
"I had a ballooned out artery and I asked (the doctor) 'Is this because of drugs?' And they said no, this particular type of brain aneurysm you're born with, and at any point in your life you can just drop dead, and we only find it in an autopsy. So you could sort of look at it two ways, like considering everything I'd been through it was a miracle that I just didn't drop dead. I didn't know that I was like a ticking time-bomb."
[phone, 7/26/14]

The document of 'Double Live' released just prior to Teresa leaving had been meant to showcase the band at the height of its powers. Instead, it became a retrospective of Teresa's time spent in the band with Pinkus. The Butthole Surfers were indeed always light-years beyond their recorded output and it was so when releasing this live document as well. For, although Teresa was leaving, the boys were much better prepared this time. The band was not ready to dissolve but was ready instead, like a butterfly emerging from its cocoon, to embark on the next phase of its life.

You Don't Know Me, You Just Know My Name

Upon seeing Gibby, Paul, Jeff, and King onstage in that muddy field in Reading that August day, one could almost mistake them for a normal rock band. A singer, a guitarist, and a bass player all in front of a single, long-haired drummer perched high upon a drum riser. It was the mold of almost every other rock band in the known universe. For fans of the Butthole Surfers, however, the sight was as foreign as the soil upon which they stood; these Texans in England emerging just as the sun peaked from behind the clouds.

There were no car crash films flickering behind them, no blinding strobes, no smoke, no fire, none of the theatrics or distractions of the band's usual stage show: just four men and their music. And this was all they needed to captivate the crowd. And, along with the debris of destroyed guitars and basses that were strewn about the stage, so too laid the scattered remains of the old Butthole Surfers. The Butthole Surfers of yore, where members would leave every few months and meals were almost as scarce as paychecks.

When the destruction was complete, after the feedback of 'The Shah Sleeps in Lee Harvey's Grave" whined to a halt, the new Butthole Surfers plugged in new instruments and danced on the pieces cast about as well as the corpse of what had been.

"Ladies and gentlemen, the most dedicated band in the history of Texas Rock'n'Roll…The goddamn Butthole Surfers!"

This new stripped-down Butthole Surfers unit would become a solid rock freak out. Not the sloppy, lo-fi, southern-fried punk of their early days, or the experimental art damaged drug orgy of yesteryear, but, more a fire-spitting comet of hardcore psychedelic rock, shooting across the intergalactic space somewhere between Hawkwind's "Motorhead"; Blue Cheer's "Second Time Around"; and Steppenwolf's, "Foggy Mental Breakdown".

They were playing in front of more people than they ever had, barring perhaps the Pandora's Music Box fiasco back when Kramer and Teresa were in the band. And, while the fans that caught this wave would never get to meet TA-DA the Shitlady or be called upon to guess how many hairs were growing out of Gibby's mole, they would still be tossed flotsam into previously unchartered territory. The band was now a skeleton crew of the damned, yielding medieval swords that were every bit as scary as anything Ray Harryhausen could conjure. The reckless abandonment and naïveté of their early tours was gone to be sure, but the new, leaner Butthole Surfers was no less committed to warping minds and destroying brain cells.

They not only survived the Reagan Revolution intact, but flourished during it, and launched a revolution of their own from their kitchen studio. Despite the revolving door of bass players and the brief hiatus in 1986, the core constituents of Gibby, Paul,

King, Jeff and Teresa somehow managed to weather the tide of the censorship, bloated patriotism, and religious fanaticism, to emerge battle hardened.

The irony of it all was that the band seemed more poised for success under regime of Ronald Reagan than they seemed to be under George HW Bush, and in front of the throngs of people at the Reading Festival.

What had been a simmering stew of southern psychedelia with Teresa was now a raging torrent of psychotic space metal. They were faster, meaner, and angrier than ever, fueled in part, no doubt, by the desperation of being a band nearly a decade into its existence and still sharing the same house. And though Teresa had moved out and was no longer a Butthole Surfer, the nights spent with her would live on in the hearts of all who had seen her. Like folklore, the memories are recounted in glorious recantations by those sea-faring souls who had sailed there, lost in other-worldly melancholic remembrances. But a new vessel was being readied for the journey onward. There were dangerous seas ahead and some souls would inevitably be lost in the whirlwind.

Among those who were jettisoned was Corey and Touch & Go. For, just after their appearance at Reading, the band would release their final record on the label. Touch & Go and the Butthole Surfers had become nearly synonymous through the 1980's, but the 1980's were drawing to an end, and the times they were indeed a-changin'. After so many years and so many records, the four remaining members of the Butthole Surfers were outgrowing the label they had called home for most of their career.

At the time before *Another Man's Sac* was released, Touch & Go had been, for all intents and purposes, a straight-edge hardcore label. Its roster was comprised of a mere handful of Midwest punk bands, all of whom were friends of Corey's, and none of whom garnished any sort of living wages for him or his small staff of employees.

By the spring of 1984, with most of the bands on the label broken up or wallowing in hardcore oblivion, Touch & Go was nearly bankrupt. Corey was struggling to stay in business and his resources and knowledge were limited to little more than the punk bands he and Tesco had become friends with while touring with the Necros and Meatmen.

The one band on the label who, upon their acquisition, stuck out like a sore thumb, was not a straight-edge band from the Midwest, but was very high and from Texas. Before too long, the Butthole Surfers were also the one band on Touch & Go that was actually generating any sort of income.

As for the band; prior to teaming up with Touch & Go, they were fighting to get their music released on Alternative Tentacles and distributed by Subterranean. Struggling to get paid for the EPs they had already produced and languishing with several record's worth of material being held in hock at Bob O'Neil Sound Studios.

When the two forces of the Butthole Surfers and Touch & Go merged, the planets seemed to align themselves. Fate smiled and after years of toil, the Butthole Surfers went on to become the highest grossing independent act on the road and Touch

& Go one of the most highly regarded independent labels in the country.

With *Another Man's Sac*, Touch & Go saw its first ever profits, and the subsequent acquisitions of bands like Scratch Acid (who Terry Tolkin brought to the label on the Buttholes' recommendation), Killdozer (who Corey brought to the label on the Buttholes recommendation), and Big Black, would help solidify Touch & Go's reputation as the purveyor of the new 'noise rock' scene. With guidance and administrative help from Terry and his pal Chris Gordon, and an infusion of cash from Corey's dad, Touch & Go survived to become a stalwart of independent music.

Terry's brainchild, the 'God's Favorite Dog" compilation, steered the label into a new realm of punk rock that was every bit as visceral, but equally as diverse, and infinitely more lucrative. As the bands that graced the grooves of the compilation began churning out more material, Touch & Go's reputation was cemented, and before long the label that seemed doomed was competing with institutions like SST, Twin Tone, and the label they coaxed the Buttholes away from, Alternative Tentacles. And there was no other band on Touch & Go more lucrative than the Butthole Surfers.

But not long after their final release on Touch & Go, it seemed like the 50% commission promised to them after expenses was being gouged into to fund other projects Corey wanted to launch. Though the mushrooming popularity of the Buttholes had kept the label afloat when its demise seemed almost certain, payments to the band had slowed to a trickle. The whole scenario harkened back to the times when Alternative Tentacles had all but ignored the Butthole Surfers to focus on the Dead Kennedys, just prior to them walking away from that label.

Terry began to realize that the expenses Corey was accruing had little to do with the promoting the Butthole Surfers, and that other bands Touch & Go was recruiting seemed to be getting better deals. Gibby was no slouch when it came to business dealings, but it didn't take a former staff auditor at Peat Marwick to know that profits were not being fully or accurately accounted for, and that the money his band was earning was not being fairly distributed.

While perhaps not clear at the time of their final release, tensions and frustrations would slowly mount between all parties involved over the subsequent year, and these, along with other personal issues, began to take their toll on Terry and Corey's friendship. Before long, they had all but ceased speaking to each other.

Terry's final decision to leave Touch & Go left the Buttholes feeling like they had lost the one person who was looking out for them. As Touch & Go prepared to move its operations from Detroit to Chicago, the Butthole Surfers seemed prepared to move their operations elsewhere as well.

Though the climate in the country was changing, the die had been cast, and it seemed that finding a label after leaving Touch & Go was not going to be quite so easy. The Butthole Surfers had proven they could make money, but they still were untouchable by most labels' standards. Most major newspapers would not even print their name, let alone review their records, and commercial radio wouldn't even think about speaking it over the airwaves, let alone add their music to their format.

It is hard to convey in the present climate, the level of adversity and downright antagonism the band needed to overcome in the time before Nirvana's success. The new decade brought with it the same problems as the old one. The Butthole Surfers' moniker seemed to be a curse that few labels could overlook, for it assured that they would be barred from just about every resource of a label's promotional tools. With Touch & Go, the band could at least ensure their newest material would get released, even if their share of the profits was less than equitable.

Few other independent labels had the distribution of Touch & Go, and few A&R representatives were willing to go to their bosses and tell them they wanted to sign a band who called themselves the Butthole Surfers. They seemed stuck in a strange state of limbo: straddling the line between acceptance and rejection, independence and slavery, and mainstream and obscurity. Even the most ardent fans struggled with the duality of wanting to see Gibby smashing a flaming cymbal at Madison Square Garden while still yearning to keep the band a secret from the rest of the straight world.

The Butthole Surfers were the band that record company employees listened to when they punched out at 5 o'clock on their commutes home after their day of pushing Michael Bolton records. They weren't the band one could sign to a major label, and their swan song on Touch & Go was proof.

Widowermaker was a scant four song EP which culled some of the newer tracks they had debuted over the previous year. Three of the songs were written by Jeff: "1401" (aka: The Colored FBI Guy), along with "Bong Song" and "Helicopter. The other song, a maniacal romp touting the joys of 'Booze, Tobacco, Dope, Pussy, and Cars' was a more recent addition to the sets; debuting in the UK at some warmup shows they played just before the Reading Festival. Brought in by Paul, the song foreshadowed the band's evolving direction as a quartet: Massive riffs at blazing speed and frantic solos with notes bending and groaning and drenched in delay. All the elements of the quartet were showcased on the EP, but one.

With King at his place in Austin and not in Driftwood, he found it difficult to get out to the country to record at a moment's notice. So instead, Jeff and Paul tried to program the drums on their Alesis drum machine. While they were not entirely unsuccessful at their endeavor, King's absence from the project was conspicuous. The record is less organic than *Hairway to Steven*, and a bit less cohesive as well, but with their last studio effort over a year and a half prior most fans were just happy to get something new to sink their teeth into.

The band, it seems, was less focused on releasing 'Widowermaker' and more focused on hearing the rumble of their RV engine chug across the interstates of America. It had been nearly a year since they had embarked on a coast-to-coast tour of the US and it was about time to remedy their absence. A new EP gave them the excuse to tour, re-introduce themselves, and ruin the ears and damage the minds of America's youth again.

With Teresa's tenure now a fading memory, testosterone levels soared. The band blazed through their sets at lightning speed; stopping briefly for Gibby to strap on his Telecaster, or to take a swig of beer, before scrambling through another eight or nine songs. Lights and films still accentuated their shows, but as Jeff and King became sole commanders of the rhythm section, shows became like dust fueled joy rides on rain slicked mountain roads. Between solid granite and the abyss of mind warping insanity, they teetered. The rain slicked stage on which they played in Reading was merely the starting line of the harrowing drive.

After a short respite to recover from the jetlag of the flight back to the U.S., they took off for LA, then headed south of the border to Tijuana for a couple of shows with the Red Hot Chili Peppers.

The Red Hot Chili Peppers had been together since 1984, and had been brought up playing the seedy punk bars in and around LA for the better part of their early career. They had been able to maintain their 'indie credibility' despite having never actually been an indie band and were now experiencing some mainstream success, despite not being quite a mainstream band.

Their latest record 'Mother's Milk' was climbing the Billboard Pop charts and would shortly be certified Gold, something that seemed implausible at the time. 'Mother's Milk' was not the meteoric success of Nirvana's *Nevermind* (that wouldn't come until after the release of their next album, *Blood Sugar Sex Magick*), however the album solidified the foundation set a year earlier by Jane's Addiction on *Nothing's Shocking*, that music outside the mainstream could actually shift units.

With the first single from the LP, "Knock Me Down", taking off on MTV, their shows were beginning to sell out quickly. The LA show with the Butthole Surfers had to be moved from the Roxy (capacity of 500), to the Palladium (capacity of 3700) to accommodate the crowd, and the two night stand subsequent, at the 1000-person capacity Iguana's in Tijuana, still left many disappointed fans standing outside the venue.

While these types of scenes were not entirely foreign to a band like the Butthole Surfers, this night had them sandwiched between two bands, RHCP and newcomers Mary's Danish, who like the Red Hot Chili Peppers had major label backing.

The Butthole Surfers were still on an indie label; setting up their own equipment and touring without even the benefit of a road manager or financial support. The dichotomy of the way the bands were treated was difficult to overlook.

They had been bossed around by Mary's Danish, who thought King was a roadie upon seeing him setting up his drum kit alone and the club's management wanted nothing to do with them. Being one of the most successful independent bands in the United States meant nothing in Mexico, nor to the bands that had an army of people catering to their every whim. That was not the Butthole Surfers.

They had crossed the border early that afternoon and spent the day much of the day in Tijuana imbibing themselves on over-priced alcohol prior to soundcheck.

King:

"...we were smart enough to not bring weed across the border, we were also dumb enough to compensate by drinking extra early at the 3000 bars around the club before the show. So, we had our drunk on early and were extra surly for the occasion." [7//28/2004]

Their soundcheck was a mess. Monitors weren't working, and the soundman was nowhere to be found. Things didn't improve by show time and the pleas from Gibby to turn up the stage monitors during their set were completely ignored. The soundman was seen chatting with a friend and must have gotten agitated by the band's continued insistence. Instead of turning the monitors up, he turned them completely off, according to Paul, too preoccupied to pay attention to any band that didn't have major label distribution.   Finally, in a complete drunken rage, Gibby hurls his beer bottle in the direction of the soundboard, and the real mayhem ensues.

King:

"...all hell broke loose. A bunch of bouncers descended on Gibby and took him outside, the rest of the band followed. The rest is a foggy memory, but punches were thrown and there were Federales on the scene. Gibby disappeared in the mayhem.

We knew we had to get the fuck out of there quickly. Our soundman (Ric Wallace), *our roadie/projectionist* (Danny Flaim), *and the surviving band members managed to keep our heads down and pack up our stuff pretty quickly and get it on the bus to head back to the safety of San Diego.*

The question was - where was Gibby? Last anyone in our crew knew, he was surrounded by Federales and hauled away. Back in San Diego, there was no sign of Gibby - no calls, no nothing. I was freaking out. I called the US Consulate, to ask if they could find Gibby in a Tijuana jail. They called me back and said they didn't know of his whereabouts. At 3 am, Gibby came back to the motel we were staying. He said he was able to pay off the Federales on the spot and walked across the border and hung out at a bar on the other side." [email: 7/28/04]

Figuring it a stroke of luck to all be reunited on home soils, they felt it best not to push their luck, and the following evening's performance was canceled. They then headed up the coast toward San Francisco for the next gigs. Mayhem seemed to follow the band, with Teresa or without.

The rest of the tour went relatively smoothly, however, and culminated in November headlining a slot at a World Music festival at New York's prestigious Brooklyn Academy of Music.

The 'Night of 1000 Bands' Festival featured the band atop a bill that included the World Saxophone Quartet with Senegalese Drummers, Bobby Previte and a 9-piece Orchestra, and Aster Aweke. It was a far cry from a riot in Tijuana, and the billing both validated and exemplified the Butthole Surfers as a band that could not be pigeon-holed. It also epitomized the struggle that many record company executives might have in trying to tether the band to any contrived labels.

Still, it was nearly impossible for the straight world of contemporary artists and critics to ignore the Butthole Surfers. Even those not ready to accept the band into their opera houses had to acknowledge them as artists of some sort. The New York Times' Jon Pareles even printed their name in his review, albeit just one time before resorting to calling them "The Surfers" for the rest of the article.

"The Surfers may be the best psychedelic rock band that never played during the 1960's." (New-Music Festival; The Festival's Finale: 11 Bands on 4 Stages", NY Times, 11/20/89)

And while this type of review could send shivers down the spines of their old punk rock fan base, it also could coax out a sly smile knowing that no matter how hard the art critics tried, they could not completely ignore the Butthole Surfers without being deemed completely out of touch.

Whether it was at a shithole in Tijuana or an opera house in New York City, the band could fit in with any crowd. Perhaps it was more like they were outcasts in every such environment, but there was no denying the fact that there were few in the industry who could ignore them.

Jeff, Gibby & Paul, Dallas, 11/9/89
© Patrick Huckabee

They existed on this other-worldly plain for most of their career. They were outside of any label yet encapsulated nearly every genre of popular music at once. It was apparent they were not going away. And if the loss of Teresa meant the band would chart a new course, then that is what they would do. Perhaps the days of the onstage sex shows and mannequins stuffed with cheeseburgers were things of the past, but that was nostalgia of yesterday. This was a new Now! Explosion.

No band could sustain this level of madness for a decade and survive. Not even the Butthole Surfers, who did it longer than anyone else in the history of rock music. Whether by choice, or by necessity, there were few who could deny these men of the honor of being, if nothing else, the most dedicated band in the history of Texas Rock'n'Roll.

Revolutionary Men

The 1980's ended quietly for the Butthole Surfers. They successfully pulled off their first tour without Teresa and got back to Texas awaiting their next move. With the success of *Hairway to Steven*, labels continued to sniff around the band like dogs would another dog's asshole, but none seemed ready to make the band their proverbial bitch.

Then, in a stroke of fortune, a call came from Terry Tolkin, who told them about a new job he had gotten at Rough Trade Records, and a proposal that must have seemed too good to be true.

After leaving Touch & Go Terry briefly returned to working at Caroline Records, where he had pulled a stint years prior. His first venture at the label was putting together a Neil Young tribute album called 'The Bridge'. The record was a testament, not only to his vision but, also his musical connections. 'The Bridge' was the first such tribute album of its kind and the list of luminaries covering Neil Young songs not only brought attention to the wealth of diverse independent bands, but also brought about a resurrection of the artist himself. After nearly a decade of being a ignored, Neil Young was finally being recognized for his influence upon the younger generation and his return to prominence led to an article in the December 1991 issue of 'Pulse!' magazine dubbing him the 'Godfather of Grunge'

While at Caroline, Terry was offered a job doing A&R at Rough Trade Records' American branch in New York City. Having always brought bands and labels together, yet having never had the official title of 'A&R Representative, it seemed like a calling fulfilled. He took the job at Rough Trade and started his own 'No. 6' record label as well. Knowing the Butthole Surfers were in the market for a new home, he made them his top priority.

After some negotiating, Terry was able to secure an unheard-of offer of $100,000 from the suits at Rough Trade as an advance. He was also able to get Paul and Gibby & Jeff separate deals for their own solo ventures. This kind of money was certainly enough to lure them away from Touch & Go Records for good. It was the offer of a lifetime, and they jumped at the chance to make some real money for their artistic endeavors.

Rough Trade had distribution that rivaled the biggest names in the industry, and with its main offices overseas, it meant the band wouldn't need to look for a sister label in the UK or Holland to get their records into stores there. They could focus on the art of making music rather than the business of shopping themselves around for distribution.

The jump from Touch & Go did not sit well with Corey, however. He was sure the band was making the wrong decision and he let them know it. It was Corey's view that he had worked harder than anyone else over the years to get the band's material released in the way they wanted, and Rough Trade would not be good to them.

He obviously felt he had nurtured the band to success through his commitment and conviction. Though impossible to know Corey's take on it, it seems feelings were hurt and relationships were forever changed once the band decided to leave Touch & Go. These sore feelings no doubt foreshadowed what was to yet come.

Corey's blood must have reached its boiling point as he watched his old friend Terry negotiating the signing of the band that was the bread and butter of his label. Touch & Go had solvency now, though. They had a catalog full of classic records by this point, even discounting the Butthole Surfers back catalogue.

Corey and Touch & Go had been there when Alternative Tentacles had all but ignored Gibby and Paul's phone calls and the band would be forever grateful for that. But, now, it was Touch & Go whose complacence was holding back the band. They decided to bid Corey a fond adieu and set their course for what they had hoped were the greener pastures of Rough Trade Records.

Rough Trade had been founded in 1978 as a record store in south London before it began promoting and releasing bands on its own label. The extensive list of cutting-edge artists they had released over the years read like a who's who in underground music: The Pop Group, James 'Blood' Ulmer, The Red Crayola, Pere Ubu, The Smiths, Stiff Little Fingers, and one of Paul's all-time favorite bands, The Fall.

Rough Trade created a network of record stores across the UK that they dubbed the Cartel that enabled small independent labels and bands to market and distribute their records nationally. It was like a grass roots musical movement that afforded labels like Factory, 2- Tone, and Fundamental Records the distribution they could never have gotten otherwise. Rough Trade's latest venture was to bring their Cartel across the pond to American shores.

Terry had been in the Buttholes corner for years and had seen Rough Trade's business dealings firsthand. He knew they had money to spend, for, he recalls, it seemed they pissed it all away on the most ludicrous endeavors. Perhaps signing the Butthole Surfers could be counted among them, but there was certainly brand recognition in their name, and a commitment that the Butthole Surfers would work harder than anyone to promote themselves. All this, coupled with a rabid fan base that was salivating to get their hands on anything the band released seemed like a formula for success.

But, what appeared like a winning formula on paper was actually a nightmare for the band. Unbeknownst to the boys, the label, the distribution network, and record shops had often been at odds with one another, as independent artists like Joy Division, the Smiths, and The Specials made records that sold more than Rough Trade to afford to distribute. The owners were eventually forced to sell the shop to pay off their debts and continue the label, but it seemed the die was cast since the early-1980's.

Between November of 1990 and March of 1991, Rough Trade was going through some of the worst financial and managerial woes since its earliest inception. The label released no less than three full length LPs by the band: one by the Butthole

Surfers, another by Gibby and Jeff's JackOfficers side-project, and a solo album by Paul entitled 'The History of Dogs'. They began this deluge with a single that included a cover of Donovan's classic 1968 hit "Hurdy Gurdy Man", backed by "Barking Dogs"; the manic tape loop they first played as an introduction to their shows on the 1988 tour.

Rough Trade had high hopes that by releasing a torrent of Butthole related material, they could save themselves from the bankruptcy which seemed inevitable to just about everybody besides the Butthole Surfers. Though it was a great time for fans, who after years of waiting finally had a windfall of product to dig into, it became a major headache for the group.

The huge expenses to get all the product shipped left Rough Trade reeling and its books even deeper in the red. The attempt to salvage what was left of the label by catching the wave of the Butthole Surfers did little but prolong the inevitable. Rough Trade went belly up just a few scant weeks after the release of *piouhgd*: their first album since *Hairway to Steven* nearly three years prior.

Rough Trade's demise not only left the band without a label by the time their next tour began, the wildly successful Lollapalooza festival, but also left them without any new product available to peddle at all. The records that hadn't yet been shipped were left in a warehouse or liquidated to pay Rough Trade's massive outstanding debt. Rough Trade had banked on the Butthole Surfers records to turn things around, but with management fleeing, and Smiths records not selling like they once used to, the modest success of *piouhgd* did nothing to change their downward trajectory.

As for the band, the release of the EP *Hurdy Gurdy Man* could be viewed almost as a tongue-in-cheek poke at the new wave of 'hippie' bands that permeated much of the Rough Trade catalogue in their later years, and which had permeated the alternative scene since Jane's Addiction had opened the flood gates to the new field of flowery, neo-psychedelic bands.

The Shoe-Gaze, or Dream-Pop movement as it was sometimes referred to in England, was all too often non-confrontational, pompously bloated, and limply derivative; In other words, nothing like the Butthole Surfers. And yet these bands, too, seemingly owed their existence to the Butthole Surfers, who was one of the only bands that had been waiving their proverbial freak flag high while most of these kids were programming their synthesizers in New Wave bands.

Seeing a Donovan song lighting up request lines for the first time since 1968 gave the band a snicker at the very least, and although the video was played on MTV, and put onto the soundtrack of a major motion picture starring none other than rubber-faced funny man, Jim Carrey, the band never did bother put it back into their live sets. As stated before, the Butthole Surfers were light years ahead of their recorded output and the peace and love of the new retro-hippie movement was as foreign to them as a pair of Birkenstocks. They were taking on this new Love Generation with a battle axe, not a daisy.

And although the band's Rough Trade catalogue was completely liquidated,

Corey saw a pretty major boost in back catalogue sales. With no one at Touch & Go keeping track of any money owed to the band, least of all Corey, it was anyone's guess as to the amount of Butthole Surfers records Touch & Go was selling, or how much the band was supposed to get paid.

Despite the success of *Hurdy Gurdy Man*, the record wasn't in stores, and the band, at the height of its popularity was completely without a label by the time they were asked to go out on their most ambitious tour to date.

It was the summer of 1991 when Jane's Addiction decided that their farewell tour, prior to a planned breakup, would be a going away party they would throw for themselves. Put together by front man Perry Farrell to pay homage to their own existence, as well as to all the bands who had influenced them over the years, they humbly acknowledged the Butthole Surfers as one of them. The concert was a huge risk at a time when alternative music was thought to have limited commercial appeal, but Perry had just the vision, and ego, to pull it off.

Lollapalooza would not be so much concerts as they would be traveling circuses. Shows featured a main stage of underground stalwarts as well as a side stage for emerging artists. All would play amongst a host of vendors, interactive attractions, and grass roots organizations at outdoor venues across the United States.

Games and food and hours and hours of music made Lollapalooza the concert event of the summer. And even if many of the people who bought tickets had never heard of half the acts on the bill, tickets sold out at most markets where the tour stopped.

Lollapalooza's surprise financial success soon became a calling card to major labels everywhere that the underground music they had been neglecting for so long, and the big corporate profits they sought, could perhaps get naked and share a sweat lodge together. It was a testament to just how far the record industry had come in just the scant two years since Warner Brothers had released 'Nothing's Shocking', let alone the last decade since the Butthole Surfers had played their first shows as the Dick Gas Five.

Jane's Addiction's latest single, "Been Caught Stealing", was now in heavy rotation on MTV and was getting adds on commercial radio stations in major markets as well. Kids, many of whom were in search of rock bands who packed the punch of the few rap acts they dug, were ready for something else. Something to take them away from the bloated, pretentious rock bands they had been spoon fed for so long. The time was right for a new revolution in music.

A month after the Lollapalooza tour wrapped up, they would get what they had longed for. In September of 1991, Geffen Records released Nirvana's *Nevermind*. Its release seemed completely inconsequential at the time, but the explosion of the record's first single, "Smells Like Teen Spirit" changed the landscape of rock music forever.

It's impossible to know exactly what recipe Nirvana brought to the table that hadn't been explored by countless other acts throughout the 80's and early 1990's, but for some reason, most likely the luck of sheer timing, kids latched onto *Nevermind* like pitbulls onto a slab of meat. Finally, they heard music that captured, and even celebrated, the way they were feeling: awkward, insecure, confused, and angry.

Nevermind melded punk aesthetics and pop hooks, while also tearing a page out of the 70's power rock handbook. Tube amps, vintage guitars, and fuzz boxes: these were not the devices of punk rockers, generally, and were certainly not the stuff of punks prior to the few brave bands like Sonic Youth, Mudhoney, Dinosaur Jr, and of course, the Butthole Surfers had made them so. Now they would become standard fare on the mainstream pop charts as *Nevermind* overtook Michael Jackson's 'Dangerous' album at the top the Billboard TOP 40 charts.

Nirvana had been a band that had opened for the Butthole Surfers on the Seattle stop of the tour that yielded most of the *Double Live* album. They were largely ignored by the crowd that night in 1988. The Butthole Surfers were the stars that everyone had come to see shine so brightly. The Butthole Surfers were the band that had commanded the spotlight and upon whose unyielding work ethic was almost as awe inspiring as the spectacle of their live experiences.

But, the Butthole Surfers were from Texas and not Seattle, where the scene was easy to pigeon-hole and even easier to market. The cookie cutter bands that followed in Nirvana's wake sat like ripened fruit on a tree waiting to be plucked and eaten up by major labels. Soon, Washington State's most lucrative export was no longer apples, but came in the form of retro-rock bands who wore flannel shirts and jammed upon regurgitated, watered-down Black Sabbath riffs.

Many of the bands who went on to become the new darlings of the Seattle Grunge Scene, like Nirvana, had been virtually ignored in their opening slots for the Butthole Surfers, in the years prior to their success: Soundgarden, Green River (from whose ashes Pearl Jam and Mudhoney would rise), and the Screaming Trees among them. And shortly after Seattle was plundered of its independent music scene, major labels began looking outside of its city limits for the next cities to pillage. The Butthole Surfers, the only band on the Lollapalooza main stage who were not signed to a major, put Driftwood, Texas, and the solitary inhabitants of that town's scene, squarely on their radar.

Talks had gotten underway with major labels prior to Lollapalooza kicking off in Phoenix, Arizona, but nothing had been finalized on paper. And so the Butthole Surfers, who were playing on the main stage of one of the hottest summer concert tickets of 1991, were not signed to any label, be it a major or an independent.

Jane's Addiction and Lollapalooza's financial success put the corporate rock community on high alert and with the absolute supernova that *Nevermind* became shortly thereafter, the fate of independent music was sealed. Bands who were once thought to be unsignable were now being courted like rock stars. By the time Lollapalooza was over, and the Butthole Surfers played their final show of 1991, a New Year's Eve outing at Houston's Vatican, they were officially Capitol recording artists.

Summer Has Come and Gone

The Butthole Surfers on the same label as the Beatles, Grand Funk Railroad, Pink Floyd, and the Beach Boys. It was surely a sign of the oncoming apocalypse. The Butthole Surfers on a major record label. It was unthinkable. For longtime fans, the thought was almost too much to bear. Most had seen ticket prices for their favorite bands skyrocket and venue sizes grow increasingly larger and impersonal, now the Butthole Surfers were joining the ranks of the new alternative elite.

The mistrust of all things corporate had to be quelled in hopes that, by a major label even acknowledging Butthole Surfers existence, it was an admission of guilt for denying them for so long. An admission of guilt is, after all, the first step to recovery.

Somehow the idea of such vehemently independent artists as fIREHOSE, Swans, and the Meat Puppets all signing to majors was easier to digest than was the thought of the Butthole Surfers doing it, though, it was almost easier for fans to accept than it was for the band themselves. For, as much as the band had always wanted to make some real money, expand its fan base, and spread the word of their own gospel to all reaches of the universe, the idea of being on a major conjured up the worst of all demons.

When asked by MTV VJ Dave Kendall backstage at the first Lollapalooza show about the future of the band remaining independent, Gibby, almost prophetically, chided:

Gibby:
"Yes, it's true we will be on a major label soon, which means you'll probably never hear another word about us in a year or two." [MTV interview 7/18/91]

This fear and mistrust of the corporate rock machine came from the old punk that still remained deeply ingrained in him. Even though many of the other bands they knew had already jumped ship from their indie label digs, Gibby's lament remained deeply cynical, slightly paranoid, and completely and utterly justified.

The old punk bands that had been granted the honor of major label contracts in the days before Nirvana had done so with an understanding from both parties that with the combination of the band's work ethic and their small but rabid fan bases, the label would garner a steady income. These bands didn't take much money to support so a label like Warner Brothers could shell out a relatively small advance to the likes of a Husker Du, or Sire the Replacements, and be guaranteed a small return on their investment.

The bands themselves were left relatively autonomous and the label did little else than release the records and offer some tour support. The labels relied on their mainstay, bread-and-butter artists to finance their smaller ventures which helped give them at least some façade of street credibility.

Things became very different in the days after the success of "Smells Like Teen Spirit". So-called Alternative Bands were not just added to the cache of huge pop artists, they were the huge pop artists themselves and as such were actually expected to sell, and sell big. The former underground artists were not wallowing in some back corner office waiting to be seen by the company executives. They were being courted and taken out to expensive dinners in LA, all while sporting torn jeans, greasy hair, and faded t-shirts. They were now be wined and dined as the new cornerstones of the label.

For Capitol Records, they saw the potential to market the Butthole Surfers based not only on their success on the Lollapalooza tour, or "the Hurdy Gurdy Man" single, but also with the success of Ministry's "Jesus Built My Hotrod" single.

Released in November of 1991, the single featured Gibby on lead vocals, and saw him prominently featured in the promotional video. "Jesus Built My Hotrod" was the latest in a string of modestly successful Butthole Surfers ventures and they couldn't be ignored by the majors for much longer.

Ministry started in 1981 as a new wave band from Chicago mimicking the tepid UK new wave bands of the day, right down to Al Jourgensen's fake British accent. Over time however, boredom, drugs, and the influence of bands like the Butthole Surfers led to a complete transformation in Ministry's sound, and ethos, and now a decade after their formation, they were reaping the rewards of this transformation.

Without that first taste of mainstream commercialism, Capitol might not have listened to their A&R Reps who promised they could sell a band like the Butthole Surfers. It seemed, however, what was being said by believers might be valid: the Butthole Surfers could remain true to their art and be still be commercially viable.

The truth was that Capitol president Hale Milgrim was a self-described music junkie and an actual fan of the band. He even owned a copy of Daddy Longhead's *Cheatos* CD (Jeff's 'one-off' side-project released in 1991 on Touch & Go), for his own personal enjoyment. This blew Jeff's mind. If Hale was a big enough fan to keep track of the band's side projects then he was certainly the kind of champion the band needed to quell their fears of major labels and perhaps even enable Gibby to relinquish his own iron-gripped control on it, allowing him to focus on his art rather than the business of the band.

It was just this type of support and belief that inspired them to say 'yes' to Capitol's offer. With the president of the label's confidence in them, they could operate as their own bosses and make their music in a vacuum as they always had with

Touch & Go. This wasn't a sellout, if there even was such a thing in this day and age, this was a joining of forces.

The Berlin Wall toppled and the world was becoming more unified and now the insular walls the band placed around themselves to protect themselves from the greed mongers and evil-doers would topple as well. The Butthole Surfers were safe in the loving arms of a gentle giant. With the label president almost as excited as the band, the contracts were signed with hope and joy in their hearts. It was a signature this time, not an oral agreement, and just like that, the Butthole Surfers were in the big leagues.

They Came In

There was always the feeling that the Buttholes would someday be playing shows at coliseums, even when they were crammed onto the stage at CBGB's, the 9:30 Club, or the Fast Lane. The movie screens slowly rose to reveal a wall of strobe lights behind them which seemed to dance in time to the music in a maddening, pulsating wave, spelling out words and furiously flashing lines and patterns. Multi-colored laser lights fluttered about the stage in an electric St. Vitus Dance. With each new tour they had a new gadget, new equipment, and a new way to fuck with the minds of the audience. It seemed that at some point they would no longer be able to be confined to the small venues they had played for so long.

And yet when the reality hit that the Butthole Surfers might actually be playing stadiums instead of the dingy punk clubs they had called their home away from any sort of home, it brought fear and sadness to the hearts of long-time devotees. Punks, like the hippies before, had a certain idealism that if they could convert the masses to their viewpoint that the world would become a better place.

But now that the masses had been converted, there was a feeling of being violated, exploited, marketed and sold. With the Buttholes being one of the last bands to hold out to sign to a major label deal, there was a feeling that the last straw had been dropped onto the camel's back. The industry had finally reached into the deepest depths and corrupted the last vestiges of independence left. There was no way that the Butthole Surfers could remain the band they had always been and be on a corporate label.

But the Butthole Surfers were never a static, concrete block. They were constantly changing and ever fluid. Evolving, devolving, morphing and reforming. Not just the fact that they seemed to have a new line-up every other week, but with their creative output as well. One could never predict what the next song on any record would sound like, let alone what the next release might bring.

It was more the narrow mindedness of the punks that held so tightly onto the past, and to the notion of what should be expected. These codgers would remember "The Shah Sleeps in Lee Harvey's Grave" and forget "Hey", remember 'Lady Sniff' and forget "Negro Observer". No doubt that if a record like 'Rembrandt Pussyhorse' had been released at this time, the Butthole Surfers would have surely been pinned as 'sellouts', trying to water down their sound to cash in with accessible hymns about creeps in the cellar, or lamenting mournfully upon the whirling hall of knives.

There was no real way for the Buttholes to win this game that punks used to play of deeming who was worthy of the title of the pigeon-hole of punk rock, so the band didn't bother playing the game at all. Punk, after all, was dead. The band just continued being the Butthole Surfers and left the question of whatever it meant to be a punk, or a Butthole Surfer, to the critics and cynics.

There was work to be done. There was a record to plan. After finally penning the deal with Capitol the band remained couped up in Texas for a spell: writing and laying down rough tracks and whittling down the list of potential producers and huge professional studios that would be afforded to them as Capitol recording artists.

They finally settled upon a studio called The Site, just across the valley from George Lucas' own Skywalker Ranch in Marin County, California. It was an idyllic setting in the rolling, golden hills outside of San Francisco, to remind them of the lazy days they used to spend in the countryside while living at the old ranch in Driftwood.

After they recorded *PIOUHGD*, one by one, they each had begun abandoning the old house, finally leaving band business to band business and life business to life business. First was Jeff, who went back to his native Atlanta to get married, before returning to a suburb of Austin to settle down with his new bride and his Jack Russell Terrier, Lincoln.

Paul was next. After Gibby's untrained pooch, Mr. Cigar, shit and pissed all over the carpet and floors, Paul bailed on the house to shack up with his new fiancé. When her roommate started dating Gibby, Mr. Cigar was back in the picture too, so Paul decided they should both move out into an apartment of their own. Gibby himself was spending more and more time in LA trying to build an acting resume, and the house in Driftwood was left vacant almost as much as the house in Winterville had been.

With the studio picked for the next recording, the next job was to find a producer. Bill Laswell's name was bounced around, as were some others, but in the end, they settled upon famed former Led Zeppelin bassist John Paul Jones. Did he have an impressive resume of production credits under his belt? Had he any clue about the Butthole Surfers? Who gave a shit! This was someone they would have to deal with for the arduous weeks of recording and tedious mixing process. If they had at least something in common, the band was ready to give it a whirl.

It was a conference call between John Paul Jones, the band, and the brass at Capitol that sealed the deal in the end. They began talking about dogs, and John Paul Jones talking about his shih tzu. His dog, he noted, looked just like the one that the Harts owned on the TV detective show, 'Hart to Hart'. The combination of his love of dogs, and reference to the shitty American TV the band loved so much made him the perfect candidate for the job of producing their next offering.

With everything in place, they picked up and headed to Philadelphia to play the first of four shows they would play as artists who were involved with a label of any sort, major or otherwise. They had played just one show since Lollapalooza had wrapped up nearly a year prior. Much of the time off was spent laying down demos, and dealing with the new, infinitely more lucrative business of the band: tying up the contracts and preparing to enter a real studio with a real producer.

There was no tour planned, but rather, a modest trip up the east coast in the waning days of spring 1992. The brief trip culminated with an AIDS benefit at the Roseland Ballroom in NYC. It was to be their first big show headlining a large alternative bill of signed bands and the boys would get their first sour taste of rock stardom.

The 'Hoaui Party' was a benefit concert held during the New Music Seminar festival in the name AIDS awareness, as well as a memoriam for New Music Seminar executive director Hoaui Montaug, who had committed suicide a year earlier just after being diagnosed as HIV positive.

It was nearly a decade since the disease had been first discovered, and a diagnosis of HIV positive was still basically a death sentence at the time. Much of the focus of the two previous presidential administrations was on military spending, flag burning, or controlling what records kids put on their turntables. With AIDS being thought of as a "gay disease", or one that only affected junkies, hookers or Haitians, it was largely ignored by the rich, white power elite. Before long, though, as Americans watched actor Rock Hudson wither away before their eyes and saw innocent teen Ryan White expelled from his middle school after being diagnosed due to a tainted hemophilia treatment, some much needed financial and legislative light was being shone on the virus.

The benefit concert was a big deal and was heavily promoted: an example of how rock musicians cared and looked after their own. It was MC'd by the B-52's Fred Schneider and rapper Ice-T, who had first met the Surfers during their stint together on the Lollapalooza tour. The media and industry folks were out in full force to show allegiance to the cause. Updates on the Seminar shows, and specifically of the 'Hoaui Party', were broadcast all over MTV News, and huge color posters adorned the subways and sidewalks of the Big Apple; with Butthole Surfers name appearing predominantly atop a bill that included Soul Asylum, Prong, and Diamanda Galas. It was the sweet fruits for all the hard work and dedication they had shown over the last decade of line-up changes, lack of money, and grueling road schedules.

But what should have been a chance to help a good cause and bask in their own hard-won successes quickly fell to a pile of shit when Diamanda Galas, among others, began vocalizing complaints that the Buttholes received their full $15,000 payment for this so-called benefit gig. The accusation painted the band as heartless and hypocritical and they oddly were shown as the new faces of the corruption of the underground music scene and of corporate greed gone amuck. They hadn't even released a record with Capitol and were already being vilified in the press.

Now, instead of paying homage to a friend and celebrating their newfound good fortune, their publicist was in damage control mode, forced to deal with explaining the band's financial arrangements to the world and left scrambling to defend a deal that managers and show promoters had agreed to long before setting the gig up in the first place.

It was a battle the band could never win. Defending what seemed to be an extraordinary amount of money for a single concert was futile, even to those who knew about the truckloads of lights and equipment they needed to haul from Texas to NYC specifically play this one gig.

The 'he-said-she-said' lack of drama played out on MTV News over the course of several days leading up to the event. The Lifebeat AIDS awareness organization, and the promoters of the concert defended the band, and Diamanda Galas herself remained strangely silent after slinging her accusations, but the damage had been done. After all of this, the show was then plagued with monitor difficulties that left Gibby visibly shaken, kicking the mic stand over in disgust repeatedly throughout the performance. They managed to salvage the set and most of the crowd at the sold out event left satisfied, but the Buttholes returned to Texas this time a bit flustered, unwashed and somewhat slightly dazed.

What should have been a celebration was a sham. Festival shows and co-headlining bills were always a horror, but this was a new low. The boys moved forward quickly to put the whole ugly episode behind them. They were far more focused on the future and recording the record they had been longing to make for the past 5 years but couldn't pull off as an indie band. The remainder of 1992 was spent recording the LP, and its release in March of 1993 marked the end of the longest dry spell in their history to date.

Clean It Up

Independent Worm Saloon was a sprawling introduction of the Butthole Surfers to the new alternative masses who had heard Kurt Cobain mention two of their LPs as among his 50 favorite records of all time in some interview or other. What the album might have lacked in its experimentation and diversity it made up for in its sheer brute power.

It was a guitar rock album in a time full of guitar rock albums, which turned off some of the older fans and critics, who had always expected the band to buck the current trends, rather than follow them. But for those who remained fans after Teresa's departure, it was the record that had been held back for the last 4 years. It culled together the material they had been performing live for years, but which had remained unreleased before now.

Though a consummate rock album, *Independent Worm Saloon* was full of many of the same trademarks upon which the band had built its reputation. Tribal drumbeats, this time played by King and not programmed or fed through a midi device, chunky bass riffs rumbling under Paul's signature solos, all of which swirled around Gibby's voice modulator, often tuned down to a growl, or sped to a frantic, high-pitched squeal.

It was a serious rock record, yet still held onto their trademark sense of humor, which immediately set it apart from the self-righteous, ego-fest that alternative guitar rock had quickly become since Nirvana's success. The Butthole Surfers had been a focused guitar rock outfit since at least the time they had become a four-piece unit in the summer of 1989. They had just been doing it in the live setting, and not on record. 'Independent Worm Saloon' finally brought their recordings up to date with their current sound and still managed to bring some new elements to the foreground.

In the time before the record's release, other bands had the chance to capitalize on the new wave of guitar rock that the Butthole Surfers had basically started, but which they had not yet committed to wax (or rather the 0's and 1's of this new digital age). Now the Butthole Surfers were finally catching up to the trend they had hatched.

For those newer fans who didn't know any better, there may have been the misconception they were merely cashing in, or no more trailblazing than Pearl Jam or the dozens of other bands exploiting the new alternative feeding frenzy; They were incorrect.   No doubt that when Kurt and Courtney Love met at a Butthole Surfers gig in LA in May of 1991, they took home with them more than each other's phone numbers, but some musical inspirations as well.

Once *Independent Worm Saloon* was released on March 23, 1993, Capitol's promotion team went into hyper-drive and it clearly served the band well. The video for the first single, "Who Was In My Room Last Night", began lighting up request lines at MTV's loud rock program, 'Headbanger's Ball', boosted by Gibby and Paul's acoustic performance on the program, and also at brave commercial radio stations across the country, many which still refused to pronounce the band's name over the airwaves.

"Who Was In My Room Last Night" held close to the things that had made "Jesus Built My Hotrod" a success for Ministry, for they were the same things that made the Butthole Surfers the band they had become: Huge chugging riffs and pounding speed induced beats all set behind Gibby's incoherent, rambling screeds.

The song rocked harder than most everything else coming out on a major label at that time, and the formula was nothing to be ashamed of. Surely it would be expected that the record company would latch onto the song that already exemplified the band's biggest successes to date. The Butthole Surfers didn't need to change their ways and the record could still sell. It was a dream for the A&R folks, the fans could live with it, and for new Capitol president Hale Milgrim, who believed in the band before it could have been fathomed they'd find a home on a major, the Butthole Surfers had what it took to produce a hit record.

Independent Worm Saloon finally revealed the quartet in its full glory. They recorded nearly enough material to produce a double album and were thrilled at the support they were getting from Capitol. John Paul Jones loved the driving, high-speed rock numbers, but didn't quite get their more spacey and noisy psychedelic material, so they threw those onto a 10" record they released to radio and record stores to promote the LP, to satisfy those cravings.

Independent Worm Saloon cleaned out the closet of songs they had been playing for years. It also showcased material that they hadn't yet played in a live setting. One song they had written while cooped up in the studio was entitled "Ballad of Naked Man", which featured Jeff's debut on lead vocals. They were even able to coax the old Led Zeppelin bass player out of the booth and into the studio to play on it. They just let loose and had fun. It was a real joy not to have to worry about rushing to get the product done so they could get out on tour to avoid starving. They could just jam and relax and create.

Shortly after the record was released, however, as the promotional teams worked the album to MTV and commercial radio stations, a Billboard article came out that questioned the future of Hale Milgrim as Capitol president. Milgrim initially had no comment on the matter, but soon thereafter came the awkward chatter buzzing around the company water cooler that became too uncomfortable to ignore.

It seemed that Capitol Records' parent company EMI disagreed with Milgrim's philosophy of developing talent slowly, opting instead for the one-off, big-hit formula that earned boatloads of cash, but which often fizzled by the time the follow up LP was introduced.

The latest hit machine for Capitol was MC Hammer, whose 1990 album, *Please Don't Hurt 'Em*, earned three Top 10 singles. Within a few short years of his massive success, he was broke with many of the 10 million albums he sold collecting dust in the $1 bins at local mom & pop record stores across the country.

For his part, Milgrim did his best to deny the rumors of his friction with

Capitol, but by the time the tour to promote 'Independent Worm Saloon' was booked, Milgrim's contract was bought out, leaving the Buttholes without one of their biggest supporters at the label.

EMI brought in new president, Gary Gersh, who was the former A&R executive that signed Nirvana to Geffen Records. Once in charge, it seemed as if he was under strict orders from the brass to buckle down and streamline the cache of artists who didn't make money and the Butthole Surfers were being watched with hawkish eyes.

Gary Gersh was being heralded as a genius for hedging his bet and signing Nirvana, and his move from lowly A&R Rep to head one of the most successful record labels in the world exemplified how clueless most major labels were about what was happening in the world of music. No focus group could have predicted Nirvana's success. No producer could have crafted them. None of the formulas that any record executive could have devised to ensure a hit record produced *Nevermind* as a quotient.

As a longtime friend and supporter of Thurston Moore and Sonic Youth, in addition to Nirvana, it seemed as if Gersh would have been at least sympathetic to the Butthole Surfers' plight, who struggled longer than any band on earth to have a seat at the table. But with summer approaching, and the tour supporting 'Independent Worm Saloon' on the horizon, he had his own ideas on what would make the tour successful, and they were polar opposite to the band's ideas.

Jeff's idea for the tour to include their old friends the Meat Puppets and Ween as openers was immediately nixed. Instead, the tour would be packaged with Atlantic Recording Artists, Stone Temple Pilots, a band that had gotten infinitely more successful than the Butthole Surfers by sticking strictly to the industry formulas for success.

Capitol's plan now was to capitalize on the Butthole Surfers brand recognition, which was, for all intents and purpose, their inclusion on the Lollapalooza tour. In a nod to the success of that tour, as well as to the notorious lack of ingenuity of the record industry, most of the concerts on the so-called "Bar-B-Que Mitzvah Tour" would be held at outdoor venues, and would feature dunking booths, funnel cakes and games to manufacture a true carnival atmosphere.

Jeff:
"They asked me who I wanted to tour with and I told them the Meat Puppets and Ween, and I remember (manager) *Tom* [Bunch] *saying, "well, that would be another theatre gig, instead of going to stadiums..."...and I thought who in our crowd would want to go to a fucking stadium?...that's about the time when the business side started to affect the other side of things."*
[phone interview, 6/20/2014]

❧

A prepackaged lineup wasn't quite what the Butthole Surfers had in mind for their first tour as Capitol recording artists. It demonstrated a huge lack of confidence on the part of the Gersh and Capitol. It appeared that he lacked the belief that the band could pull off a successful tour on their own, something which should have been blatantly apparent that the band could do, for they had done it for many years going back to the old days at Touch & Go. The whole thing was a real kick in the groin that left Gibby, in particular, groaning with that dull sinking feeling in his gut.

❧

Gibby:
"It's kind of a Lollapalooza kinda mentality which will probably fall right...right flat on its face...Not my idea, I hope it's a success!
['MTV's Headbanger's Ball', June 12, 1993]

❧

The sense of bewilderment from Gibby and Paul during one of their first interviews as Capitol artists was palpable and infectious. As host Riki Rachtman scrambled to try to find positives about their newfound successes it was obvious that they themselves were not feeling quite as optimistic about the plans laid out for them by the suits on the top floor of the Capitol Records building.

They were, however, excited about the new record, and they were willing to put on their big boy britches and show their game face, despite the wounds from the 'Hoaui Party' still oozing puss. If Capitol was willing to fund it then the Butthole Surfers would hop on for the ride.

And although Ween and the Meat Puppets weren't on the bill, Capitol did allow them to grab some other old friends in fIREHOSE and the Flaming Lips to join them on the tour in their stead, which made sitting through STP's sets slightly more tolerable.

And while the outdoor venues meant that their smoke machines would be rendered mostly useless, and the beaches and lakeside settings would leave their projectors and equipment encrusted with grit and salt, they held on to their high hopes and tried keep positive despite the hassles and obvious misgivings.

Never had the band needed a manufactured carnival atmosphere to be conjured for them to promote their shows. It was assuredly always there. A decade since the release of *A Brown Reason to Live*, however, they were once again the proverbial new kids on the block, and, although they weren't quite ready to be sculpted into model citizens, they were willing to put forth a good faith effort at their new label's behest.

News of an impending descent of the Butthole Surfers upon one's hometown always left fans feeling like they had just sucked a big balloon full of nitrous oxide. The lightheaded giddiness, coupled with throbbing waves of anxiety, echoing with a slight bit of flange. Fans danced down city streets en route to the proceedings, shouting "SATAN!"; spilling their beers and hurling synchronized leg kicks into the air. There was revelry that would have made Caligula himself blush, and the long respite the band had taken only increased the level electricity in the air.

"I'm goin to Hollywood…They'll see that I'm so good…"

But with everyone at Capitol suddenly becoming experts on how the Butthole Surfers should act (*'tone down the potty references, guys'*), the fun was getting drained out of things. Artists can rely on critics and editors for feedback, but the pre- packaged tour, the silly marketing angles, and countless banal interviews with the clueless mainstream media left them bored and uninspired. Playing every night was no problem, but the days were long and filled with endless questions about how they came up with the name Butthole Surfers.

"I won't care how I feel…And I'll get to fuck Brooke Shields…"

All of this might have dampened prospects for a triumphant return to the road, but the band was concentrating on bigger and better things. The prospect of leaving their homes and wives for a summer-long excursion was certainly made easier by not having to work every aspect of the tour. They could get on the bus and go rather than having to worry about booking, promoting, and financing the whole thing themselves.

Gibby, for his part, reluctantly accepted relinquishing his role as business manager, tour manager, and banker. Although he had vast experience playing those roles, he was freed from having to fist-fight promoters to get paid the money they were owed or having to call from the road to book the next gigs.

"And I'll just sit and grin…The money will roll right in…"

Gibby at Aquafest Stage, Vancouver, 7/7/93
© *Bev Davies*

In relinquishing the business of the band, he should have been able to focus on being an artist. But the frustration of feeling stifled and marketed to a record buying constituent he had little in common with, and even a smaller care for, became an increasingly difficult pill to swallow. The band played on, but as the tour progressed, oblivious crowds booed. Venues were often left half empty due to STP fans leaving en masse while the Buttholes were onstage.

Jeff:
"...To see Gibby go from being in charge of everything to not, I think affected the way he made some of his choices...like, 'if I'm not in charge, 'fuck it'." [phone, 6/20/14]

Gibby's mindset, and inevitably the shows themselves, began to deteriorate. Being outdoors only meant Gibby got to watch the headlights of cars as parking lots emptied during his set, and while he worked his ass off to perform. His mind and heart were in a bad place and all he wanted, desperately, was to be somewhere else.

It had been during the recording of "Jesus Built My Hotrod" that Gibby began dabbling with heroin and smoking crack cocaine. Ministry's Al Jourgensen had been a functional addict for years and the two of them together let the warming comfort of the nod wash over them as both bands stood on the edge of the true and life affirming success.

But now, those pillowy-soft, nod dreams of success and fame gave way to the harsh downer of regiments, schedules and countless industry dicks who knew, even better than Gibby himself, what was best for the band he had nurtured and starved for. Gibby found himself retreating more and more to the soft, warm cocoon of heroin rather than railing against the bastards as he always had in the past. To his credit, perhaps he didn't want to upset the apple cart or the other members of the band by fighting the powers in charge. These best intentions, however, paved the road to his own private hell.

Gibby had always been the outspoken prankster, but as Capitol lost confidence and interest in the Butthole Surfers, he was feeling his doubts as well and began sinking deeper and deeper into his anger and depression. Life-long friends were fearful of his condition. It had only been a few months since the release of *Independent Worm Saloon* and yet Gibby was already questioning the success he had strived to attain. Potentially more successful than if he had continued his career with Peat, Marwick, Mitchell.

"And I would give you some…If you only would have treated me nice

On this tour Gibby took his Gibbytronix box out of the dark recesses off to the side of the stage, where he toiled alone in the dark corner, and out to center stage on a console that stood beside his mic stand. Now, he was able to witness the audience douchebaggery firsthand, for those few who remained in attendance for their set.

More often than not, concerts were populated with the violent jocks and the frat boys they raged against when they were young punks opening for the Big Boys, the ones who used the music as a backdrop for their drunken idiocy. The revelry of these mainstream rockers finally seeing a General Admission show after so many Journey gigs played out on the dance floor in the form of shirtless jocks throwing aimless fists and hurling leg kicks mashing anyone who stepped too close. Or worse, gangs of burly meatheads picking fights with anyone who stepped into the pit. Music was not the answer it was the excuse, or rather the soundtrack, for their beatings, like a bit of the old Ludwig Von during the Ludovico treatments. This was not the dream we had envisioned when we thought punk rock could change the world.

...And you'll wish that you did...And you'll feel pretty stupid..."

Before long, Gibby began openly berating the crowds who, in turn, taunted and threw shit at the band. He played sets with his back turned to the audience in disgust, as Miles Davis had taken to doing when audiences shunned him for not being the trained seal they wanted him to be. A broadcast of "Who Was In My Room Last Night" on the nationally syndicated "In Concert" TV program shows Gibby leaning on his mic stand and facing King and the movies as the massive stage is engrossed in strobes and a high tech laser show. The crowds were either so bombarded by the assault, or too wrapped up in crowd surfing, to know or care, but anyone who took notice could see Gibby was unhappy, and there were still two full months of shows left to play.

"It's fun to be a star...It's nice to have a car...

In an attempt to hang out with STP and get acquainted during the first days of tour, Gibby partied with their lead singer Scott Weiland. Soon, Weiland too was using heroin and falling into a bad place in the grips of addiction. Tensions in the two camps mounted. After the tour ended, Weiland appeared on the Howard Stern Show shouting out Gibby by name, blaming Gibby for his own blossoming drug problem. The after-show partying often found the two bands wandering aimlessly backstage while their respective lead singers were off in separate rooms shooting up.

Yeah you'll have to admit...That I'll be rich as shit..."

Gibby's growing disdain for the huge venues and the clueless jocks that made up much of the audience only fueled his anger, which only fueled his desire to escape. Perhaps he thought he could get out his aggression and discontent by covering "The Money Will Roll Right In" by the Bay area hardcore band Fang, but it did little to help his bruised ego, and by the end of the tour he had a full-blown addiction.

"And I'll just sit and grin...The money will roll right in..."

The concept of success was now in question: A huge advance and a fully staffed promotional team, sold out venues with 10-foot-tall marquees touting the BUTTHOLE SURFERS name in lights, they were never dreamed of when they were playing at Studio 29 or the Raw Power & Light Co. Some money to buy beer and cigarettes or pay rent, or perhaps the blessing of a brief respite from the road to return to their collective home in the country. These were simple rewards.

Paul in Vancouver, 7/7/93
© Bev Davies

Now with each affording their own separate homes, recording sessions in multi-million-dollar studios, and shows in amphitheaters and stadiums, they were finally reaping the rewards for the dedication they had shown over the last decade of their existence.

But success also meant lawyers and managers, A&R Reps, and company executives, publicity and marketing agents: The same type of people Gibby ran from when he decided to quit Peat Marwick to become a Butthole Surfer. Roadies and lighting techs and street teams and lackeys the band had no idea about all relying on the band for their paychecks.

It was clear the Butthole Surfers couldn't be the alternative darlings the label was trying to make them into. They needed to bring back some sanity to the equation after the 'BBQ Mitzvah Tour' concluded. Perhaps, given the chance, they could prove to Gary Gersh that they could be a success on their own without the need for packaged bills with the latest industry alterna-darlings.

Jeff:
"What was really bad for me at that point was the guy who was acting as our

276

manager drove me and those guys apart. If it would have just been me and them together, I think it would have been a different scene. Supposedly, he was back on cocaine, and he was saying one thing to me and another to those guys...He definitely drove a wedge between many of the folks in the band..." [phone, 6/20/14]

But again, tour managers and managers and promoters had their own agendas and the band had seen what happened to the slow and weak like Hale Milgrim. They needed to produce and produce big. Shift units, get out the street teams, pump up the word-of-mouth name recognition. After playing the part of opening band for some Pearl Jam dates, it was time for them to headline the second leg of the "Independent Worm Saloon' tour.

This time it was the Mighty Mighty Bosstones that was chosen to share the bill as co-headliners. Paul and Jeff had never even heard of them prior to the pairing. This package made even less sense than the coupling with Stone Temple Pilots.

'They kicked into their first song and they started dancing around the stage and it definitely wasn't our thing', recalls Jeff. He looked over to Paul, who was standing across from him on the other side of the stage, aghast. After putting up with Pearl Jam's egos and the months on tour with STP, this was just too much to bear. What the hell were these guys doing? What the fuck were the suits at Capitol thinking?

Though the tour found them playing indoors at more intimate venues, where their stage show would actually be effective, the tour was over almost before it began. After a handful of shows together in Florida, Georgia and Virginia, an altercation (reportedly over MMBT's feeling that the 50/50 split of profits was unreasonable) left each band giving a resounding "fuck you" to the idea of spending any more time on the road with each other. Mighty Mighty Bosstones went back to Massachusetts, or wherever, and the Buttholes played the following two-night stint in Philadelphia by themselves.

Though they performed with the fire and intensity of a band that didn't have to sit through a Mighty Mighty Bosstones set, the tour was done before they were able to recoup their losses. They closed 1993 with week-long jaunt with none other than Nirvana, playing stadiums from Oakland up to Vancouver. They were colossal venues, but this time, infinitely more successful than the first leg of the tour. They had become quite friendly with the boys in Nirvana, who like themselves couldn't really understand the business of fame or the reality of how famous they had become, but who tried as best they could to deal with the endless barrage of bullshit. The difference with Nirvana's success was that they were afforded the luxury of being able to tell the record company what they wanted and have it magically appear at their feet. The Buttholes could barely get anyone at Capitol to open their office door.

In retrospect, 1993 had been a meteoric ride for the Butthole Surfers. They had spent the previous decade slowly and steadily recruiting new freaks into their ranks, and now, with a professional promotional team behind them, they were being recognized as the elder statesmen among the new crop of new "alternative" bands. Likewise, by all fiduciary standards, 1993 had been the most successful year in the band's history, hands down. They lit up the night skies in a streak of fire and rock, but the meteor was gradually and inevitably beginning to break apart as it entered earth's atmosphere and measured time and space.

The stone-cold reality was that Gibby was a junkie and Paul was watching his band, and more importantly his lifelong friendship, dissolve into dust. Paul's success wasn't limited to his guitar playing, but also his production work. That year he produced his first record that wasn't for his own band. 'Too High to Die' became a huge hit record for the Meat Puppets and its success allowed him to walk away after the Nirvana gigs, the Butthole Surfers last scheduled commitments, with other prospects that were potentially more lucrative, and certainly more fun than propping up his lead singer for another grueling tour.

King was also busy running his Trance Syndicate Record label that he had formed in 1990, and which was now the home to a growing stable of bands. His choice to live apart from the band had saved him from much of the drama and ill will felt between Gibby and Paul in particular, and though the future of the band was uncertain, he had his label, and a side project called Drain to keep him occupied while all the unpleasantries sorted themselves out.

Jeff, who had been left to play the middleman more often than he was playing the bass, also decided to form a side band with his old friends Jimbo Yongue, who by this point had moved to Austin, and workhorse drummer Rey Washam. His new outfit allowed him to escape from the drudgery that had become the Butthole Surfers and get back to what he loved: playing dirty, southern-fried psychedelic music in dingy rock clubs. Daddy Longhead, the 'one-off' side project he recorded while still very much a Butthole Surfer, began playing and practicing steadily and soon became his focus as priorities for the Buttholes subsided.

Capitol had little to offer the Butthole Surfers as far as what was next. They proposed a tour with Motley Crue, who had reformed with John Carraby on vocals, instead of Vince Neil. Not exactly what the Butthole Surfers had in mind, probably not Motley Crue either.

Jeff:
"That was it. That was the one that killed me. I remember two of us wanted to do it, and two of us didn't (I was one that didn't), and that's when Tom really started to clamp down on me. I knew Motley Crue was gonna get $70,000 with

John Carraby instead of Vince Neil, and I'm already seeing money lost. So they're [Gibby, Paul & King] gonna have a bad taste in their mouths, again...and for me, business-wise, it was just bad all the way around. We had already fucked up that shit with the Mighty Bosstones and now we're gonna go back out on this losing tour...we all had been heading in different directions: King was buying a house, Paul was doing production, and Gibby was trying to see if he could get something going, it just seemed the time was right." [phone, 6/20/14]

So instead of a tour with Motley Crue, the band took some time to handle other, more personal, matters. Gibby was beginning to feel the pains of addiction and checked himself into the Exodus Recovery Center outside of Los Angeles. There, he was reunited with Kurt Cobain, who was admitted shortly after Gibby had arrived. Kurt was in even worse shape and was enrolled in the program at the prodding of his wife, label, and friends. Within days, he went outside to smoke a cigarette and jumped the wall enclosing the property of the voluntary facility. He flew back to his home in Seattle and within days was found dead of a self-inflicted gunshot wound to the head.

Kurt's death and Nirvana's demise left fans mourning, and the music industry reeling. Without Nirvana as a beacon, marketing teams were left scrambling like rats on a sinking ship to find the next trend to latch onto. Alternative rock had been their cash cow for the previous three years, and now its future to generate huge profits was in disarray. Who would be the next voice of the new generation?

Shortly after Kurt's suicide, the new epoch of fans, dubbed "Gen X", discovered an artist who, like the Butthole Surfers, spent years in squalor in NYC: playing gigs at local clubs and coffee houses and recording songs on a cheap tape deck in his bedroom. Upon his return to his hometown of Los Angeles, he recorded his song "Loser". The sparse acoustic track was then remixed by a couple of his friends and made into a white boy hip-hop, blues number. It was picked up by a local radio station in LA and caught the attention of some A&R folk at Gary Gersh's old haunt, Geffen Records. The track caught on like a bad cold, and soon the mild-mannered Beck Hanson became the unwilling and unwitting replacement for Kurt Cobain and Nirvana.

Beck's early material culled from a vast array of influences, from punk rock to blues and folk to found sound assemblage, and just about everything in between. He honed his chops playing covers of Mississippi John Hurt songs for spare change but spent hours on end of jamming and recording in his room. Before long, he had a vast and varied catalogue of material, the ranged from blistering hardcore romps to lo-fi country ballads, often using two boom boxes to' multi-track' his recordings. His ethic owed more to the golden era of experimental punk than the new era of pompous rock bands that had been marketed since Nirvana's emergence.

Mainstream music of the 1990's was more like the 1970's had become prior to punk rock shaking things up. Big dumb rock dominated the airwaves and the Billboard charts and anything else was overlooked or ignored. The formula for success was in place and it was adhered to like flies on flypaper by both labels and the bands looking for mainstream acceptance. Beck's homegrown melodies were eclectic, earthy, and unpretentious and were the perfect antidote to the barrage of cookie-cutter bands that had been unloaded like yesterday's trash by major labels looking to score the next "Smells Like Teen Spirit"

Labels knew little about alternative music and seemingly signed everyone in an effort to figure out the tastes of music fans. Beck was one of the artists who would have probably been subjected to the same grueling and miserable existence the Buttholes had come accustomed to over the previous decade, but instead became a star, and the poster child of a generation of so-called 'slackers'.

Beck harkened back to the time when the Butthole Surfers were recording in their kitchen, creating house music versions of classic 70's rock anthems and splicing together bits and pieces of tape to create their own sonic explorations. It seemed that, in the absence of the Butthole Surfers of yore, the world was now ready for the band they had been in the past: experimental, trippy and completely unaffected by any trends that came, went, and faded into the lexicon of pop culture nostalgia. Using the better part of a century of American music as a canvas, they slung together patterns and textures that was the musical equivalent to a Jackson Pollock painting.

This brave new world passed by outside while Gibby shook and sweated out his junk sickness, and upon his release into straight society it continued to rotate and revolve. It had been more than a year since 'Independent Worm Saloon' and there was seemingly little prospect that the band would ever play together again at all. Even if there was a chance of getting back into a studio, most of the fun had been sucked dry. Paul and Gibby were barely on speaking terms, and they had recorded nearly all the songs they had in the can during the sessions that produced 'Independent Worm Saloon'.

Inspired to create, write and play music again, Jeff formally announced to the rest of the band that he was leaving for good. He had a whole album's worth of material already written for Daddy Longhead and with the Butthole Surfers on life support, the time had come to give up the ghost. Gibby was spending most of his time hanging out in LA, Paul was busy producing, and King was the patriarch of the younger bands on Trance Syndicate Records, who all owed a debt to the Butthole Surfers and were packing clubs around Austin.

It seemed increasingly unlikely, with all the awful craziness of the previous year, and complete lack of enthusiasm at Capitol, that they were going to call everyone back together to the same locale. Even if they did, Jeff had decided that another big budget, polished Butthole Surfers package tour, and the drama that it brought, was no longer worth the trouble.

☙

Jeff:
"I remember Gibby said to me, 'What would you like to see happen in the band?' and I told him that I'd like for us to all get together again in the same room and write songs again. And, they were at the point where they were into just passing around discs to each other and not be in the same room...and play songs like that..." [phone interview, 6/20/2014]

☙

While a simple one, the request for everyone to get together in the same room again was more than Gibby, Paul and King could muster. Jeff was saddened, but with his new project gaining steam, and the Butthole Surfers in a bizarre state of limbo, he got returned to the underground with his integrity firmly intact.

The southern fried prog-rock blues experience of Daddy Longhead, and later Honky, was in stark contrast to the more professional brand of stadium rock the Buttholes were becoming. Jeff needed to bring it back down to the small bars and honky tonks where he spent his time when not being whisked to shows in a huge custom bus with an entourage of industry dicks in tow. It was nice to bring it back to the streets and back alleys once again.

With many of the alternative bands on majors, the void they left in independent scene was filling up with cool acts that had always been relegated to small labels in the past. Bands like KARP from Olympia, Washington, the Jesus Lizard (formed out of the ashes of Scratch Acid), and Oakland, California's SLEEP, whose mammoth hour long epic "Jerusalem" (later retitled "Dopesmoker") was a completely uncompromising magnum opus to weed. These bands were the newest breed of punks. They eluded the majors by breaking the rules and punishing the listener with an aural sledgehammer. It was far better in the underground than in the bratty, spoiled world of corporate rock. Like college basketball in relation to the NBA, it was nice to see bands having to fight for their art, and not resting on their laurels and financing their drug habits with a hefty advance from the label.

Jeff helped to mold the Butthole Surfers into the band they had become. He helped form them from their unrefined and undefined lump of clay into Rodin's Gates of Hell: with mammoth riffs and sticky, purple nugs as his hammer and chisel. When he began his tenure on bass, he was being called "Jeff the black-haired guy" in press articles: just another lackey in the cavalcade of souls who occupied the role of bass guitarist for the Butthole Surfers.

He seemed destined to become merely another footnote in their history. But, now, eight years after his first show, where he tapped on contact mics stuffed in his jeans as a JackOfficer, it was glaringly obvious that there was no other bassist who had contributed more to the sound, image, and success of the band as did JD Pinkus.

Bill Jolly had helped make the band infamous within the confines of Texas, and Terence got them out of Texas and out onto the road, but Jeff brought them up from the streets and out into the cosmos. It was nearly impossible now to think of what the Butthole Surfers would have become without Jeff Pinkus on bass guitar.

In years past, any change in line-ups or internal band business played out in their living room or in the back of their RV. Now, it was playing out in industry papers, on the internet, and out in the public domain. The enigma that had lent itself to many of the legends about the band was gone, and with much of the news about the band being negative, it seemed almost better to look away than to see our heroes reduced to ghosts.

The label spin regarding Jeff's departure, of course, cited 'musical differences', as labels tend to do, and the band seemed to be falling victim to the very fate they had feared before signing their names to that contract three years before: almost exactly as Gibby had predicted during that MTV interview backstage at Lollapalooza. That was back when Hale Milgrim was still in charge and Capitol was still excited about signing them. Now, Gary Gersh seemed to be doing everything he could to avoid them.

Signing to a major label did more to kill the Butthole Surfers than the years of squalor, hunger, and destitution. A year would pass with little more than a peep from the band's camp. There were no prospects for a record, nor a tour, nor was there even inspiration enough to get back in the same room together. It seemed as if the Butthole Surfers might finally be over.

What Do They Know about Love?

The Butthole Surfers laid languid and enervated. Their friendships suffered and their inspirations were few. Paul was left feeling betrayed and Gibby was straggling around LA and taking bit parts in movies. He spent his nights hanging out with the bad boy movie actors who, like himself, had some spare cash and a penchant for opiates. King was too busy with his own record label to be bothered.

The band was always on their minds, but their hearts were not reciprocating. Finally, though, after nearly two years spent completely apart, with the few scant recordings released piecemealed together, the remaining 3 members of the Butthole Surfers felt enough of a spark of inspiration to write and record together again.

The initial press releases announcing the Butthole's upcoming sophomore effort for Capitol Records entitled 'Oklahoma!' were a pleasant shock and surprise for the fans who remained faithful, many of whom believed they heard the last notes from their musical heroes.

Any idea of a punk rock ethos was almost laughable at this time. With William Jefferson Clinton in the White House and the economy rebounding after years of stagnation, it seemed that many of the voices of opposition had fallen silent. With the majors snatching up even the most alternative of alternative bands, independent labels were struggling to survive. Independent labels were left to build up new artists from the ground up and before long, many of those bands ditched them and headed for the majors as well.

America was in full recovery mode and there was little reason to complain. Almost all the bands who had survived through the 1980's were now millionaires. They were the new faces of rock's mainstream. There was little reason to rock the boat when life was good, the house was paid for, and records were flying off the shelves. It seemed the death of conservatism and rise of the Baby Boomers left most of the artists and visionaries lulled into a dreamlike state of contentment. There were few reasons to buck the system when the system was providing a decent living and the ways and means of putting food on the table, even to those as outside the mainstream as the Butthole Surfers.

There was still plenty to be pissed off about: global allies in NAFTA and the G8 gave big business a chance to affect policies of big government, Republicans and Democrats continued to play their cat and mouse games, shutting down the government over petty gripe,; and brutal genocides in both Rwanda and in the former Yugoslavia were ignored as the world watched on TV. Despite it all, most musicians and artists had lost all interest and inspiration to rabble rouse. Abbie Hoffman was of the same generation as the Clintons, but his was the politics of fools. The new left was far more ameliorating to the real power brokers on Wall Street and in China. They took a page from Reagan and realized the financial benefits of playing nice with their corporate overlords.

The music scene reeled once again as Jerry Garcia's death killed the Dead and brought a plethora of nouveau-hippie bands trying, but failing miserably, to fill the void left in their absence. It was the same old glossy drivel the industry had tried to push on the kids like high fructose corn syrup throughout the 70's and 80's. Peace signs equaled dollar signs. With a baby boomer president, we were now treated to Fleetwood Mac blaring out of the White House windows instead of Wayne Newton. It might have rocked a little harder, but it was equally nauseating.

The Buttholes tried to keep visible in their absence by releasing 'The Hole Truth and Nothing Butt', a fan produced live bootleg compilation that King repressed on Trance Syndicate. Then came a Christmas themed 7" picture disc. It had been two years since they had played out live, though, and they still didn't have a bass player to replace Jeff. Their fan base had scattered, some grew up, some returned deep into the underground scene looking for the spark of vibrancy still left in bands who were struggling to make ends meet. Of the newest fans of 'alternative music, few remembered that it was the Butthole Surfers we had always looked toward to save us from the doldrums and banality of so-called mainstream rock.

Now the Butthole Surfers were mainstream rock. When Capitol felt the name 'Oklahoma!', could bring about lawsuits from the estate of Rogers & Hammerstein, the band acquiesced and renamed their new offering 'Electriclarryland', which Capitol ok'd with little fear the Hendrix estate would even bother to care. It certainly wasn't the best sign that we were going to be delivered the 90's equivalent to *Locust Abortion Technician*.

But, the band was older and the silly simple requests to change the name of their record didn't seem like the most important thing in the world, even if the advanced cassettes had already gone out to radio and press. Perhaps it really wasn't a big deal, 'Electriclarryland' is probably the better name anyway, but the knowledge of the Butthole Surfers were, yet again, caving to label demands brought a big sigh from those few fans who still cared.

Still, the Butthole Surfers had other, more pressing things on their plate, ones that would test the limits of their indie credibility to a breaking point. One that would shock fans in a way that not even an on-stage fuck show at Danceteria could. They decided to sue Corey Rusk and Touch & Go Records.

Everybody's Talkin' 'bout Lawyers

It was December of 1995, and the remaining members of the band were putting the finishing touches on the record formerly known as 'Oklahoma!'. It was also around this time when the papers were drawn up and filed with the Illinois State legal system. Those same papers had already been sent off to Corey Rusk, requesting a change in the original oral agreement between the two parties.

The letter requested a new deal of profit sharing from the original handshake deal of 50/50 to an 80/20 split for the band on all monies earned on the sale of their Touch & Go product. After 3 years' time, this deal would expire, at which time the band would then take back control of their entire Touch & Go catalogue.

The band, through their manager, Tom Bunch (the same Tom Bunch at TAB Productions, that booked the 'naked Houston' show so many moons before), had attempted to contact Corey several times and each attempt had been ignored. Corey later admitted that he wanted to hear from the band and not from their representatives, since he made the original deal with them, not with Tom Bunch.

The band admitted in the press that Tom's method of handling the task might have exacerbated some of the hard feelings still left over from their initial split from Touch & Go. But, they also note that Tom was indeed their manager at the time, and the man they paid 15% of their earnings to in order to handle their business affairs. Corey had an obligation to reply to the renegotiation request no matter what his personal feelings may have been toward Tom Bunch or the band.

It had been more than 5 years since the band's last release on Touch & Go and the request seemed like a fair one to Paul, King, and Gibby. The Butthole Surfers were able to boost sales of their back catalogue at least twice in the previous 5 years since leaving the label: once with the success of "Hurdy Gurdy Man" and then again with "Who Was In My Room Last Night". This is discounting their success at Lollapalooza and the increased popularity of the CD format, which had music fans replacing their entire LP collections with the new 'rich man's 8-track'.

Aside from their own successes, Ministry's use of Gibby for "Jesus Built My Hotrod", and Kurt Cobain's recognition of the band as a personal inspiration certainly drew more people to check out the best of the Butthole Surfers catalog, all of which was on the Touch & Go label. The Butthole Surfers continued to be the label's mainstay act for years after they stopped releasing records for them. Corey had moved on to promote his newer label stalwarts, leaving the Butthole Surfers recent successes to promote their own back catalogue. Still, he continued to earn 50% of all the money made on the sales of Butthole Surfers product.

With the Jesus Lizard's output and Steve Albini's post-Big Black outfit Shellac now in full swing, as well as a host of up-and-coming bands, Touch & Go had a new cache of groups to keep itself in the black, along with the Butthole Surfers back catalog. Promoting the Butthole Surfers was completely unnecessary. Corey could leave that work to the promotional staff at Capitol to do on his behalf.

Along with a distribution deal with ¼ Stick Records he acquired, Corey and Touch & Go became one of the most successful indies still in operation. It flourished despite the plundering that occurred at most indie labels since Nirvana dug up the underground scene. Corey had learned the business of selling music since the Buttholes had left the label and was able to survive and thrive based on his newfound business savvy.

When he finally got the cease-and-desist letter from the band's representatives and was told to immediately stop selling Butthole Surfers product, and to immediately return the band's master tapes, the battle lines were drawn. He was not going to let the Butthole Surfers get away with their aggression without a fight. The letter from Capitol's suits was an affront to his indie sensibilities. The band had agreed to the 50/50 split back in 1984 and now they were asking for an 80/20 split more than a decade later, along with a termination time limit: All this with the backing of their expensive corporate lawyers? Perhaps it was the realization that one of his biggest money makers was cutting off his meal ticket, or that he honestly felt betrayed, but in either case, he was ready to take the challenge.

Corey was hurt and angered, and he jotted a quick note back to them stating that the deal they had agreed to was final. The deal, he argued, would be in place for a duration of at least 15 years (the time that it takes for a normal licensing deal to expire), and that he, being the license holder, would keep the records that the Butthole Surfers made as his own. Furthermore, there would be no negotiation on Corey's part for any change that hadn't already been agreed to between the band and himself those many years ago.

The band was shocked by Corey's reaction and his inflexibility. The fact was, Corey was making more money on each record than each individual band member of the band was making. The Butthole Surfers art was being held hostage and their livelihood was being denied them. With little else they could do in the form of recourse, options were fading. With both parties at an impasse, the outcome, it seemed, would need to be settled, not by the parties themselves, but by the Illinois Northern District Court. Corey hired attorney Santiago Durango former guitarist of Naked Raygun, Big Black, and Arsenal to handle his affairs.

It was the beginning of a four-year knock-down-drag-out brawl that left the Buttholes becoming the punching bags for nearly every independent label and artist who hadn't yet died of starvation or a heroin overdose. Once the darlings of the underground, the bastions of independence, and the yard stick used to judge one's level of coolness, the Butthole Surfers were now the lowest of all corporate shills whose only motivation could be to destroy any and all of the last vestiges of punk rock.

Was this the same band who had struggled to get Alternative Tentacles to notice that they existed? Was this the same band that was courted by Corey to join the sparse ranks of bands who were then Touch & Go artists? The Butthole Surfers, then, just wanted an outlet to release their material as a way to make a few bucks while being stymied by Alternative Tentacles. Some way to get their tapes out of hock from the BOSS to put out their next record.

They had developed a true friendship with Corey. He was one of the few people at the time who had any faith in the band at all. Thus began their tenure with Touch & Go, with a simple oral agreement of a 50/50 split between band and label. What seemed to be an easy way to get their material out was now a shackle around their necks that would take the better part of a decade to remove. Back in 1984, no one could have dreamed that the Butthole Surfers would survive long enough to witness underground music become mainstream, or that the band would ever be courted by a major record label. Who could have even imagined it? Certainly not the Butthole Surfers. And even with all his faith in the band, surely not Corey Rusk.

As the Butthole Surfers matured into the highest grossing independent band in the world, it still seemed impossible to believe they would reap their profits from a major record label, let alone achieve even the modest successes that they had seen up until this point in 1995. It was only through their epic tour schedule, dizzying work ethic, and their faith and resilience that they garnered any success at all; these, as well as Corey's undying belief in them. And yet, despite their gratitude for his support during those lean times, it was now time to cut off the trust fund.

The Butthole Surfers' success was earned on the roads of America. They amassed followers little by little along the path to their New Jerusalem. With each performance they inched one step closer to the Promised Land. A covenant was forged between these acid drenched Gods and their loyal disciples. The News the band delivered in the form of a new studio release was merely the Word; the scripture; A testament to the religious experience. Their shows were true religious experiences. Though the experience could never be reproduced with quite the same rapturous joy in the scriptures, the 'Words' were proof that the miracles were real.

Corey could certainly testify to the miracles found in the Word of the Butthole Surfers, for he earned 50% of the profits on each sale of their back catalogue, despite having little else to do but to breathe their name in public. When the band was on Touch & Go he pushed them like Elmer Gantry at a country revival, selling them like snake oil to a bald man. But now, the Butthole Surfers records sold themselves, and any of the money that was made from the sale of the Butthole Surfers previous releases was put back into promoting the next Girls Against Boys record, not financing the next Buttholes venture.

As bad as things were between the two camps, and as they so often seemed to be for the Butthole Surfers since deciding to leave Touch & Go in the first place, the equation was about to get even more complicated. The Butthole's successes up until this point had been fairly modest, but that was about to change, and the sales of their back catalogue were about to spike like never before.

With the release of *Electriclarryland* in May of 1996; and the success of the single, "Pepper"; the album breached the Billboard Top 40 Charts, and by August of that same year, the album was certified as Gold by the Recording Industry Association of America, selling over 600 thousand units in just its first few months.

It was an astounding revelation for a band that, mere months earlier, were, for all intents and purposes, non-existent. Paul recalls the recording of 'Electric Larryland' much in the same way he recalls the recording of their earliest material.

Paul:
"Our first few records were recorded while we were barely a band, and our last few records were the same." [email, 3/2014]

It had been yet another triumph of will that further exemplified the resilience of their friendship, and as a band. But again, instead of being able to celebrate their successes, they were left lamenting them. The boost in sales of their back catalogue due to the success of "Pepper" brought absolutely no money their way, not even the 50% they had seen before. Now, all profits were being held in limbo, tied up in the United States legal system.

An RIAA certified album, along with the bitter and contentious lawsuit, brought out indie heavyweights from Steve Albini to their old pals Ian McKaye and Tim Kerr of the Big Boys decrying their name. The Butthole Surfers were the new sellouts: heartless and greedy corporate rockers.

Cries of the "Beckhole Surfers", and scorn from critics and fans; many of whom were faced with the harsh reality of having to make excuses for all the fuss they once made over a band who was now in the Billboard Top 40, left them cold and alone. New fans bought records but did not build a solid base of support. While many just liked the song, they weren't in the band's corner believing in them. It was lonely at the top. And now, suing their former record label and threatening to drive it out of business had made them pariahs.

The very subject of the Butthole Surfers became toxic. In Holland, the same place they were once heralded as "sensations of the Pandora festival," a DJ prefaced a broadcast with: 'in the 80's the band was interesting, now they're just dull'.

It would be difficult to convince people that their new messiah, Beck, had spent his first US tour closing shows with a song called "Jimmy" (aka: Jimmy Carter); a song in which feedback blared, and fires were often ignited about the stage; as often happened when the Butthole Surfers played their own magnum opus, "Jimi". Most would have been alarmed to discover that it was not he, but the Butthole Surfers, who had reignited the rock'n'roll rituals which became so commonplace in music at this time.

Now, the Butthole Surfers were accused of being copycats by critics who were either too young to have witnessed the band in their prime, or too old and crusty in their punk rock belief system to admit their influence on most every other band in the world that was worth a damn.

With a marketing machine like Capitol now behind them, they were reaping the rewards of all their hard work. But success is relative, and the band, or what was left of it, began to realize that some of their happiest memories were when they were scratching and scraping to survive, when they were playing shows and booking tours with a fire and a purpose.

With the hornet's nest busted open, they now had to tour behind a record that had reopened so many old wounds. They would have almost rather have hidden their faces in their pillows and locked the doors at their own respective homes than to have to face the roar of the crowd.

The real shame is that *Electriclarryland* is a great pop record. They returned to a more straight-forward punk rock sound, that mixed elements of trance, electronica and even dance music into their bag of tricks. The record was much more diverse than *Independent Worm Saloon*, and more reflective, as well. They still had the hard driving rock songs in 'Birds' and 'Ulcer Breakout', but the album was, for lack of a better word, peppered with more nuanced tracks like "Space" and "Let's Talk about Cars", and the diversity of that material gave it a more well-rounded appeal.

As for "Pepper", the song which gained them their status as a 'one-hit wonder', it was Gibby's lovelorn reflection on a simpler time: the early days of the punk rock scene back in Dallas. Like Richard Linklater's film, the love letter to Austin weirdness, *Slacker*, (featuring a cameo by none other than Teresa Taylor herself in the movie's most memorable role), "Pepper" was a guided tour through Texas' old scene; mentioning fellow scenesters and friends like Chit Cherie and Bobby Soxx by name. The song incriminated the guilty parties and lamented on the many joyous and sad times, as well as the untimely demises Gibby experienced while still trying to find a career that didn't involve being a staff auditor at America's largest accounting firm.

"Pepper" journeyed back to the days when Superman's Girlfriend, VDegenerates, Terminal Mind and Sharon Tate's Baby were the local legends, and the wild times when Gibby was dragged out of a PIL show in Austin by his hair. Back then, that was the worst of his troubles. Now, he was fighting his own demons rather than a gang of bouncers, and his old friends at Touch & Go behind a bevy of attorneys.

"Pepper" reminisces on simpler times, like the perfumed whiff of a t-shirt worn the previous night, flooding back the avalanche of memories of the night before. "Pepper" whisks us into that dream-like daze of a morning's hangover. It lingers in a calm, post-LSD melancholia where senses peak and muscles tingle. The fragrance carries you back to some distant time that only survives in the wispy haze of flickering cognitive photographs.

With this new offering to the public came, not a daydream of reminiscence, but rather a real and sobering reality: those of the obligations of another tour and all

the

Mark Farner
© Pat Blashill

temptations that being out on the road would bring, especially for the struggling Gibby. In light of all the other horrible weirdness going on in the Butthole Surfers camp, the road was not really where they wanted to be.

Paul, like Gibby, was also in bad shape, but for other, far more personal reasons. His mother had recently been diagnosed with terminal cancer and would pass away while he stood on an outdoor stage at a scheduled appearance in Tulsa, Oklahoma.

A calm breeze passed around his head and Paul knew even before his dad, Paul Walthall, Sr, broke the news to him over the phone after the show. Mark Farner, the legendary terrier and band mascot, who soared high above their heads in the pages of SPIN magazine passed away, too.

Farner had been the sixth member of the band and had seen them at their worst. She endured longer than all their bass players combined and loved them no matter what happened. She guarded equipment and scared promoters into coughing up cash. Later, she would revel at the house they all bought together in Driftwood, almost as much for her to scamper happily as for the band to record and play. Loyalty repaid. She had been stuffed into the Lady Killer and various vans, RV's, and busses for most of her life, as had her owners. She, like they, had surely earned her place in the sun.
290

But as Paul embarked on a tour behind a record that would shortly go gold, the walls of his life were crumbling around him. Large venues were selling out across the country, but his heart lay in mourning. His heart was with his mom, and on being home, not on being a Butthole Surfer: and certainly not being a Butthole Surfer for the other 22 ½ hours of the day in which he wasn't out on stage. There, he could forget his troubles and wield his mighty battle axe against the forces of reality. Offstage, unarmed, he sat defenseless to the seemingly unending barrage of long drives, bad interviews, and of course, Gibby's demons.

Paul:
"I never think of tours as album tours, but the tour we did summer of '96 was brutal. My mother was terminally ill, and I was flying home after shows to spend time with her. She passed away when I was on stage in Oklahoma during an outdoor show. I remember feeling a cool breeze and knowing what had happened before making the phone call home. That tour was no fun."
[email Dec, 2012]

Offstage, where the dream ended, was the darkness: the distance from his mom and his family; his best friend and co-founding bandmate barely on speaking terms; and the storm cloud of fear that he might wake up on any particular morning and find Gibby dead of an overdose.

It was outside the Viper Room in Los Angles three years prior. During a performance of Gibby's one-off side-project "P", which he had formed with some of his Hollywood pals (including actor Johnny Depp), where Gibby's friend River Phoenix collapsed and died on the sidewalk. It was just on the other side of the wall as the band staggered through their set. Gibby's trajectory seemed sadly on the same course. He was getting better, perhaps, but it was a daily struggle, and even more of a struggle for those, like Paul, who had his own grief which to contend.

Like the end of Werner Hertzog's *Stroszek,* carnival animals dance and a solitary player piano plays a solemn tune. An unmanned pick-up truck drives in circles like a whirligig. An unoccupied ski lift, too, spins around and around: bringing nobody to nowhere. The tour bus wheels spin as well. They spin around in circles as the bus circles the United States and stop only for the animals to dance and surf the crowd. What should have been the pinnacle of their existence was their nadir. What used to be important now seemed meaningless. And what used to be their way to escape all the world's problems seemed, almost, to be the cause of them.

This new version of the Butthole Surfers was no longer the tight-knit group of friends who had spent previous decade as a battalion against the insanity. Now, they were a commodity fulfilling contractual obligations until they could get back home to their friends and loved ones and latest inspirations; ones the band seemed to be keeping them from, rather than being the vehicle for. But, they got on the bus and got out on stage and the fans cheered and welcomed them back. After three years of waiting, the Butthole Surfers were finally back on stage.

For the *Electriclarryland* tour, King grabbed Owen McMahon, bassist from CHERUBS, a band in his Trance Syndicate stable. Kyle Ellison was added as a second guitarist. They weren't much of a band anymore and even took most press photos as a trio of just Gibby, Paul and King.

The U.S. leg of the tour started in Austin in June of 1996, and by August, had them featured in their network television debut, in a rare triumphant appearance on Late Night with David Letterman; where so many years prior Sandra Bernhardt had bragged about her wild night with the Butthole Surfers as stage managers fumbled for the bleep censor.

It was indeed a lifetime ago, it seemed, since they were that band struggling to make ends meet and living on handouts and hard work. They were older now, and despite Rome burning all around them, at this Letterman appearance at least, they seemed relaxed and to be actually enjoying themselves for the first time in ages.

At the tour's conclusion, they put down their instruments and parted ways. It was November and, combined with the European dates prior to the US tour, they had been on road for nearly the entire half of 1996. It was time to take care of the business of life and leave the business of the Butthole Surfers in the hands of the managers and lawyers.

Circling back home to Austin for their final night of the tour, they let go of all the baggage of the previous year and just played with abandon. They got back to being the band they thought was lost. One that didn't need to live up to label expectations, album promotions, or sales numbers. They eased into their set with a loose trip hop improvisational jam they called "It's Jazz, Man", with Gibby using his Casio and voice modulator to spin a pseudo-DJ set before Paul broke into the opening strains of "Cough Syrup".

"She played for the angels, I played for the tribe…the summer had exploded and the bases were all loaded there was big money on the line…"

The second song of the night showed the crowd the "Pepper" that was not a 'copycat' hit song or 'regurgitated Beck track', but a song that was fit to stand among the Butthole Surfer canon of rich and varied material without need for comparison or compromise. Paul's extended solo was graceful and beautiful and left even the long-time fans in attendance baffled and blissing.

Their closing noise jam stretched nearly a half-hour in length, and featured Sean Lennon and the rest of his bandmates in Cibo Matto joining the Butthole Surfers onstage for the madness. The show faded out in a near full circle with "More Jazz, Man"; trippy beats provided by Gibby on his keyboard before dissolving into chatter and the crowd cheering for their struggling heroes. It was the best show they had played in years and would also be the last they would play for years.

It had been nearly two years since Kurt Cobain had killed himself and grunge was becoming out of vogue, but the Buttholes proved they were not following any sort of trend, but rather that the trends had followed them. The Butthole Surfers were always there, doing what they did, it was the industry and newer fans that had finally caught on to it, and not the Butthole Surfers catering to any pigeon-hole du jour.

As the lights faded into darkness and they packed away their instruments, it seemed unclear as to whether the Butthole Surfers would ever play together again. Despite their success with "Pepper", and the sales of *Electriclarryland*, the suits at Capitol were still unimpressed. The band had achieved a Top 40 hit, and still could barely get their label to listen to them. Capitol didn't even bother to release a follow up single from the album.

Paul:
"Gary Gersh became president at Capitol, and he and I never hit it off. After our album went gold, he called us into his office to celebrate, then made us wait outside of his office for half an hour. Then, during the 'celebration,' he came up to me and said 'Hi, I'm Gary Gersh, and I really respect what you do.' I started thinking maybe he did respect what we did, but he came back to me a minute later and said 'Hi, I'm Gary Gersh, and I really respect what you do,' not remembering he had just told me that." [email, 12/18/12]

Instead, Capitol insisted on treating the Butthole Surfers like a band who needed to be clumped in with more lucrative acts to prove themselves. They were paired with Moby to produce "Tiny Rubberband" for the 'Spawn' movie soundtrack and were thrown onto a silly 'Saturday Morning Cartoon' compilation, covering the theme to the 1970's animated classic, "Underdog". Their last two efforts for Capitol had garnered more financial success than the label could ever have dreamed, even if most of the profits were still tied up in the Illinois legal system.

They had proven that they could rock with the kids and proven that they were willing to compromise with Capitol for the greater good of artist \ label harmony. But it was becoming increasingly apparent that the relationship was too often one sided and strained.

They had grown tired of making "big dumb rock albums," says King, and as inspirations finally began to flow for a new project, Paul and Gibby and King dropped the baggage which had been heaped upon them and began recording demos for fun. Now it was time to make a record for themselves and no one else, not for the new fans, nor the old fans, and certainly not for the suits at Capitol.

It was unclear who might be listening anymore, anyway. It made more sense to abandon all codes, rules and laws and simply create beautiful music. Having achieved some semblance of fame, as fleeting as it can be, and a true hit song, which is even more fleeting, the band got back to what they knew best: producing an uncompromising work that would completely change the direction of what they had become since signing with Capitol.

As 1997 played out, and rock music suffered from the hangover of the post-grunge doldrums, the Butthole Surfers began tinkering on their most imaginative and avant-garde work since *Hairway to Steven*. With the working title of "After the Astronaut," their newest batch of songs mixed the frenzied industrial elements found on Al Jourgensen's Wax Trax label, with the sweeping textural soundscapes of Brian Eno, The Orb, or Massive Attack. It was a complete 180-degree turn from what they had been producing, and inevitably, upon its unveiling to the suits at Capitol, they hated it.

Capitol had gotten spoiled reaping the rewards from a band they never would have signed had there not been a grunge movement, or if Gary Gersh was in charge instead of Hale Milgrim. Nirvana was gone now, but the formula for success had been forged. Major labels had little time for bands that wanted to change direction or experiment with new material. Now that the Butthole Surfers were actually shifting units, there was no need, from the label suits' point of view, to change a winning formula.

At best, Gary Gersh and the Capitol heads tolerated the band Hale Milgrim had courted six years previous. There was no love lost between the band and their new home, but with records selling, Capitol couldn't find enough of a reason to drop them. The record that the Butthole Surfers were calling 'After the Astronaut' would give them the out they were looking for.

The band had been shackled by packaged tours and industry tedium, touring had become a complete drag, and the lawsuit with Touch & Go dragged on into its second year; leaving sales of their old catalog in the defendant's hands. The recent death of Paul's mother, and strained relationships left feelings dour. If the band wasn't quite feeling like being a band, then Capitol was finding even less of a reason to finance the demos they were given for the new record.

The Butthole Surfers had far exceeded the expectations that Capitol had for them. Now, however, it was time for them to produce their art on their own terms. To shut their studio doors and close off the outside world: To tinker and toil and turn the knobs. Take the rocket into space and view the world outside their window in the third person.

This is Domino Excavator… on an exploratory satellite, number 5-8-12…

The world below reeled with lawyers and businessmen. With old friends who unfairly judged them and bad mouthed them in the press and with new fans who had already traded in their *Electriclarryland* CDs for the newest Marilyn Manson release. It was lonely at the top.

"If one party becomes a fucking jerk, no contract is going to help. The Butthole Surfers wanted more money. What's at issue is one party let their greed totally upset the balance of the relationship." - **Ian McKaye**
['Touch and Go v. The Buttholes" by Josh Goldfein; Chicago Reader, 4/16/99]

It seemed as if only one party adhered to the gag order imposed by the court, as Corey's pals jumped to his defense. And yet, high above the clouds, in the rarified air, the blues turned to a peaceful black stillness…

It seems that the people are very sad, everyone is just sort of confused right now…it seems as if some sort of device has been detonated here…and uh…there's a lot of confusion…

And so, our three remaining astronauts climbed into their craft, with a bobble-head statue of Jesus bouncing wildly on the console as they bounded into the cosmos. They looked curiously out the porthole window and surveyed the devastation below…

There are absolutely no ambulances… no ambulances, at all, in the area…

'After the Astronaut' brought the live show into the studio and fed it through synthesizers and midi devices. Though not sounding quite like anything they had ever produced in the past, the record returned them to their classic ingredients that made *Rembrandt Pussyhorse* so successful: manic, off kilter guitar solos, warped time signatures, found samples, and the use of Gibbytronix; the voice modulator that Gibby had been using less and less of since he had started to actually write down the lyrics to his songs.

Somehow they got control of the …transmitter…it's just…bodies everywhere…just bodies.

With little left to lose, they went back to having fun; utilizing the years of knowledge of engineering, mixing, and producing their own material to create a piece of art unlike anything else in their own, or anyone else's, canon of work. There was just one problem: It was never going to see the light of day.

Complete Separation

The February 2, 1998 release date came and went without a peep from the band or the label. Rumors of artwork woes and legal wranglings circulated. As advance cassettes leaked out to press and radio insiders, there was still no word as to when the record would get its proper unveiling to fans.

The initial delay, it was rumored, came from Capitol's fears of a lawsuit from the estate of Malcolm X, due to the lyrics of the song "The Weird Revolution". Though none of the lyrics appear to be attributable to the slain civil rights activist, the ideas and tone of the rhetoric are straight out of X's notebook. Instead of a cry against the racist system of capitalism and jurisprudence, Gibby tweaked the rant to become a rail against 'the normal society which completely freaked him out'. It is an anarchistic tirade that Gibby delivered with passion and vehemence worthy of Shabazz himself, even if not actually attributable to him.

Then, rumors circulated about artwork delays. Weeks turned into months and soon after, rumors of legal tussling between the band and label began circulating. Still, both camps remained silent as to when fans could expect the album's release. It seemed the label was determined to hold the record in check indefinitely.

The record was long ditched before another Capitol recruit, the Marcy Playground, found the art that was proposed to be the disc's back over among the cache of artwork in the archives. Capitol's art department simply gave it to them. Even if the album ever gets a proper release one day, the original art would be unavailable.

Mark Ryden (artist):
"I was hired by Capitol Records to do a new Butthole Surfers album cover. Paul Leary specifically wanted the image of an Indian woman with an alien baby. He was into the idea of combining Indians and Aliens. I did a painting of that image, but then also did a painting for the back cover, which was my own concept with that theme. I did the image of the Indian and alien cowboy at the campfire. Capitol and the band got into legal disagreements and the band left the label. The album project with my art was killed. Years later Capitol was doing a project with Marcy Playground. The name of the album was "Shape Shifter". My back cover image fit this perfectly. The art department and I decided to use it. I was very happy this painting would finally get used for something. I don't believe Marcy Playground even knew it had been intended to be a Butthole Surfers back cover." [email, 12/22/2014]

© Mark Ryden

The endless gripes, feet dragging, and complications at Capitol soon turned into bad blood, and as the label was silent as to when or whether the record would ever come out, the Butthole Surfers became angrier and more frustrated that the brilliant record they were so proud of languished unreleased. Finally, King broke the silence in the local press.

King:
"We haven't been happy with how Capitol has worked the last two records and

aren't confident they would do anything different for the new one (especially considering it's one of the more experimental records we've done). Therefore, we've refused to give final permission to Capitol to release this (fortunately we have such a thing in our contract). While there is still no release date, we're still hoping on a release sometime this year - it just may not be on Capitol."
[Austin Chronicle, 2/13/98 edition]

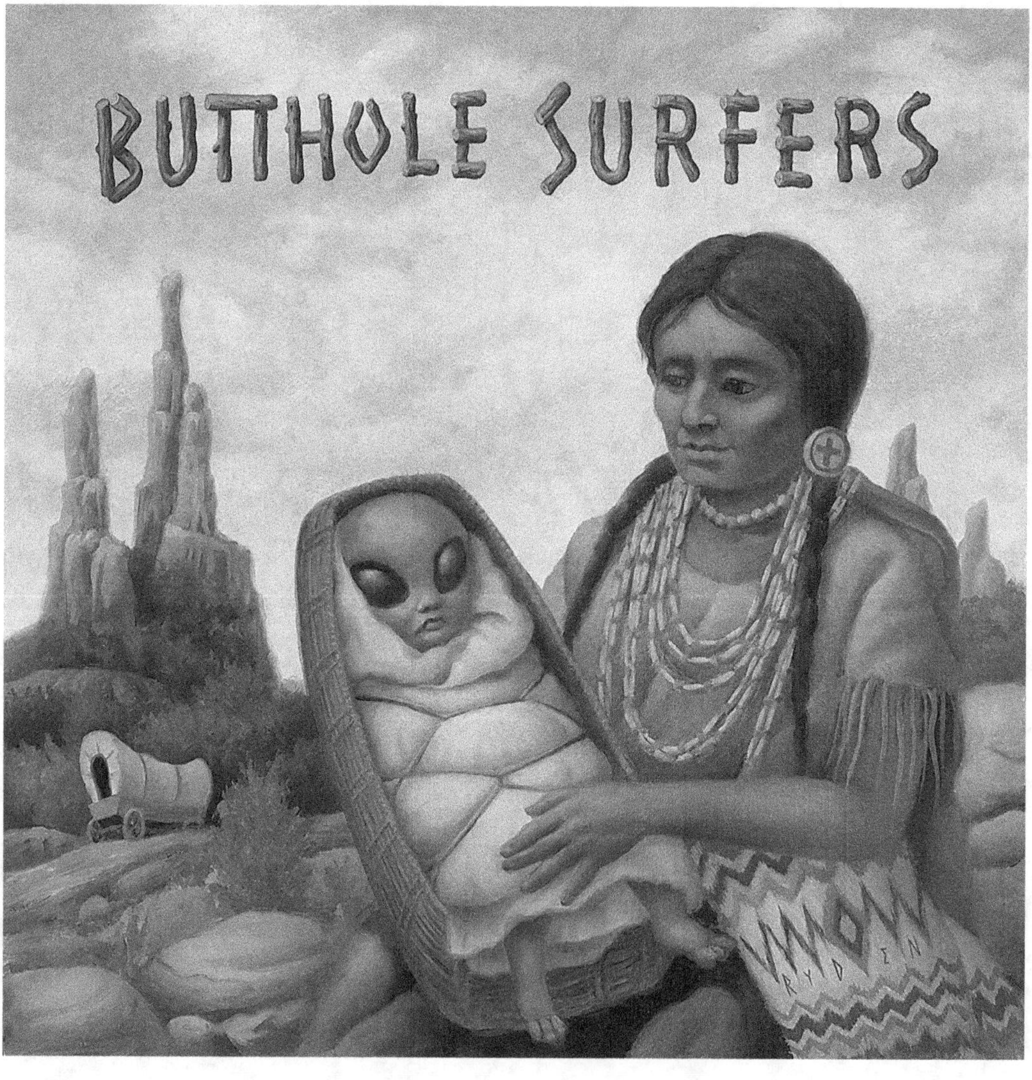

The Cover of After the Astronaut
© Mark Ryden

Capitol seemed to have a different idea regarding their contract stipulation. After all their difficulties since signing with Capitol, the band still managed to fulfil their obligations. They continued to give Capitol new releases without a proper bass player, with their lead singer teetering on the brink of an OD, and with Paul and King busy recording and promoting bands other than the Butthole Surfers.

But the Butthole Surfers were now a TOP 40 band, and Top 40 bands need to remain TOP 40 bands or else. There is nothing a TOP 40 band can do to lose, until they drop out of the TOP 40. Then, everyone has advice as to what needs to be done to keep them on top. Starving artists are not for labels like Capitol to support and failure to comply with their demands would not be tolerated. The method to eliminate the artists that didn't comply was simple yet effective: refuse to release the product until the band makes all the concessions the label wants them to make.

It is what caused Prince to change his name to "The Artist formerly known as Prince", then to "The Artist", and then to an unpronounceable symbol. Yes, even an artist as popular and prolific as Prince was not immune to this fate. Terminate the enemies. Make them an offer they can't refuse. Play by our rules or your records don't get released. The name of the band is off limits. The publishing rights to the songs remain in the labels' hands, making them too, off limits. And those same lawyers that were once on your team helping you to get the money that was rightfully yours, are now working to get the money they felt rightfully theirs. Turn around is a bitch. It is a cruel game and the losers lose all.

Capitol was setting the Butthole Surfers up to fail. The band was left with a record Capitol didn't want and a contract they could never fulfill. It was indeed lonely at the top and even lonelier in the middle. They had few friends in the industry left to console them and their label seemed content, not with letting them go, but with letting them die.

As the tug-of-war waged on, the band finally received word that another struggle was finally coming to an end. There was a ruling on the 4-year long brawl with Corey and Touch & Go. The ugly skirmish that left them estranged and cash poor was finally over.

In the two years since "Pepper" had been released, half of the profits from the sale of their back catalogue were frozen in limbo. With Capitol dragging its feet on releasing 'After the Astronaut', there had been a huge dent in their collective wallet. Faint, but distinct, prayers could be heard muttered that they might finally have something go their way

The court case wasn't all about the money in their eyes; I t was about control of their music and their livelihood. Like the old blues musicians before them, the Butthole Surfers gave a handshake and a backslap to a friend who wanted to release and distribute their material. They were young and hungry and desperate and needed a break. They were more than willing to share half of their money for the chance of having product to peddle at shows to enable them to buy a meal instead of picking it from the dumpster behind some restaurant near Terry Tolkin's apartment in Little Italy.

In the early days of the Saturday Night Fish Fry and smoke-filled juke joints, negro blues artists sold their songs for enough money to eat, buy some booze, fancy clothes, or maybe a car, while the white artists that released the songs they wrote sold millions and became international superstars. There was little recourse, and most wallowed in obscurity and poverty after the relatively small lump of money was spent.

In this new age of mainstream alternative rock, an independent label that shook hands with a band maintained the rights to nearly a decade's worth of material for a minimum of 15 years. Yes, it was a new era, and for the bands who finally signed to a major label after years on an indie, the precedent could have been devastating.

For the judges who carefully reviewed the points in this case, it was irrational to believe the intent behind the statute was for artists to lose the rights to their back catalogue based on an oral agreement made when the band was living out of their van. They compared the deal between Corey and the band to the one made with Richard Berry by Flip Records of his then unknown song, "Louie Louie". Berry sold his song for a mere $750 dollars to pay for his own wedding. The wedding no doubt was lovely, but the song went on to be, few would argue, the most famous, and most covered, song in the history of rock'n'roll.

Berry was left wallowing in obscurity, divorced, and living on welfare with his mother in South Central, Los Angeles by the mid-1980's. He finally won back the rights to his song when a wine cooler company wanted to use the song in a commercial, making him a millionaire in the last decade of his life.

Despite the cries of 'sellout' from the indie elite, the case between the Butthole Surfers and Touch & Go established a precedent for artists, like Berry, to hold the rights to their own material, especially when entering a deal as rubes and with little leverage to negotiate. The fact had always remained that the band would have never agreed to release a single record on Touch & Go if they thought their entire catalogue would be held in perpetuity.

The hubris of Corey in refusing to renegotiate the deal was not cool to talk about, but it couldn't be ignored, neither by the judges, nor by those who understood the legal consequences for other artists had the band lost the case. The paranoid indie elite feared that every band that had signed with a major would turn around and sue their former labels for back royalties. In fact, not one did. The case didn't set a precedent for bands to sue, it set up a structure so that labels didn't own an artist's rights for life. Perhaps the era of the 'handshake' deal was dead, but in all honesty, most notions of an oral agreement as a record contract died long before this case, especially for multi-album deals. As Yogi Berra once noted, and the judges repeated in their verdict, 'An oral contract isn't worth the paper it's written on.'

The irony that this case was ending as Capitol refused to release any the new Butthole Surfers album seems lost on the indie elite. Touch & Go was holding up the Butthole Surfers from being paid for the material they had already released, much like a major label does to an artist they've grown tired of supporting. Touch & Go wound up looking like the victim of big corporate lawyers, but closer inspection shows that, while greed might not have been his motivation, it was the consequence of Corey's own inflexibility.

When the verdict was handed down by the Illinois Federal Court of Appeals, Touch & Go was immediately ordered to return the band's entire catalogue to them, a ruling worse than what the band had initially offered to him in good faith before this ugly ordeal had begun. He was also ordered to pay compensation of $100,000 dollars in lost revenue since the case had first been filed. It was a bittersweet victory, but after so many losses, it was victory, at last.

Touch & Go was granted the right to keep all the product they already had in stock, so Corey rented a giant compactor and crushed all the remaining CDs and LPs left in the warehouse. *"Talk about a rift in the scene, man!"*, says Michael Gerald, of labelmates, Killdozer, now a tax attorney in Los Angeles.

"I certainly understand where they were coming from, what they did, and why they did it," he says about the Butthole Surfers. "I still consider [them] to be my friends, and I feel the same about Corey". Still, passions run deep when the subject of the court case is brought up. Tim Kerr, painter, and former guitarist of the Big Boys, who still lives in Austin "politely declined" to be interviewed. "I don't have much respect for them after the whole Touch & Go stunt." [message, 8/15/12]

There was little way for the band to win as denizens of a major label who were fighting against an indie label as revered as Touch & Go. Even if the Butthole Surfers were the reason the label became so revered in the first place. "

Michael Gerald (Killdozer):
"[The Butthole Surfers] were easily one of the most influential bands of the era, They had a lot to do with T&G being the label it was in the 80's – they were the reason we wanted to be on T&G, and I doubt if we were the only band that felt that way." [interview, 4/11/14]

Yet, even after receiving the verdict in their favor, it was hard to reconcile the joy with the sincere regret that it had to come to this point in the first place. After so many failures and heartbreaks, they could now finally celebrate, in some small way, a victory of any sort. With one court case behind them, they could focus their energies on their current label woes and on trying to get Capitol to release their latest record.

Two years turned into three years, and it was becoming obvious that the record known as "After the Astronaut" would never see the light of day. It would oxidize in Capitol's vaults, much like the tapes of Captain Beefheart's *Shiny Beast* or Brian Wilson's *Smile*: unreleased and unheard by the masses who didn't seek out a bootleg copy.

Like *Smile* and *Shiny Beast*, *After the Astronaut* was a groundbreaking work that would have shattered conceptions of what corporate rock music could achieve, and perhaps re-establish the Butthole Surfers reputation of making beautiful music without regard for marketability or trends.

Also like those records, by the time the Butthole Surfers untangled themselves from the web of lies, lawsuits, and lack of interest from Capitol, and finally released the record on Disney subsidiary Hollywood under the name 'Weird Revolution' in August of 2001, it barely resembled the masterwork of the original recording.

All the original recordings were remixed, bludgeoning the nuances under pounding house beats and slick mastering. The most experimental pieces, no doubt the ones that made Capitol the most squeamish, like the poignant and ethereal "I Don't Have a Problem", and the foreboding Middle-Eastern chunk of hashish, "Junky Jenny in Gaytown", were scrapped and replaced with songs Capitol would have creamed for.

'Weird Revolution', in contrast, included "the Shame of Life", which gave co-song-writing credits to white-rapper, Kid Rock. If Capitol wasn't going to release their album as it was intended, it seemed, the Butthole Surfers were satisfied to go for the gold and have another big hit under their belts as their final 'fuck you and goodbye' to Gary Gersh, now ex-manager Tom Bunch, and all the others who had given up, stabbed their backs, or sold them out.

Instead, with 'Weird Revolution' came the end of the Butthole Surfers. They toured behind its release in the fall of 2001, with wunderkind Josh Klinghoffer on second guitar \ second drums, and Nathan Calhoun of Austin stalwarts, Chaindrive filling the empty bass slot. The tour ended, and they went their separate ways. It was understandable that the band would aspire to the same success they tasted with "Pepper", if not only to show Capitol the mistake they made by abandoning them, but for many old fans, it was the final compromise they could bring themselves to embrace. The Butthole Surfers, after so many years of bowing to no man, changed their 'Oklahoma!' to *Electriclarryland*, submitted themselves to the myriad package tours, and collaborated with the rock stars the likes of Trent Reznor, Kid Rock, and Moby: the very artists they would have ignored at their creative peak. They recorded songs for Tom Cruise and Leonardo DiCaprio movies and played the major label game like nice former indie artists should. While old fans wanted to see the Butthole Surfers become famous, they wanted it to happen on their own terms, not on the terms of a major record label. The band had played nice one too many times and gave up on a record that was at once beautiful and challenging.

So, when the band presented *After the Astronaut* as their next record, it made sense that Capitol thought they could dictate the terms of its release. And, when the

Buttholes decided they had finally given up caving to Capitol's demands, the label simply held the product hostage, claiming the record unsellable, and refused to release it. The band held firm and left Capitol records in a flurry of lawsuits and renegotiations. It seemed the best time for them to release a record that refused to follow the established rules. The time had come to reclaim their credibility by force. Fans deserved a record like *After the Astronaut*. Instead, they got *Weird Revolution*.

Replacing the record's strongest material for "obvious hits," one which proudly stated they "loved the girls and the money" seemed like a betrayal for those few who stuck with them through the turbid and tempestuous times. It gave their critics a way to quote them and write them off at the same time. The next single, the treacherous "Dracula from Houston" stole its riff from the Velvet Underground's "Sweet Jane" and featured a sappy, sing along chorus that was cold and vacuous.

Weird Revolution lacked the very beauty and the subtlety that made *After the Astronaut* their best effort since leaving Touch & Go. The introspective and poignant soundscape of "I Don't Have a Problem" was replaced with the uninspired "Shit Like That". The eerie back ally nightmare of "Junky Jenny in Gaytown" and frantic "Imbuya" were both discarded, and the new mixes of "Intelligent Guy, "They Came In", and new 'title' track all lacked the power and mayhem of their 'After the Astronaut' counterparts.

It seemed that after sticking to their guns and keeping their record intact, they proceeded to water down the mix, drop the songs without commercial appeal, and replace them with songs they thought would be obvious hits. The results are almost always the same. The songs were neither hits nor inspired. It was a huge letdown after years of waiting. And in what had become serendipitous in the life of the band since signing to Capitol, the tour supporting 'Weird Revolution' started mere days after devastation of the 9/11/01 attacks. No one was in the mood to celebrate, not even a Butthole Surfers tour. Another short tour in 2002 found them in much better sorts, but like T.S. Eliot's "The Hollow Men", the world of the Butthole Surfers didn't end with a bang, but with a whimper.

The previous five years had been filled with appeasing company brass, a quagmire of legal tussles, an exodus of old friends and fans, and a band that was hardly a band at all. After Jeff Pinkus moved on, they seemed to have lost focus, as well as the will to fight for their own art, even after the trouble of winning it all back from Touch & Go.

They became known as one-hit wonders, forgotten by the casual fans they courted for success rather than remembered for their groundbreaking and genre bending work of the previous two decades. With the internet becoming accessible after the band was on Capitol, and their enigmatic history fogged in a cloud of bong smoke and scatological humor, their legacy was in jeopardy of being a footnote of all the bands they influenced: remembered more for the time the band was being torn apart by major label demands, managerial woes, illicit drugs, and destroying their indie credibility. The decade they spent building their dreams on endless tours and consciousness altering albums might only be remembered by the few whose memory wasn't completely destroyed by the ravages of lysergics.

Jane's Addiction is often credited as the band that kept the spirit of punk alive while incorporating the hedonism and spirit of free love aesthetics of the 60's. Nirvana is credited with changing the face of rock music, and Beck as the voice of a new generation, even as he rapped through a bullhorn and overlaid tracks of half-speed, Quaalude-induced guitar solos.

And if the Butthole Surfers were indeed a footnote in the history books of rock music, it would at least be some recognition. An acknowledgement that, for a time when underground music was dying, they were one of the brave few bands to keep it on life support long enough for Nirvana to bring it back from its coma.

The fact is, nearly ALL the memories of the band in its prime have faded from consciousness, as if they were just a fleeting dream. The Butthole Surfers are hardly referred to by the critics or rock historians, sans the brave few who feel like arguing for hours on the band's merits, and of their impact on the world of music.

If 1991 was the year that punk broke, as David Markey's film suggests, then 1987 was the year that punk wandered, floundered and flustered, and laid prostrated. Had the Butthole Surfers not been there to remind us of its importance, there is no telling if the bridge to Nirvana would have been crossed, or whether the Red Hot Chili Peppers would have been under it to reap the rewards.

With the band's reunion in 2008, which included both Jeff and Teresa back onstage, there was enthusiasm again, and the spark of hope not seen since the early daze. Time has done her work to try to diminish the legacy of the Butthole Surfers. History has distorted the facts, making many believe that the Butthole Surfers were little else than a gimmick and a tour bus. A one hit wonder among the cacophony of one hit wonders, or just a plain joke, merely existing as a band to get out of having real jobs.

But for those of us who saw it, the power and the glory; the ones who saw beyond the rock history books and deeper into our hallowed Self, there is a realization of just how important a band they were, and still are. For it is impossible to see the multitudes of bands who exist outside of the mainstream today and not see that it was the Butthole Surfers who laid the stony foundations their music is often built upon.

Beyond the music, the *formula* of how the Butthole Surfers achieved their success is one that underground bands, labels, and promoters have held dear to like that of Coca-Cola. They confirmed the theory that, with hard work and steadfast determination, any band can be successful. Any dream could become reality if you dragged it out of your brain, into existence and out on the road. If you remained true to yourself and your art, critics and cynics be damned. It was the idealism of punk rock, with the pragmatism of Noah building the ark. The waters ebb and flow; you just keep hammering. God is on your side.

And yet, even with the benefit of hindsight, the band's legacy remains muddled and tainted. Fans who recount how high they were at the shows, or how "freaked out" they were by the films only serve to diminish the band's already sullied reputation. The band is often written about in this context, leaving out the fact that the band left the burden of enlightenment upon the participant. The onus was on you to process the mass media blitz that bombarded you. The duty was yours to rationalize and reason and to establish your place within its context. The band wasn't going to tell you what to think or sum it all up neatly in an interview or on their record sleeves. With the freedom the Butthole Surfers proposed, came a responsibility.

If you weren't completely freaked out you were probably dead, but the type of freakout the band attempted to produce was more than wholesale theatrics. It was a warning, A battle-cry, a catharsis, a breaking of the will and a rebuilding of the spirit. It was not just some fodder for the acid-imbibed to get their rocks off, but a type of shock treatment for the complacent and mindlessly contented to fight against the powers of greed, violence, corruption, and propaganda.

The Butthole Surfers seemed to have the same dystopian fears as Orwell and Huxley. They embraced the human condition like Voltaire's 'Candide', and held the same philosophies as Pavlov and Jung. They utilized the same techniques that the military used to draw information from prisoners of war, and the same psychology and methodology that advertisers used to sell consumers their products.

The concepts and methods they executed were culled from the highest level of human intelligence, only now, the ministers of propaganda stood for truth and justice, not in a revolt against them. All we as the ticketholders had to do was walk away with something other than a hangover. Most of us dropped the ball.

Thankfully, one person who had been turned on and been enlightened and realized was a named Paul Green. Paul had become a legend of sorts for being the inspiration behind the movie, 'School of Rock', and his real-life School of Rock had turned a whole new generation of kids on to bands whose music might have been accessible to only the coolest kids who looked back at who influenced the bands that influenced the bands that they were listening to today.

By 2008, the Butthole Surfers were all but forgotten. We had trudged through two terms of a president born and raised in the great state of Texas, but barely had heard a peep from the most dedicated band in the history of Texas rock'n'roll.

George W. Bush, Texas oilman, former owner of the Texas Rangers baseball team, and son of Reagan's former vice-president and CIA chief, George HW Bush, won the national election by the smallest margin in history in 2001, but our own Texans were still eerily quiet. Perhaps they had fallen victim to the Extraordinary Rendition program the Bush administration had ramped up since the attacks of 9/11: whisked from their homes and brought to some CIA 'black site' in Eastern Europe to be beaten like mules for their 'Un-American activities'.

Such were the times immediately following the attacks on 9/11. And, somehow, the fate of a late-night home invasion and kidnapping by our government seemed far more likely, and palatable, than word that the Butthole Surfers had broken up of their own volition. The bond that held them together through the most difficult of circumstances is one that was deeper than blood: it was sweat, and tears, and filth. It was poverty and art and vision. A breakup would seem as likely as divorcing a brother or parent. But when Gibby and Paul started bad mouthing each other and internet rumors and dirty laundry started to fly to and fro, it seemed as if the band was truly done for good.

Thankfully, Paul Green had little idea of the state of the band at the time, other than they hadn't played a show together in 7 years and it would be great to hear, and see, them play their material again in the live setting. Having a mutual friend in Mickey Melchiondo (aka Dean Ween), Green asked if he'd contact Gibby with hopes of resurrecting the music of the Butthole Surfers with his School of Rock kids.

A short tour in homage to the music of the Butthole Surfers was accepted by Gibby, and once again, the music of the Butthole Surfers was played live, this time to a whole new generation of rock fans. The tour was such a success that Gibby asked the remaining Buttholes to join him on a reunion tour which would feature also feature the School of Rock All-Star kids.

Everyone agreed except for Paul Leary, who wasn't quite sure he was ready to relive the last experiences he had had with the band. Jeff, Teresa and King seemed ready to go without him. But a Butthole Surfers without Paul Leary is no Butthole Surfers, and if it went down without him, it would have been a disaster. The shows were announced, and tour was scheduled and there was still no word from Paul at all. Finally, a week before the tour's kick off, it was announced publicly, first that he would be making an appearance at one show, in NYC, and then finally, the whole tour.

The shows were a huge success, and since then, they have pulled a couple of tours without the School of Rock kids. Teresa left again (a trifecta!), but the four boys remained steadfast. They pulled off a couple of tours as a four piece: with Jeff on bass, the way it's supposed to be and were stronger with each venture.

A Halloween concert that featured a mind-bending performance of *Locust Abortion Technician* in its entirety proves the album, and the band, are still as viable and vibrant as ever, and are capable of the brilliance of yore. It was comforting to know that the Butthole Surfers were back in the fray; fighting the good fight, even if the good fight is no longer against "old cancer butt", Ronald Satan.

Seeing the Butthole Surfers live again harkened back to a time when they were here for us when we needed them most; at a time when punk rock was dying, glam-metal and pre-packaged boy bands ruled the airwaves, and the Moral Majority ruled the country. It seemed as if we might all concede defeat. The PMRC had their sights on the Dead Kennedys and Frank Zappa, and any art that was controversial was dubbed obscene and blasphemous. It seemed the ship was sinking and we were all going to drown in the frigid seas of bloated Patriotism at the hands of religious zealots.

But the band played on, untouched by the icy waters. The Butthole Surfers seemed to levitate above it all. Not merely walking on its glassy surface but flying high above it.

And as Washington continues to fail us and society seems steadfastly determined to crumble and fail, perhaps we can build upon the foundations laid by artists, writers and bands who warned us, and who railed against the forces of evil at a time before it was easy. A time before anonymous screen names and Tweeting and blogging. A time when singing a song or taking a photograph could get you arrested or hauled before a congressional tribunal. A time when being radical meant true sacrifice and having the heart of a troubadour.

And if history does indeed repeat itself, then maybe the lens with which we see the past can become clearer over time, or at least give us some context: remind us of our responsibility and our own place in the world. Perhaps we can become enlightened and view it with the wisdom of someone who has lived it before, as if in some past life, and confront it with the knowledge and experience necessary to exit victorious.

Perhaps, like Siddhartha, we gain more wisdom along The Path and see things in their proper context, in contemplative reflection and of our relationship to the present moment. All the hard work, vision, and yes, the mistakes, reward us with, not only insight on our current state, but a solid foundation upon which to build a future. It gives solace to know that the Butthole Surfers might be a part of that future, for they were certainly helped build the foundation.

They held a mirror to our faces and forced us to look at ourselves: the horror and humanity, the triumph and foibles. What was revealed wasn't always pretty, but I, for one, am a better person for it. I know because I saw it. It was as real as a vision of Christ, and it loomed over me like a monstrous shadow ever since. I saw in it my own life, death, and rebirth. My true Self in relation to the world around me.

…and it was wicked ass…wicked ass…wicked ass…

Gibby & Jeff, 10/12/09, Vancouver
© Bev Davies

Logs

My fascination with the Butthole Surfers began after hearing an on WNYU-FM's 'New Afternoon Show' in July of 1987. My brother and I laughed hysterically as they flagrantly boasted about their own drug use, mocked Oliver North, and tortured the listeners with an off-the-cuff version of Gordon Lightfoot's, "The Wreck of the Edmund Fitzgerald". All this madness with the backdrop of the PMRC clamping down on artists and as stores were refusing to stock anything which might be deemed objectionable.

My brother flippantly asked if I wanted to go to the show they were playing that night at the Cat Club and I quickly got changed and washed up.

I had been a casual fan of the band since the first EP but had never really delved into the rest of their catalog. Upon seeing them live however, my 16-year-old, straight edge mind was completely blown. I needed to hear more. I bought every record I could find, searching for "Johnny Smoke" and the 10-minute, aptly titled "Psychedelic Jam", both of which were indelibly etched into my brain. Upon buying every record I could find, I fell completely in love, but I also realized that neither of those songs were on any of the albums I purchased. I was confused.

I figured I would need to search out a live recording to see if I could find either of them there. Well, I did, but I also found about a dozen or so other songs I hadn't heard on any of the records. Was I missing something? I was confused again.

As my love blossomed, I began collecting more live recordings, often finding songs I had never heard, despite owning their complete discography. What became The Anal Obsession website started out as a handwritten document, later transcribed into an MS WORD, as the Live Discography, or LIVE DISCO. It all started merely to archive my growing collection of live cassettes and attempt to figure out what all these songs were. Still, it was difficult to keep track of line-ups and the slew of unreleased material that comprised most of their live sets.

As my love for the band became a slightly unhealthier, and I began to accumulate some trade lists from folks around the globe, I began to archive recorded shows which I didn't yet possess...it became a sort of a checklist of recordings I needed, as I was fully enraptured by now. I then decided to start actively hunt down tapes by taking out classified ads in FLIPSIDE and Maximum Rock'n'Roll magazines looking for traders and collectors who might have the same interest in the band as I.

It was through these ads that I met Erik Denning and his pal Carlos 'Cake' Nunez from LA. Both had been huge fans of the Butthole Surfers and were afflicted with the same addiction from which I was now suffering. Their tape list became a huge inspiration to me to get the LIVE DISCO going in full swing. I soon began searching for folks who had recordings they didn't have, so I could go trade more and obtain more.

But as my collection of live recordings grew, it only seemed to add to my confusion, which would only add fuel to the fire of my curiosity about the band. Line-ups never really seemed to jibe, songs were played once one year, then not again until years after. It was a big ball of confusion, and the more I tapes I amassed, the more questions I had.

At some point during all of this, I was contacted by Paul Wehle, who was as interested in getting things sorted out as I was. He asked for a copy of the Live Disco, and we began to write up the history of past incarnations of the band. Looking back, it was woefully and comically inaccurate, but still, few had attempted such a feat and it was the best we could do with our limited knowledge and resources at the time.

Paul (Wehle) and I kept in touch for several years, trading war stories, getting leads on new tapes and gathering info and contacting anyone and everyone we could find contact info for. The LIVE DISCO was now becoming a comprehensive resource, even as the band themselves had been relatively quiet. Then, in a stroke of complete and utter weirdness, the Butthole Surfers became a TOP 40 band. Soon after, they'd be labeled a one-hit wonder. The band that had inspired us to do all this work was destined to be relegated to the used bins at the local record store. But, Paul and I knew that the band was far more important than being a footnote in the history of rock music.

As the internet became the preferred mode of communication, Paul and I were able to find many key players in the band's history, and I also began get some really positive feedback on the Live Disco, which I had been sending out to a couple of people a week. Apparently, word of mouth spread like wildfire in the digital realm and friends of friends who had heard from their other friends that it existed began contacting me out of the blue about the document, which was now stretching out to over 50 pages in length. Then over 100. Now several hundred.

Soon, folks began writing and telling me about how important the band was to them. How they had seen them at such-&-such a place on such-&-such a date and it was mind altering and life changing. With their info, I began adding live concert dates to the DISCO without knowing whether the show was recorded or not…a damn behemoth was taking form.

The volume of people getting in touch and the vehemence with which they professed their love was impressive. It was becoming obvious that the Butthole Surfers were, as Paul and I had always believed, an important band to a lot of people.

Eventually, through the Butthole Surfers Forum page, I was contacted by Jason Ramke from Australia, who said he'd like to host the Live Disco off his webpage. I began the arduous task of digging out all the old lists and emails, letters, pictures and flyers which I had accumulated over the years, and which were scattered and saved on various floppy discs and CDs, various drawers, Rubbermaid buckets and boxes and bins which were strewn around my house. Magazine articles and photos and setlists of shows I had collected from the stage: it was getting ree-goddamn-diculous. Posting them all in one spot needed to be done. Despite the wealth of material littering my house, I was able to get most of it posted within a month and, in September of 2005, the Anal Obsession was officially unveiled to the public.

After the site was up and running, we began searching out and trying to contact some of the faceless masses who we had heard about in articles and interviews, some of whom the band themselves barely remembered. After all, it was often many years after the fact, by this point, and with their records not listing studios or band members, who could honestly blame them for forgetting? But the people who had lived through their tenures in the band, or had dealt with them intimately, would never forget their antics, and their recantations were often priceless.

Through their stories, a narrative began to develop. When I was finally contacted by former bass player Bill Jolly, the lost time in Texas between late-1982 through the summer of 1984 was finally revealed. I now had the inspiration to start putting it all down in the narrative that had never been properly told before, and the result is what you have in your hands. More than 25 years in the making.

Though several books and articles have shed more light on the band, all have been incomplete, missing key elements, or just plain factually inaccurate. It's not the fault of the author. The "facts" found here are based on the recantations of literally dozens of people, cross-referencing each account with other accounts which sometimes completely contradicted each other. Stories about particular gigs were checked against recordings of the show in question. No stone was left unturned in my attempts to make this the most factual account of the band ever told.

There are some key players who were not interested in participating in this project, for their own individual reasons. Some details were left out to protect the privacy and relationships of those involved. I only hope I was able to give every viewpoint a fair and accurate voice and bolster the reputation and legacy. Lord knows they have had their detractors over the years. I obviously have my own viewpoint but tried not to have any agenda other than to put the band into some context of the time. By doing so, I hope to show the adversity and triumphs so often downplayed or simply forgotten to the folds of time and negative press.

For those who were there and witnessed the band in their prime, the images are probably still burned into the fabric of your minds, and hopefully reading this will shake off the cobwebs and bring you back to that strange and grotesque time. To those who weren't, or who think the band was little more than a gimmick, I hope this book at least gives some pause for reconsideration. Much love and respect.

Fin

Gratitude

I would like to give endless and eternal thanks to these amazing people, whose input, inspiration, and insights throughout the writing process were invaluable:

First and foremost; huge thanks must be extended to brother Paul Wehle, whose tireless help gathering information for the Anal Obsession, the foundation for this narrative, cannot be overstated. Thanks Pablo!!...

Furthermore, thanks and blessings go out to Paul Leary, King Coffey, Teresa Taylor, Pinkus, Cheryl Dyer, Terry Tolkin, Bill Jolly, Mark Kramer, Kathleen Lynch, Scott Stevens, Scott Mathews, Quinn Mathews, Juan Molina, Brad Perkins, Terence Smart, William McConnell, Adriane Bahr, Steve Fitch, Kevin Leman, Kytha Gernatt, Michael Gerald, Alan Tubbs & Mary Hestand, Jimbo Yongue, Meg Fox (roach) , Andrew Mullin, Tom Flynn, Paul Smith, Ken Salerno, Bobby Beeman, Ric Wallace, Marky Ray, Trevor Malcolm, Bill Daniel, Krk Dominguez, Carlene Heitman, Suzanne Ferguson, Michael Overn, Bev Davies, Amy Yates Wuelfling, Ryan Richardson, Charles M Young, Chris Laygo, Greg Fasolino, Patrick Huckabee, Carlos "Cake' Nunez, Danny Flaim, Mr. Horribly Charred Infant, Scott Bevers, Dirk Vandenberg, Mike Watt, Bill Doherty, Greg Prato, Pat Blashill, Chris Schneider, Michael Corcoran, Laurie Stevens, Flloyd Heacock, Robert Carillo-Cohen, Jessica Goldfinch, Frank Fusco, and Kevin Purcell. Much respect to Gibby Haynes.

Credits and copyrights:

1) Depeche Mode – lyrics: Sacred, from the LP 'Music for the Masses' © 1987, Mute Records; all rights reserved.
2) Charles M. Young's Review (Playboy Magazine, Aug. 1985, p.32)
3) Some of the LP catalog numbers and discography photos were obtained with help from the DISCOGS record database.
4) The comparison of Gibby to Col Kurtz can be first attributed to Michael Corcoran in his article "Can Your Pussyhorse Do the Dog" - Thrasher Magazine (March 1987).
5) Details and accounts of the infamous Danceteria show come from several sources, including: Mr HCI of Happy Flowers, Kramer, Macioce, Cheryl Dyer, and Terry Tolkin A video of the evening's performance filmed by Michael Overn provided setlist, wardrobe and general antics in the chapter "Long Haired, Drug-Crazed Hippies".

6) Some of the City Gardens recantations are credited to Amy Yates Wuelfling, and her book, 'No Slam Dancing, No Stage Diving, No Spikes: *How City Gardens Defined an Era.*", Further documentation of that afternoon comes from Ken Salerno's pictures, and an audio recording of the event taped by Bill Doherty.

7) Alan Tubbs helped iron out the early NYC days, as did an article by Martin Pincher from DeTox magazine entitled THE BAND THAT NEVER WAS.

8) Fang – lyrics for "The Money Will Roll Right In", from the' Land Shark' LP, ©1982, Boner Records, courtesy of Tom Flynn.

9) Other lyrics attributed to Gibby Haynes, all rights reserved.

10) Kramer's quotes are copyrighted to him, and used with his permission. Blessings!

11) All session and song info which has an asterisk is unconfirmed…all songs in brackets are working \ unknown titles.

12) **No part of this book may be reprinted, in whole or in part, without express written consent from the author...so drop a line to me, at notsaved1401@gmail.com , we'll chat...:)**

Photographers

Some of the photographs in this book are by professional photographers who make a living from their art. Please support them by visiting their sites; going to their gallery exhibits; dropping them a kind word; or best of all, purchasing some of their works for your own viewing pleasure.

Michael Macioce
www.macioce.org/

Bill Daniel
www.billdaniel.net/

KRK Dominguez - http://krkdominguez.com

Bev Davies - http://members.shaw.ca/bevdavies

Edward Colver -
http://edwardcolver.com/

Pat Blashill
http://www.patblashill.com/

Ken Salerno
https://www.facebook.com/ken.salerno.9

Please support the Seaside Heights Animal Welfare Organization in any way that you can!

About the Author

James Burns is from Bellmore, NY, and currently lives in Saugerties, NY with his wife and kids. He's been running the Butthole Surfers Anal Obsession archive for more years than he wants to admit. He is available for birthday parties, bar mitzvahs, and business luncheons. You can contact him via email at notsaved1401@gmail.com

www.ingramcontent.com/pod-product-compliance
Lightning Source LLC
Chambersburg PA
CBHW081924120726
47997CB00010B/3028